IF WE WANT TO WIN

IF WE WANT
TO WIN

A LATINE VISION FOR A NEW
AMERICAN DEMOCRACY

EDITED BY DIANA CAMPOAMOR

THE
NEW
PRESS

NEW YORK
LONDON

Requests for permission to reproduce selections from this book should be made through
our website: https://thenewpress.com/contact.

Published in the United States by The New Press, New York, 2021
Distributed by Two Rivers Distribution

ISBN 978-1-62097-680-7 (hc)
ISBN 978-1-62097-691-3 (ebook)
CIP data is available

The New Press publishes books that promote and enrich public discussion and
understanding of the issues vital to our democracy and to a more equitable world. These
books are made possible by the enthusiasm of our readers; the support of a committed
group of donors, large and small; the collaboration of our many partners in the
independent media and the not-for-profit sector; booksellers, who often hand-sell New
Press books; librarians; and above all by our authors.

www.thenewpress.com

Book design and composition by Bookbright Media
This book was set in Minion and Myriad Pro

Printed in the United States of America

10 9 8 7 6 5 4 3 2 1

CONTENTS

PREFACE

When my son Pablo was nine, we moved from Miami to San Francisco. One day, he came home from school and asked me, "Mami, are we Chicanos?"

"We're not," I said. "We're Cuban Americans, but what does it mean if someone thinks you're a Chicano?"

"It means we're poor and live in a ghetto," he blurted without pause. At the time, I worked with a group of Chicano Ivy League-educated public interest lawyers, many of whom came from modest but loving families, and vibrant and richly diverse communities. They were powerful, skilled, resourceful, and effective. What narrative was driving the message Pablo received? It was the same that decades later would label Mexicans as rapists and gang members, and justify putting children in cages. In the absence of authentic narrative, prejudice and negativity fill the void.

This book is meant to help remedy the lack of accurate portrayals of who we are as individuals, families, and communities. These omissions are a form of disempowerment—in essence, a message that we don't belong. But if we are to take a leap into a new democracy that empowers everyone—if we want to win in the global realm of democratic ideals and human rights—we must include everyone. Indeed, Latines are actively writing the next chapter in the story of the United States and the Americas.

Born at a moment of historic social and political change, this collection of essays seeks to offer authentic portrayals, shape policies, and advance social justice. Latine experts are too often overlooked or underrepresented in U.S. public discourse, and in these pages Latine thought leaders share strategies for change in this decade. If we are to get past the racism, xenophobia, and polarization that have diminished our democracy, we must write a new story about the Americas, one where all our voices help us to win the challenges confronting our societies, our planet.

Through these essays, we contribute to that renewed vision by including the Latine presence in our shared American story. We weave our policies and personal narratives into the fabric of the United States. We write from the perspective of practitioners who work, day in and day out, not only in politics and voter engagement, but also in the arts, the environment, social and racial justice, philanthropy, and immigration, as well as about the ties between U.S. Latines and their countries of origin. And we call on other activists, especially from communities of color, to lift their stories for inclusion in this new American narrative that is emerging from the wreckage of the recent past. (We have included, in the back of this book, an activists' guide to writing your narrative for social change.)

Suffice it to say that there is no one Latine story that represents our diversity and, indeed, no common term that is accepted by all communities. The reader will note a number of terms currently in use, from Hispanics—a controversial term for some because it refers to the legacy of colonization by Spain—and Latino to Latinx and Latine. We selected Latine for the title of this book because it is gender neutral, is a new trend both in Spanish and English, and reflects the preference of the younger generation that we hope will read and use this book.

Who are we, these Latine communities we write about? We're 61 million Americans, or 18 percent of the 2019 population, according to the U.S. census. Most of us are native-born Americans who speak English as our first language. We are 52 percent of the U.S. population growth in the decade from 2010 to 2019, according to the Pew Research Center. In that period, the South added 4.7 million Latines, an increase of 26 percent. In Western states, the number of Latines increased by 3 million, or 14 percent, while in the Midwest and Northeast our numbers increased by 18 percent, 900,000 and 1.3 million, respectively.

Among U.S. Latines, Mexican Americans are the overwhelming majority at 62 percent. They live mostly in the West and U.S.–Mexico border states, but there are more than 800,000 in the Chicago metro area, where Latinos are now the largest racial or ethnic group. In the New York City area, there are 2.5 million Latine people, or 29 percent of the area's population. Of those Latines, there are 29 percent each of Puerto Ricans and Dominicans, followed by Mexicans, with 14 percent, and Central and South Americans combined, with 23 percent, according to the American Sociological Association.

People of Puerto Rican origin, including those who live on the island, are a much smaller but still second-largest group nationally at just under 10 percent of Latine. By 2018, Florida (at 1,128,000 people) had surpassed New York (1,113,000) as the leading state for Puerto Ricans. But Puerto Rican populations have also grown in Indiana and Washington state, according to a Hunter CUNY Center for Puerto Rican Studies report. Based on UN population data, Worldometers.info showed the population of Puerto Rico having declined a stunning 22 percent from 3.67 million in 2001 to 2.86 million in 2020.

People of Cuban and Salvadoran heritage are each 4 percent of the U.S. Hispanic total. Florida is home to the largest share of them, with 1.5 million Cubans, followed by California, New Jersey, Texas, and New York. Many Salvadorans have settled in the Washington, DC, Maryland, and Northern Virginia areas, as well as Southern California. Dominicans largely reside in the Northeast, such as Rhode Island, Connecticut, and Pennsylvania, as well as Florida. They make up 3.4 percent of U.S. Latines. The immigrants and their descendants from other countries of Central and South America represent the remaining 16 percent.

As we look at the future, the browning of America becomes more evident. Census projections show that by 2045 one in four

Americans will be of Latine descent. Two of our largest states are leading the trend, and their Latine voters are increasing their share of the electorate. California is already majority minority; Texas was expected to become majority Hispanic by 2022.

Given the pandemic and its devastating impact on the nation, it is no surprise that Latines' top election issues were COVID-19, healthcare, and jobs and the economy. Although former President Donald Trump succeeded in drawing Latine support by raising the specter of communism in Florida's voter-rich and heavily Cuban American Miami-Dade County, and also gained fans among rural conservative Latine voters in Texas's Rio Grande Valley, most Latines favored President Joe Biden. Latinas and other women of color lined up solidly behind Biden. While Latines made up one in eight eligible voters nationally, an impressive 40 percent of those Latine voters were eighteen to thirty-five years old, NBC News pointed out, citing census data.

On a personal note, my granddaughters, Mayelí and Soraya are U.S.-born "Blatinas" (equal parts Afro descendant and Cuban American). Mayelí will turn thirty-seven years old and Soraya thirty-four in 2045, when this will be a very different country. Consider this: That year, the nation will become majority minority, with Latines, at 24.6 percent, the largest ethnic group, followed by Blacks (13.1 percent) and Asians (7.9 percent), according to a 2018 Brookings Institution analysis of census data. Non-Hispanic Whites will be slightly less than half of the population at 49.7 percent. It is a terrifying prospect for some, and, for others, a pluralistic society is something to aspire to, the win-win for our shared planet.

In a nation of immigrants where over 14 percent of the people are naturalized citizens, the percentage of naturalized citizens among Latine is 34.8 percent, according to 2019 census estimates. Since more than a third of Latine were born abroad, we maintain close ties to our countries of origin. The overwhelming majority of us (71.4 percent) speak Spanish, according to a 2017 Pew Research Center estimate. In fact, RosettaStone.com ranks the United States third (tied at 41 million people with Argentina) among the countries with the most Spanish speakers, behind Mexico and Colombia.

In past decades, bilingualism was seen as an impediment to assimilation. That trend has been reversed, and multilingualism is seen as an asset in education, business, and arts and culture. In a global economy, Spanish-language proficiency, binational experience, and a strong connection to hard work, extended family, and growing civic engagement are assets for economic prosperity and democracy. Binational, bicultural citizens overwhelmingly contribute to families abroad and are keenly interested in the politics of their home countries. For the United States, they are natural citizen diplomats, promoting better economies and advocating for the rule of law, free press, and transparency, and for closer ties with the United States.

Remittances sent home by Latin American immigrants in 2019 reached almost $100 billion, according to a 2020 report from Inter-American Dialogue. "Remittances represent a notable share of GDP for the most politically unstable countries in the region," including the Northern Triangle of El Salvador, Honduras, and Guatemala, among other areas, according to the report. The flow of money from immigrants to their home countries helps generate greater economic stability in Mexico and Central America.

On this side of the border, U.S. Latines welcome the administration's efforts to bring justice, fairness, and dignity to immigration policy. Few would argue against immigration reform that emphasizes human rights, even while providing programs that welcome immigrant workers, artists, scientists, and others who will strengthen our democracy as the aging workforce continues shrinking as expected.

Instead of U.S. corporate interests guiding U.S. foreign policy in the region, we should put people first. Our foreign policy needs to balance corporate interests with people, families, equity, and democracy. Although corporate interests certainly matter, they can also undercut small farms and local businesses that support the working poor of Latin America. In contrast, individuals who send money from the United States to their families have a much greater interest in the growth of democratic ideals and political stability, as well as in seeing an end to drug violence and corruption in those countries. It makes sense that the Latin American Diasporas influence and participate in U.S. foreign policy toward their countries of origin.

Joe Biden traveled to Latin America a record sixteen times while he was Vice President, according to Inter-American Dialogue. While still a presidential candidate, he proposed an ambitious $4 billion plan to address violence, poverty, and corruption in Central America. As President, Biden has called for the restoration of U.S. hemispheric leadership based on principles of respect, responsibility, and partnership. Members of the Latin American Diasporas need to hold him to his promises and offer realistic models for economic development to help forestall the migration of those who would like to work and safely support their families in their home countries.

As an example, instead of providing funds to governments, which fail to rigorously monitor the flow of cash, the United States could consider matching remittances to nonprofits in Latin American countries. If immigrants knew their contributions in their home countries would be matched by the United States, they would likely give money to fiscally responsible organizations with which they were familiar. Such a program would support small local economies and, indirectly, donors' family members.

Sonia Nazario's book, *Enrique's Journey: The Story of a Boy's Dangerous Odyssey to Reunite with His Mother,* tells of a teen who left Honduras in 2007 and crossed Mexico alone on trains to find his mother in the United States. Nazario has become an activist on the topic of Central American immigration. She points out that many of Central America's immigrants are fleeing the takeover of their neighborhoods by gangs. The gang violence has too often grown out of the U.S. policy of deporting undocumented gang members, many of whom have never seen their families' countries of origin. Nazario suggests the United States expand investments in neighborhood antiviolence programs in Central America. Her research has shown this economic support has already proven successful in Honduras.

Like Nazario, we must join our voices with those of people and groups that work on foreign policy and immigration reform. We need to let our leaders and policy makers know what we expect from them.

Philanthropy has an important role to play in setting priorities in the social justice and racial equality movements in the United States. It also supports programs in Latin America that enable people to stay home, strengthen their communities through their work and family ties, and remain free from the oppression and hopelessness that force so many to flee.

It was that desire to flee oppression that brought me and my family to this country. Though mine was a somewhat privileged exodus, far from the horrendous abuses countless have experienced coming to this country, it was a jarring loss, nonetheless.

On that warm morning on August 11, 1960, my mother, in her freshly pressed linen dress, teared up as we left our home, an apartment at the top of a building my father designed, with a lovely view of Havana. My father, in a gray suit, starched white shirt, and tie, murmured to her, "*Margot, los niños . . .*," not wanting her to upset us with her crying.

I was eleven and my brother was fourteen. We were middle class, my parents were well-educated and spoke English, and my father was a successful architect, one of the designers of 1950s Havana. Yet we were leaving everything behind—our home, our school, our friends, our beloved country. My brother and I were told we were going to live in the United States for a while so we could learn English. I was trying to get excited about the adventure of it. Instead, the sense of loss for me and my family was overwhelming. The personal cost of immigration, no matter the circumstances, is always enormous.

We were leaving Fidel Castro's dictatorship, like many other Cubans, with the hope that the United States was going to help exiles like us to overthrow the government—and we would soon be back. The rest is history, and it is a history that repeats itself. Later, for instance, a wave of Nicaraguans fled the Sandinista takeover. Today, it is the Venezuelans who are in the same spot we were, stuck with a U.S. foreign policy that undervalues their home countries, manipulates their voters, excludes their Diasporas from policy making, and makes promises that are forgotten after the election. Latin Americans have remained too long at the bottom of the U.S. foreign policy agenda.

My family arrived in 1960 in Jim Crow New Orleans, with segregated housing and schools and Blacks riding in the back of the buses. In fact, my parents had to present an affidavit asserting that I was White before I could be admitted to the local public elementary school. I identified as a Cuban but also as an American because Cuba is in the Americas. But I quickly realized my peers did not see me as an American. I was an alien, an other. I was an alien protected by a loving family, but nonetheless an outsider—just like the thousands of immigrants from Latin America and elsewhere who came before and would come after me.

When did America come to mean only the United States? From my perspective, all the people in the thirty-five countries of North, Central, and South America are American. Sixty years later, I hear politicians talk about "America," and I cringe because "that" concept of America leaves me and the millions of inhabitants of all those countries out.

For a while, I thought I was a lonely, thin-skinned immigrant, who was imagining these issues. But no.

The United States didn't always call itself "America." George Washington didn't use the term in his first inaugural address nor in his farewell speech, preferring to call his country "the United States" or simply "the Union." In the early 1800s, the United States was sympathetic to the independence movements of Latin America, which resembled its revolutionary break with England. The first frequent mentions of "America" for the United States were in President Theodore Roosevelt's speeches after the Spanish-American War.

Northwestern University Associate Professor Daniel Immerwahr, the author of *How to Hide an Empire: A History of the Greater United States*, suggests the reason for the name change in a July 4, 2019, *Mother Jones* article:

> It was the United States' leap into overseas colonialism that changed things. After fighting a war with Spain in 1898, the United States annexed not only the Spanish colonies of the Philippines, Puerto Rico, and Guam, but also the non-Spanish lands of Hawai'i and American Samoa. This was its proud entrance into the imperial club, and the old names—the Republic, the Union, the United States—no longer seemed apt. It wasn't a republic; it wasn't a union (which suggests voluntary entry), and it included colonies as well as states.
>
> As at the nation's founding, writers proposed new names: Imperial America, the Greater Republic, the Greater United States. But the name that stuck was America.

Reframing the use of the term America does not rule out notions of American exceptionalism. The United States can still continue to toot its own horn about many of its accomplishments, some as yet unfinished, such as its record on human rights and its moral leadership in the continent and the world.

I don't expect our politicians to stop using the word America, but it should be preceded by "the United States of," and, in an era of polarization, "the Union" would be infinitely more constructive. This would be a giant step toward unifying the country, forming a more resilient and peaceful democracy, and building stronger relationships with Latin American countries. If people feel included, they are more likely to participate. The different Latine groups that might increase their participation because they see themselves as part of a larger "Americas" concept and not as "others," nor as targets of discrimination, would be more likely to work toward the common good.

This is a moment for Latine thought leaders to reaffirm what they have in common, focus their message, and think creatively about ways to support multinational civic engagement. In the same manner, we need to strengthen coalitions both among our diverse communities and with other groups. It is a moment of reckoning with ourselves: we have plenty of work to do to address machismo, misogyny, homophobia, and racism both in the United States and in our homelands.

The underlying premise of this book is to broaden the sense of who is American, inviting greater diversity under the Union's resilient umbrella to lead us forward as the United States becomes a minority-majority land—for the benefit of all.

Diana Campoamor
San Francisco
2021

FOREWORD

I am writing at a time of enormous civic tumult and uncertainty in our nation, at what is hopefully the end of a once-in-a-century pandemic, and at a moment of deep divisions, of unresolved structural and racial inequality in our systems. But history is replete with evidence that chaos and crisis can birth positive change, and even transformation. As an eternal optimist, I choose to hang on to this belief. My thesis is that the fields of philanthropy, nonprofits, education, and public service must behave diligently and optimistically about transformation in pursuit of social justice in our society.

At the time of writing, our nation has been brought to its knees by the combination of the COVID-19 pandemic, killings of racial injustice at the hands of law enforcement, and what was arguably the most divisive and pivotal presidential election season in one hundred years. COVID-19 has unmasked structural inequality in our health and economic systems, and the killings of George Floyd and Breonna Taylor have unmasked racial injustice. Neither structural inequality nor racial injustice is new to our nation's history—they are now just plainer and clearer in our civic consciousness.

In my field of work—the world of philanthropy—there is an existential question we must answer: what is our role at this juncture of our nation's history?

As an Afro Latino executive in philanthropy, I was compelled to reflect on the power of our authentic stories to shape a vision for the rest of the decade. What has been the unique and value-added contribution of Latinos/Latines to U.S. philanthropies, many of which have roots in a nakedly capitalist, structurally racist corporate America?

My answer to this question takes me back to my own roots. I grew up as an Afro Puerto Rican in the South Bronx in the 1960s. My dad, Charles, was an African American whose family came from Georgia and Washington, DC. After serving in the U.S. Merchant Marines toward the end of World War II, he returned to New York and met my mother at a Macy's department store in New York City, where he was working as a stock boy and she was a cashier. They later married, and he labored for thirty years as a blue-collar worker for Con Edison, the power company in New York.

My mom was born as Josefina Calderón in Puerto Rico, and she recently turned ninety-two years old. She worked in retail department stores and then as a dental assistant in New York City for many years. She was one of eight children from my grandmother, my *abuela* Agapita. Most people referred to this tough-minded, no-nonsense but loving matriarch as Doña Tea (pronounced Tay-ahh). Abuela spoke very little English, and, growing up, my Spanish was only a bit better than her English. But her love and wisdom for me was clear and abundant nonetheless—kitchen table love and kitchen table soul.

I recall a moment.

For the purposes of context, anyone who has experienced a bicultural upbringing can relate to my recounting of this set of memories. Central to any cultural experience are the issues of food and music; my household would feature "soul food"—fried fish or chicken, potato salad, and collard greens on a Saturday night—with Aretha Franklin or Nat King Cole tunes filling the air. Sunday evenings might feature delights such as *arroz con pollo*, *habichuelas* (beans), and *plátanos* (fried plantains) from my abuela's kitchen—with the sounds of Eddie Palmieri, Tito Puente, or Celia Cruz wafting into our ears.

I recall an evening of family, food, and musical revelry at our home during a holiday season—I am perhaps ten or eleven years old. My brothers, cousins, and I are munching on some Puerto Rican feast cobbled together by our abuela and our aunts—while we are observing my dad and our Puerto Rican uncles engaged in raucous conversation over a bottle of rum (and cigarettes, unfortunately, but it was a different time) in our kitchen. My dad turns to my Tío Angelo and joyfully shouts: "Hey, brother, you know why I love our people?!" He was referring to Blacks and Puerto Ricans.

My uncle turns to my dad and says, "No, Hoss, tell me why you love our people!" "Hoss" was my father's family nickname.

"Because, brother—our people got SOUL!" Joyous laughter ensues, as my dad and my Tío Angelo share an affectionate embrace.

Soul. In Spanish, *alma*—meaning some blend of love, spirit, heart, nourishing, replenishment. Growing up in the South Bronx, my best, lifelong, friends were two brothers, Chuck and Anthony Martinez, who were Puerto Rican. I vividly recall how when I visited their home—which was quite frequently—their mom, Toni, welcomed me as one of her own children; their kitchen was a frenetic, cheerful, and loving center of activity, and a plate of rice and beans was automatically put before me as a member of the family. With this spirit of unconditional love and "belonging" behind us, Chuck, Anthony, and I supported one another through our schooling-years friendship. All three of us eventually went on to college and medical school. Chuck is an ER physician in New York City, and Anthony is a critical care physician in Maryland. We remain great friends.

I contrast my upbringing and roots with the culture of the world of institutional philanthropy and private foundations. Institutional philanthropy has strong corporate and academic roots, and the making of a grant to a nonprofit organization can be profoundly analytical. Metrics, and measures, and "track record," and organizational capacity are all assessed as we enact decisions about which particular nonprofit merits being funded by our precious resources.

But this aspect of the foundation-driven grantmaking process only captures one of what I see as three critical dimensions of our mission and work in philanthropy. The "strategic" value of a grant reflects the direct service impact—number of meals for the hungry, number of shelter beds for the homeless, or the number of medical visits for asthmatics at a community health clinic. But there are two other critical elements to our work as grantmakers—and they are more nuanced, subtle, and dare I say "cultural" in their dimensions.

Each grant we make is also capable of asserting a *moral* dimension to its investment. And each grant we make is capable of asserting a *spiritual* dimension to that very same investment.

Let's take, for example, a collaborative project led in recent years by the philanthropic affinity group Hispanics in Philanthropy and its inspiring leader, Ana Marie Argilagos. Several foundations, including ours at The California Endowment, collaborated to support community organizations working along the Mexico–U.S. border in California, Texas, and Arizona. These organizations were responding to the crisis of thousands of detained migrant families and unaccompanied minor children stymied by a hostile immigration policy at the U.S. border. Hispanics in Philanthropy organized learning visits for leaders in philanthropy, such as me, to visit migrant camps and detention centers at the Tijuana–San Diego border.

The grants we collectively made to support this heroic work by the nonprofits had strategic, moral, and spiritual dimensions. Strategically, we could count the number of families receiving humanitarian and legal assistance in response to the crisis. Morally, our support was making a statement about the inhumane conditions generated by our nation's immigration policies—and that policies resulting in the detention and caging of migrant families were unacceptable. Spiritually, through our support, we were sending and affirming a critically important message to the families and children themselves: you belong, you have value, and we believe in your struggle.

This example embodies the fundamental value of the Latine

professional in philanthropy: the bringing of kitchen table love and soul—*un abrazo*—to those most impacted by the struggles of social justice. The Latine foundation program officer, or manager, or board member is culturally inclined to operate in proximity to the pain of injustice, and the lens of foundation work is framed by *sentimiento*. Yes, the value of data, research, and analysis remains in tow; but the Latinx operative in philanthropy understands the value and power of *belonging*. The struggles of our farmworker, immigrant, and migrant brothers and sisters across this nation provide a daily reminder of the need to allow soul—*alma*—to breathe through our work.

The theme of *If We Want to Win* is to capture the contributions of the Latine community, and it is indeed an impressive collection of stories and perspectives. But at this pivotal and critical moment in our nation's history—where the very fundamental question of "Who are we?" as a nation is hanging in the balance—what are we morally obligated to do, and how must we act?

At this moment, I am inspired by the story of the mythical West African creature, the Sankofa Bird. The Sankofa Bird takes forward flight by peering backward—an acknowledgment of past journeys in order to achieve needed progress. We have before us a nation—and a world—infused with the histories of colonialism, slavery, structural racism, stigmatization, and marginalization of Black, Brown, Indigenous, and all other people of color, abbreviated as BIPOC.

The path forward—to what the Rev. Martin Luther King Jr. and the late John Lewis referred to as "The Beloved Community" of true sisterhood and brotherhood—will require two things of those among us who are privileged to work in this field. First, we must channel the leadership and wisdom of our inspiring ancestors into our work—their passion, their dignity, their courage, their spirit, their agency, their soul. We can no longer afford to check these impulses "at the door"; we must remain proximate to the pain of the most impacted in our communities, as well as trust their ability to forge and shape solutions.

Secondly, it will be critical in the coming decade to act on our shared struggles as BIPOC community members through more assertive and impactful partnership and alliance- and coalition-building. The racial and ethnic disparities and inequities our communities experience—in health, education, economic inclusion, housing, the justice system, and civic participation—are profoundly and deeply structural and policy-driven in nature. Our nation needs more than piecemeal reforms; we must have transformative changes in these systems. Transformative changes to advance equity and meaningful inclusion simply cannot be achieved with business-as-usual. We must assert the voice and power of the most impacted communities—and do so together, as one family.

After all, it is what our abuelas would expect that we would have learned at the kitchen table.

Read, enjoy, and immerse yourselves in the stories that follow. We got soul.

Robert K. Ross, MD
President & CEO, The California Endowment

PART I

ENGAGEMENT IN OUR CIVIC LIFE

1 POLITICS
LATINE PATHS TO POLITICAL LEADERSHIP

HON. NELLIE M. GORBEA

In 2014, I was elected Secretary of State in Rhode Island—a state of about a million people, where about 14 percent of the population is Latine. Somewhat unusually, this was my first race. But one of the myths of campaigns is that there is a set political path that you must follow in order to get elected. Truth be told, there is no set path, and a successful strategy depends greatly on your local politics. The odds are harder for those of us not in the mainstream, but they are not impossible—Latine candidates of all ages and backgrounds can and should run for office.

And they can win.

The Changing Tide

The past decade has seen a significant trend toward greater diversity among our elected leadership at the local, state, and federal levels.

In Rhode Island alone, the November 2020 election brought significant change to the makeup of our elected leadership. The Rhode Island Senate has achieved gender parity and includes four Latine Senators, up from two. At last count, there were nineteen Black and/or Hispanic members of the state's bicameral General Assembly. The 17 percent membership of Black and/or Hispanic descent in the legislature for the first time mirrors the minority percentage of the state's population. These Latine elected leaders come from a variety of backgrounds—Puerto Rican, Dominican, Colombian, Guatemalan, Cuban, Panamanian, Salvadoran, and

Mexican. This ethnic diversity is one of the strengths of Rhode Island's elected leaders and is uncommon in other jurisdictions.

Nationally, there is an undeniable shift in the demographics of our government. Over the past decade, our country has gone from having nine Latine statewide elected leaders to seventeen.[1] In 2020, the U.S. Congress saw increases in the numbers of women and people of color elected, as well as the historic nomination of Senator Kamala Harris for Vice President. More than a century after women earned the right to vote through the passage of the Nineteenth Amendment and forty-five years after the passage of the Voting Rights Act made suffrage truly universal, we have finally seen results in who represents us.

The lively experiment of American democracy is about to get livelier.

Prior to winning greater representation, the Rhode Island Latine community was left to play only the role of advocate. We were able to garner some change, such as passage in the 1990s of an English-plus law recognizing the benefits of multilingualism, instead of English-only legislation. When passing laws was not

Demographics of Political Power, 2019

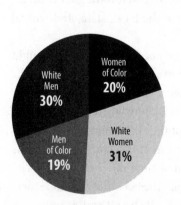

U.S. Census

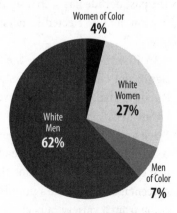

U.S. Elected Officials

feasible, we devised other strategies. Faced with an unyielding legislature, Rhode Island's Latine community successfully advocated that in-state tuition for undocumented students become the norm through an administrative vote by the Board of Higher Education.

But American democracy is meant to be a representative democracy, and there is no better opportunity for advocacy than being at the table when decisions are being made. More inclusive representation means we can finally envision and implement different policies, with solutions that have not been given consideration before.

In Rhode Island, Latine legislators have already made significant advances on behalf of all communities. This includes successfully passing legislation to protect the rights of nursing mothers at work, ensure state budgetary allocations for low-income municipalities, and create a certificate that recognizes the value of bilingual fluency in high school graduates.

In many areas of this country, Latines, Blacks, immigrants, and people of color are vastly underrepresented. Rhode Island's story should provide hope that change is possible even when we are outnumbered.

The Barriers to Representation

Amendments to the Constitution, changes in voting laws, and court cases that upheld voting rights have, in theory, opened up voting to any eligible citizen. But change has come slowly, and there are still barriers. Once the Nineteenth Amendment passed in 1920, women had the right to vote. Or did they? If you were Black or Latine in many areas of the United States, you were still denied the right to vote through poll taxes and other structural barriers. Barriers to voting are still the subject of cases being litigated all the way to the Supreme Court. Expanding access to voting, while very difficult, is only the beginning of the work that needs to happen to dismantle barriers to inclusive government.

As suffrage becomes truly universal, there is an opportunity for our elected leadership to better reflect our nation's communities.

At more than 60 million, Latines represent over 18 percent of our country, but according to a 2018 report from the National Association of Latino Elected and Appointed Officials (NALEO), we represented just 1.2 percent of elected officials for local, state, and federal governments.[2] Although the results from the 2020 election were encouraging, barriers persist—stemming from the systemic racism and sexism that are anchored in the foundations of our democracy.

But candidates from diverse backgrounds *can* succeed. From my own experience and that of my Latine colleagues, I know that the first ingredient for success is for Latine candidates to see themselves as leaders and to put themselves forward. Historically, political parties had machinery that recruited and supported candidates, especially at the local level. These days, state parties do little grooming and selecting of candidates. Individuals frequently select themselves. Currently, the main activity of political parties is endorsements, which may lead to some institutional support.

This change in American politics has had a significant impact on Latine candidates and others from diverse backgrounds. As communities of color become truly enfranchised through constitutional and legal changes to voting laws, the party ladders to elected leadership have been eliminated or altered. Changing our campaign structures from Tammany Hall politics—where elite institutions hand-picked the "deserving" candidates—might be good overall for our democracy, but the structures left behind do not encourage greater numbers of diverse candidates.

For example, it is always difficult to be something you have never seen. In many communities, where there have not been Latine elected officials, putting yourself forward as a candidate entails imagining a future for yourself that you have never seen. For Latinas, the challenge is greater. Studies show that women tend to doubt themselves much more than men do before running for office. Research has found that women need to be asked at least seven times before considering themselves worthy candidates.[3]

Latine candidates that do put themselves forward often face another immediate challenge: fundraising. Whether running for a school committee, land commission, state legislature, or statewide office, candidates either need to have their own disposable income to invest in a campaign, or need to be able to raise significant amounts of money.

Given the lack of strong political party structures and resources, a candidate's own socioeconomic background can provide an important advantage. Traditional political fundraising starts with having the candidate ask family and friends for contributions, followed by those who might want to see the candidate win, and those who have an axe to grind against the candidate's opponent.

The persistent wealth inequality in our country means that many Latines do not have sufficient disposable income or access to wealthy networks that can underwrite their campaign costs. According to the Pew Research Center, in 2016 the median wealth of White households was eight times that of Hispanic households.[4]

For Latine candidates, if they are coming from low-income communities and have not attended a prestigious university, fundraising is much more challenging. It also takes time—many candidates find themselves spending twenty to forty hours a week on fundraising as the election draws near. This is difficult for those who hold a full-time job.

Running for office can be especially challenging for younger Latine candidates. As people's view of elected leaders has grown more negative, being a young elected leader can be perceived as damaging to your career development. The excitement of being elected is dampened by the realization that ethics rules now affect how you can engage in business transactions, or even that people now see you as one more "politician." Without savings, being in elected office can be financially challenging to some young leaders and others who do not come from a background with economic wealth.

Much attention has been given to Latine candidates who run in majority-minority districts, but in Rhode Island and in other states, we are increasingly seeing Latine candidates elected in predominantly non-Hispanic White jurisdictions. The mayor of Topeka, Kansas, Michelle de la Isla, is an example of this trend. So is the election of any Latine candidate to a statewide position.

Media coverage of candidates can also play a large role in success. Candidates seeking statewide or federal office, especially, must count on more than just the "Latine vote."

The mainstream media's portrayal of Latine candidates in these races matters. Is the candidate introduced as a Latino or Latina candidate, or as a candidate who later in the biography is described as being of Hispanic descent? The first tends to alienate the candidate from the larger non-Hispanic voting bloc, in part due to fears about "identity politics" and an assumption that these candidates will only support their "own" communities. The latter allows the candidate to be presented in a way where ethnicity or gender are simply one more descriptor.

In Rhode Island's 2014 election cycle, three Latine candidates ran for the highest offices in the state—Mayor of Providence, Governor, and Secretary of State. Local media did not refer to them as "Hispanic candidates" but rather as candidates that happened to be Hispanic. Two of the three won, including me. And, although this was not the only reason we won, making ethnicity a lesser descriptor helped voters connect with us as candidates.

Changing the World: My Path to Office

I grew up in a middle-class family in Puerto Rico. My parents were professionals who had worked their way through the rapid industrialization of the island from the 1960s to the 1980s. My dad was an electrical engineer, and my mother was a freelance translator. Education was a deeply held value. On my mother's side, my grandmother had gone to college first—with a degree from the University of Puerto Rico, she became a home economics teacher at a time when women pursuing higher education were a rarity.

Over time, my parents earned master's degrees and sent their four children to study at well-known universities on the mainland. All of us achieved graduate degrees, and two of my siblings went on to earn PhDs. Although politics was not a common topic of conversation at home, I found myself drawn to student government at school and leadership activities in after-school clubs. My tenth-grade world history class made me realize that modern societal problems could be better understood when you learned their history.

By the time I enrolled at Princeton University, I was committed to helping make changes in the world. I dove into a wide variety of courses that led to my earning a degree in public policy and Latin American studies. My first job as an Education Policy Specialist for the New Jersey Governor's Committee on Children's Services Planning was a crash course in public education policy in the United States.

After a few years in New Jersey state government, I started graduate school at Columbia University in New York City. After earning a master's degree in public administration, I went straight for a job in the private sector. Trying to avoid being typecast as a career bureaucrat, I worked in public finance at a regional investment banking group in Boston.

This experience proved valuable in building the skills and understanding needed to serve effectively in government. Learning how municipalities and state governments could obtain funds for their infrastructure and growth was especially useful. Still, I learned quickly that banking was not my calling.

A few years later, I was recruited to become the first program officer in community economic development at The Rhode Island Foundation. This was the first of several jobs that helped me fulfill my vocation for community problem solving and was made possible during graduate school by a life-changing summer fellowship at The Ford Foundation.

At Ford, I was fortunate to be selected for the summer fellowship in the Urban Poverty Program by a Latine program officer, Diana Bermúdez, who became a lifelong mentor and friend. Within the field of community economic development, I learned the important role that affordable housing plays in the well-being of communities.

My experiences in economic development and public finance helped me greatly as I returned briefly to Puerto Rico for positions at the Government Development Bank and as Economic Advisor to Governor Pedro Rosselló. My two-and-a-half years in government in Puerto Rico were like a second master's degree. I learned how to hold agencies accountable, the importance of listening to various perspectives to get to the truth, and how to develop and follow a strategic plan in government.

Eventually, I returned to Rhode Island and reconnected to my community through politics. I became President of the Rhode Island Latino Political Action Committee (RILPAC) and led the creation of the Rhode Island Latino Civic Fund.

Raising money for the PAC was very challenging. By creating the Civic Fund as a 501(c)4, we were able to raise charitable dollars to take care of the civic education activities we felt were needed to develop an informed electorate in the Latine community. The Civic Fund sponsored important community debates in off-election years and eventually created a Latina Leadership Institute.

The Latine community in Rhode Island grew substantially during the 1990s. Increasing numbers of Dominicans, Puerto Ricans, Colombians, Guatemalans, Mexicans, and other Latine groups came looking for jobs and a better life. RILPAC was able to highlight this new diversity in Rhode Island by working to elect candidates who would best address the needs and opportunities of the state's Latino population. RILPAC came to be seen by non-Latine candidates as not only a provider of an endorsement and a campaign contribution, but also as a guide in navigating the politics of this newly growing, diverse demographic base.

In the 2002 statewide election, RILPAC endorsed nine candidates for statewide, legislative, and local office. Six of them won—including one Republican. Suddenly, the Latine community became important in Rhode Island political circles. A number of us in RILPAC were offered positions, and, for the first time, Rhode Island had Latines in significant administrative positions—beyond the "Hispanic Community Liaison" positions of prior years.

I accepted an offer from newly elected Secretary of State Matthew Brown to become Deputy Secretary of State and run that agency as the Director of Administration. My four years in Rhode Island government were yet another important education in how government in our state works.

Even as email was starting to take hold of our world in the public sector, at the Department of State I learned the value of establishing strong personal relationships for success in any project. Those relationships mattered whether I was developing an agencywide strategic plan or managing the agency's first-ever contract with a labor union. Engaging others in partnership as you tackle big issues is a key component of successful leadership in the public sector.

I returned to community economic development and affordable housing in 2007 as Executive Director of HousingWorks RI, which sought to make affordable housing part of the economic strategy of the state. Through my work there, I was able to use two very important tools effectively—stakeholder organizing, and clear and attractive advocacy research and communication.

I loved the opportunity to bring what seemed to be disparate stakeholders together in pursuit of a better Rhode Island. HousingWorks RI brought business, construction, labor, and community advocates together to address the lack of affordable housing. Our advocacy work proved successful in 2012, when Rhode Island passed a $25 million bond issue for affordable housing. That work built the foundation for several more bond issues, most recently a $65 million housing bond that voters approved in March 2021.

Community engagement has always been a passion of mine. Looking back, the kid who got elected to six years of student council in her school grew up to lead college organizations and then, not surprisingly, community groups.

In Rhode Island, I made sure I contributed on Boards of local nonprofits. That volunteer public service introduced me to a wide range of individuals, all of whom were doing important community work. I gained important insights on big community problems at organizations, such as the Women's Fund of Rhode Island, United Way of RI, the RI Latino Political Action Committee, Neighborhood Health Plan of RI, and Gateway Healthcare.

They also provided me with new ways to connect people who lived in Rhode Island but were separated by their lives and backgrounds. Serving as a connector has always been important to me, and it was wonderful to do this in a variety of community organizations.

Our best solutions come when there is a diversity of opinions and backgrounds around the decision-making table.

The Decision to Run for Office

In 2013, after years of helping others get elected and being asked repeatedly when I would run, I announced my candidacy for Secretary of State of Rhode Island. Like many women, Latinas especially, I had to be asked repeatedly before I saw myself as a viable candidate.

And, like many Latines, fundraising was a challenge, especially in contrast to my opponent, the scion of an old Newport, Rhode Island, family who was able to self-fund his campaign. He had his own foundation and a love for the pricey pastime of flying airplanes. He received the endorsement of the Rhode Island Democratic Party and almost every labor union.

I was quickly labeled an underdog in political circles. But I ran because I thought I was the best candidate, and I wasn't going to let a lack of funds stand in my way.

Despite the financial and political head start he had, I felt I had an obvious advantage. I knew the office we were running for, and he didn't. As Deputy Secretary of State from 2002 to 2006, I had managed the modernization of the office. I knew I could come back and quickly lead it to the next level.

I also had two decades of community involvement in Rhode Island, and he didn't.

Still, the campaign was brutal. It was the single hardest thing I had ever experienced. It was tough on my family, as well. The campaign required not just my own dedication but that of my husband and my kids, who were then three, seven, and nine years old. I will always be grateful for their support and grace under pressure.

Being the underdog candidate might sound romantic, but in political fundraising circles it does not sell. Political donors look for sure winners. I did not look like a sure winner going into the 2014 Democratic primary season.

Days and nights of calling family, friends, and acquaintances helped me raise about $355,000. My average contribution was $200 or less. We had more than 1,500 donors. Half of the total raised was spent on TV ad time over ten days.

My campaign operation was small. The consultant team— Jen Burton, Trish Hoppey, David Beattie, and Kate Coyne McCoy—worked well together and worked hard. My family all pitched in; my husband and kids traveled with me to pancake breakfasts, and my parents flew in from Puerto Rico to help me gather signatures, hold campaign signs, and help take care of my kids. Local engagement from lifelong Rhode Islanders, such as my Campaign Manager Rico Vota and volunteers like Betty Sepe, the Bernal Family, David aRusso, and many other friends who gave contributions and lent public support at a moment's notice.

Latino Public Radio, founded by Dr. Pablo Rodríguez, and the Mendez brothers' Poder 1110 (WPMZ-AM) Spanish-language radio station provided important access to Latine voters. Being fully bilingual and bicultural gave me a distinct advantage on

Spanish-language radio. My decades-long advocacy for civic engagement and commitment to educating Latines on how government works and why elections matter had made me a familiar presence.

Campaigns in Rhode Island have the distinct feel of retail politics. The state's compact size leads people to expect to meet even statewide candidates at their community events. With only twenty-four hours in a day, I felt the pressure of the never-ending fundraising call time, which cuts into your time with voters and your family.

Still, all those days of fundraising calls did help in a very important way—we raised enough money to get on TV.

The power of TV became apparent to me very quickly in the last few days of the campaign. We were able to produce one commercial that became an instant sensation with a tag line that morphed into "That's our Nellie!" The commercial was an important part of my win because it gave me widespread name recognition, bestowed my campaign with legitimacy, and helped me connect with Rhode Islanders in a fundamental way.

To succeed in the primary, I had spent all of my campaign funds knowing that, if I won, there would be public matching funds to help me make it through to the general election. I won my first general election with a vote total second only to U.S. Senator Jack Reed, a longtime elected leader in Rhode Island.

My win in Rhode Island meant that, for the first time in New England's history, a Latine had been elected to statewide office. But making history meant less to me than making change happen. Over time, I've realized what a blessing it is to be someone who can inspire young people to look differently at themselves—and the world around them.

Reelection in 2018 has given me two terms in which to advocate for the passage of voting rights legislation, obtain modern voting technology with paper ballots, and make it easier for people to vote while protecting the integrity of our elections, even during a pandemic. These efforts have led us to a record 10 percent increase in voter turnout. Over 520,000 Rhode Islanders voted by November 3, 2020, without a problem.

Our success at the Department of State has gone beyond elections. Small business owners tell me how much they appreciate the service they receive at our office. We have enabled our State Archives to provide Rhode Island history lessons and strengthened government transparency so voters can hold government accountable. Hearing Rhode Islanders' appreciation for making the Department of State work for them has been one of the most significant joys of being an elected constitutional officer.

My win in 2014 debunked one of the accepted tenets of running for office in the United States: you need to have the most money to win. It is often true that, for economic, youth, and academic background reasons, it's harder for Latine candidates to build the largest campaign war chest. However, I won my first primary, despite being outspent three to one. And I have seen many other races where this is the case. At the local level, where races can be won on thin vote margins, a candidate's willingness to out-hustle her opponent can be more powerful than deep pockets.

But the myth of money being a deciding factor for winning continues to be replayed over and over in media accounts. Early in races, when there is still no investment in polling, attention is given to how much each candidate has raised. This fundraising correlates to candidates' economic, professional, and academic backgrounds, more than to their potential to win.

But in our elections, whether you are rich or poor, you are able to cast only one vote. This "each person has one vote" system means that underdogs can win if they are able to figure out their local politics. It's hard, but it's doable.

Rhode Island's Long History of Experimentation

For many, the thought of a New England state's being at the forefront of electing Latine leaders and implementing progressive policies seems odd. Our national media reflects a bias toward covering the Latine experience through Latine majority jurisdictions.

But a closer examination of Rhode Island's history shows why, from its beginnings, the Ocean State had a greater likelihood for a more successful "lively experiment" in inclusion than its New England neighbors.

Engraved on the massive marble walls flanking the entrance to the Rhode Island State House, where I serve as Secretary of State, are the words: "to hold forth a lively experiment that a most flourishing civil state may stand."

These words hail from our colonial Royal Charter of 1663, granted by King Charles II of England to the newly formed Colony of Rhode Island and Providence Plantations. This charter was an extraordinary document for its time—it was the first to grant individual freedom of religion and provided for the separation of church and state. Both of these concepts went on to become foundational principles of our country.

This nation originated with the ideas of a handful of White, landowning men, who sought in the 1700s to create a government that responded to their needs. But what makes the United States a different kind of country is that embedded in our DNA is the possibility of a better future through experimentation for better outcomes. And, as time has gone by, the United States' "lively experiment" has evolved, and so have its people.

For the roughly two and a half centuries since its founding, our country has struggled to expand its rights and governance to include more than just White landowning men.

Waves of immigrants fight through rounds of discrimination. Formerly enslaved people struggle through bias and barriers to self-sufficiency.

Still, our country has made progress. The founding fathers would no doubt be astonished to see how the Constitution they drafted has been amended to include a diversity they would have had difficulty envisioning, and to see that their hallowed halls of power now include people like me, an adopted Rhode Islander born in Puerto Rico.

For our country to truly realize the promise of universal suffrage, election systems must change and our elected leaders must better represent the current diversity of our country. Just as the Latine community has become the largest minority in the United States, so too should our presence in elected ranks and other decision-making positions. Other states, such as Florida, New Mexico, and California, have elected Latinos to statewide offices in the twenty-first century. But, even now, they are considered rare exceptions.

A Path Forward

For other states to match Rhode Island's progress in electing more diverse and representative leadership, measured and deliberate actions must be taken.

Some of the solutions that are already being implemented, or are available throughout the country, include programs like those of EMILY's List, Emerge, and other organizations supporting candidates who are women and people of color. The programs provide not just guidance on how to run but, more important, fundraising training. Back in 2014, I benefitted greatly from EMILY's List training and support, along with my fellow trainee, now U.S. Representative Nanette Barragán. We need to ensure that Latines from our community participate in these programs—both as campaign staff and as candidates.

The Barbara Lee Foundation in Boston has done remarkable research that has helped elect women governors throughout the country. Recently, it has added information on voters' perceptions of women of color and LGTBQ women candidates. Also recently, the Center for American Women and Politics at Rutgers University has released findings on opportunities and challenges for women candidates and donors, especially women of color.[5] More research is needed to help frame our current challenges and devise ways of campaigning that lead us to a more inclusive government.

Locally, leadership-development programs are a good strategy to create the space for future candidacies. In Rhode Island, five out of the eighteen Latinas in elected office in 2020 were graduates of the RI Latino Civic Fund's Latina Leadership Institute. Three of them—Suzy Alba, Sabina Matos, and María Rivera—have served as municipal council presidents. Former Council President Rivera was elected in November 2020 as the first woman Mayor of Central Falls, Rhode Island. In April 2020, I administered the oath of office to Lieutenant Governor Sabina Matos, who became the first *afro latina* and Dominican American to serve as a Rhode Island constitutional officer.

Leadership development programs—even when not tied to the specific goal of running for office—give individuals the opportunity to see themselves differently. This is particularly important for individuals coming from underrepresented groups, who tend to lack role models and mentors. The programs frequently lead to alliances and friendships that support candidates.

Developing fundraising entities, such as political action committees in the Latine community, are also key, given the current political fundraising structures. Nationally, in recent years the Congressional Hispanic Caucus' BOLD PAC, the Latino Victory Fund, and, to a lesser degree, Poder PAC, have been fueling Latines running for office through direct campaign contributions and independent expenditure campaigns.

In Rhode Island, Angel Taveras helped write the RI Latino Political Action Committee's bylaws as a young attorney more than a decade before he became the first Latino to be elected Mayor of Providence. RILPAC's efforts led to the first Latine City Council members—Luis Aponte in Providence and Ricardo Patiño in Central Falls. Patiño's election helped pave the way for Mayor James Diossa to be elected in 2012 as Rhode Island's first Latine mayor.

Key to RILPAC's success was that it was truly a pan-Latine organization. RILPAC recognized the diversity of the Latine community. The group actively sought members among Puerto Ricans, Dominicans, Argentinians, Colombians, Peruvians, and every other Latine group, and it promoted a united front. We sought policy changes in education, economic development, public safety, and health, and we had buy-in across the Latine community because of our diverse membership.

Still, in its first cycles, RILPAC actually endorsed very few Latine candidates. The goal of RILPAC was not specifically to elect Latine candidates but rather to recommend the best candidate for the Latine and urban communities in a given race, no matter what their racial or ethnic background.

This more holistic approach made the RILPAC endorsement a coveted one by both non-Latine and Latine candidates. The conversations between Latine community leaders and candidates that were involved in gaining the RILPAC endorsement centered around the needs of and resources to help the Latine community. They also gave non-Latine elected candidates the opportunity to meet Latine community leaders in non-threatening spaces.

Many of those conversations, along with a robust effort to provide candidates with resumes of Latine individuals for appointments to jobs or Boards and commissions, contributed significantly to the numbers of Latine in the public sector today in Rhode Island.

RILPAC also gave a focus to our political advocacy. As RILPAC President in 2001, I filed a class-action lawsuit in U.S. District Court alleging that redistricting by the state legislature following the 2000 census violated the Voting Rights Act.[6] The case led to changes in legislative districts that enabled the election of Juan Pichardo, the first Latine state Senator.

Developing political fundraising entities, such as RILPAC, requires participation from Latine businesses and individuals. Latine candidates frequently face a disadvantage in that the culture of political contributions has not been developed in our community. First-generation Latine businesspeople may not fully understand how their support of a political candidate may lead to better policies that benefit the community or their own business sector. Immigrant businesspeople often come from countries with very different political fundraising models.

Of course, another alternative is to fundamentally change the existing political fundraising model in the United States. Given the traditional demographics of who is involved, the growth of dark money in politics can only serve to make it more difficult to increase diversity in public office. Consequently, candidates seeking office need to build their fundraising and support networks in the existing structures.

Latine candidates who have made it into the elected ranks have a duty to make change happen once they are "in the room where it happens." New laws or policies that promote inclusion must be successfully implemented. The structures of government, our laws, and our election systems are not set in stone tablets—they are made to be altered and adapted to changing times, as the lively experiment of our nation continues to unfold.

The work ahead to diversify our country's elected leadership at the local, state, and federal levels is daunting, but it must be done. This change will not be through prescribed or historical paths. But it can happen through innovation and a lot of hard work. It can also be accelerated through investments in education and mentorship.

Our democracy carries at its core the desire of people who seek self-governance. This is as true for those that came in the 1600s as it is for those arriving today.

Throughout my time in government and politics, I have been drawn to President Abraham Lincoln's summary of this in his Gettysburg Address. The United States, Lincoln said, is "a government of the people, by the people and for the people." Our best public policies come when there is a diversity of perspectives and backgrounds around the policy-making table.

I invite other Latines to join me in taking part in this lively experiment. We can play a leading role in the evolution of our country by putting ourselves forward as candidates and leaders. To quote Dolores Huerta and César Chávez, "*Sí, se puede.*"

I did it, and you can, too. *¡Pa'lante, juntos!*

PROFILE: RAMÓN MURGUÍA

Ramón Murguía has maintained an impressive career as a lawyer and a volunteer trustee at a number of foundations, with a particular eye for helping low-income youth and youth of color go to college.

Over the years, he has frequently found himself to be the only Latino in the room, but Murguía has always pushed his foundation colleagues to expand their narrow focus, encouraging them to set their sights on justice as a pathway to success. Throughout his career, his values of family and community, influenced by his upbringing in Kansas City, Kansas, where he still resides, have kept him grounded.

Murguía's parents raised seven children in a three-bedroom home, and, while things were tight, there was always enough. He credits them for instilling in him the values that would later shape his career: humility, strength of will, and a generosity of spirit.

His father, Alfredo, rose every morning before the sun to head to the local steel company, where he had worked ever since coming to the United States from Mexico in the 1940s. He was treated poorly by some of his White co-workers for being Mexican. Once, when pushed past his limit by a White co-worker, he punched the man in the face and told him, "You're no better than anybody, and you are no less than anybody." Equality is a family value that he passed along.

Ramón's mother, Amalia, was known for her cooking, laboring daily over traditional dishes like his favorite, red mole and homemade tortillas. She received visits throughout the day from elderly neighbors, who came to her seeking counsel, assistance, or simply her company. She never turned them away. There was always an extra seat at the dinner table, and she always had time to hear their stories and help them read and write letters to their loved ones.

After graduating from high school, Murguía received a scholarship to attend the University of Kansas, from which he graduated with a degree in business administration and accounting. He went on to study law at Harvard for three years and then entered private practice, remaining in Kansas City and specializing in corporate and real estate law.

Since graduating from law school, Murguía has served on the Boards of half a dozen foundations and is currently a trustee of the W.K. Kellogg Foundation, one of the largest U.S. foundations by asset size.

Though his background has the trappings of the American Dream, Murguía refused to portray his family's story as a predictable "rags to riches" tale. To do so, he said, is to rob the story of its grit. Rather, his story is a reminder of how much work and investment is still needed to correct for centuries of injustice that have made it unfairly difficult for people to succeed if they come from low-income communities of color such as his. He continues to challenge philanthropic organizations to do more to counter these injustices.

Leadership Lesson #1: Recognize those who contributed to your success, and pay it forward

In 2016, Murguía stood behind a podium before a crowd of people celebrating the fiftieth anniversary of the National Association of Student Financial Aid Administrators (NASFAA). In his speech, he testified to the importance of financial aid by sharing his family's story: out of seven siblings, six were able to go to college thanks to the help of financial aid.

"At one time, there were five of us in my family attending college at the University of Kansas," Murguía told the crowd.

"There were more in my family at the KU campus than in our family home."

This paved the way for them to reach positions of influence. Murguía's sister, Janet, for example, served for seven years in the Clinton White House and later returned to the University of Kansas to work as the university's Executive Vice Chancellor. She has been President and CEO of UnidosUS, formerly the National Council of La Raza, since 2005. Her twin sister, Mary, also a graduate of the University of Kansas, became the first Latina U.S. District Court judge for the State of Arizona. Today she sits on the 9th U.S. Circuit Court of Appeals. When their now retired brother, Carlos, became Kansas's first Latino U.S. District Court judge, he and Mary made history as the only brother and sister to serve on the federal judiciary.

For the Murguía siblings, access to a college education expanded the bounds of what they could dream and achieve. Murguía often says that his parents, first and foremost, should be credited for his and his siblings' success. After all, it was their hard work, encouragement, and strong example that inspired their children to go to college in the first place. But it is also true that it would never have been possible for Alfred and Amalia to put half a dozen children through college without financial assistance.

"Our parents' lesson in generosity taught me and my siblings that we had an obligation to give back for the blessings we had received as a family," Murguía said.

Murguía dove into philanthropy just two years after completing his law degree, when he was invited to join the Board of the newly created Hispanic Development Fund (HDF), a project of the Greater Kansas City Community Foundation. The Fund was dedicated to helping improve outcomes for Latino families in the Kansas City Metro Area. Its most successful strategy was to focus on Latino youth by creating greater access to a college education.

In 1987, when Murguía first stepped into his HDF leadership position, the goal was to raise $30,000 in scholarships for some 150 Latine students. In 2019, the fund awarded $600,000 in scholarships to 320 students. In the intervening thirty-four years, and with Murguía's support and leadership, the Fund has awarded over $4.5 million to more than three thousand prospective college graduates in the Kansas City Metro Area. Of all those awardees, 71 percent were the first in their families to attend college, and 60 percent have come from communities that are underserved and in the urban core. Murguía continues to serve as Chairman of the Board, and it is hard to miss the pride in his voice when he speaks about what HDF has achieved.

"I don't take full responsibility for that success," he told the crowd at the NASFAA celebration. "I do recognize, however, that my work in philanthropy has been inspired by the help that my family received when we needed it most. . . . I swear to you today, there are more families like mine that are out there, primed to finish college and do great things for our country."

He also gives back by mentoring younger Latinx leaders in philanthropy.

"I think of myself as the older generation now," he said with a laugh. "There's a different obligation I have; instead of trying to create and do things, I'm more in tune with how I help others get involved, how I create mentorship and that kind of space in my career."

When asked what mentorship looks like to him, he says, "Mentorship is about creating real relationships with people. . . . We need to know that the people we're mentoring are people who are going to care about others. So, I think it's about making sure we know one another, and getting the right people in the right positions."

Murguía's focus on paving the way for younger Latine leaders who feel deeply responsible to their communities exemplifies a mindset that is key to transforming philanthropy. Leadership must expand its focus to include all kinds of people.

"There are a lot of families out there just like us who may not have achieved the same, but who have worked just as hard. Just because people in my family have accomplished our goals doesn't mean we're done. There's still a lot of work to do."

Leadership Lesson #2: Justice for one community is prosperity for all: bring others along in the fight

For foundations, having a voice like Murguía's in the room is valuable because he reminds Board members to invest energy and capital in areas relevant to Latine communities. While the largest foundations tout the importance of investing more in communities of color, this does not always reflect the actual giving patterns of the vast majority of foundations across the country.

Based on a study by the D5 Coalition, just 6.9 percent of total grant dollars between 2009 and 2013 went specifically to funding efforts by and for people of color, and only 1.1 percent went to Latine communities—yet people of color make up an estimated 40 percent of the U.S. population, including nearly one in five (18 percent) who are Latinx, according to 2018 U.S. census data.

Murguía has always encouraged foundation leaders of all backgrounds to invest in Latinx communities. He has always argued that investing in communities of color should be seen as a necessity for the well-being of the whole nation.

"There is a role for every foundation," he said, "regardless of where your model and mission are, to be engaged with the Latino community."

> *"The next best scientists might be held in cages right now at the border."*

People of color in philanthropy, like in other fields, are often called on to be the spokespeople for entire populations. Although he brings a diverse range of skills and expertise to Board positions, Murguía is regularly called upon to "wear [his] Latino hat."

"As a foundation," Murguía said, "the most important goal we have is to improve the lives of those who need the help the most. That includes African Americans, it includes Latinos, and it includes Anglos who are struggling economically. . . . Fundamentally, that's the message I try to give at Board meetings. It's not just about Latinos, it's about improving outcomes for everybody who needs it."

For Murguía, "wearing his Latino hat" often means reminding fellow Board members that you don't have to be an explicitly Latinx-oriented funder to be outraged over injustices facing the Latine community, or to support organizations that are fighting those injustices.

For Murguía, the U.S. Immigration and Customs Enforcement raids that tear communities apart; family separations at the U.S.–Mexico border and children detained in inhumane conditions; and lack of access to basic public services and legal aid for undocumented people around the country—all of these policies pose a threat not only to Latine communities, but also to the country at large.

Foundations whose grantmaking priorities are based on issue areas such as scientific discovery and environmental conservation should be just as concerned by the violence affecting specific racial communities as foundations are whose mission is to protect those communities. He believes these injustices should not just be considered priorities for Latinx funders.

"The next best scientists might be held in cages right now at the border," Murguía commented in 2019.

Leadership Lesson #3: Keep close to your community; inspiration can be found at home

Every Sunday morning in pre-pandemic times, Murguía could be found at St. John the Evangelist Church, praying alongside the same congregation he's been a part of for his entire life.

After graduating from Harvard, Murguía chose to move back

home—back to Argentine in Kansas City, the working-class community where he grew up; back to his church; back to the place where he started out and learned all that is important to him.

When they married over twenty years ago, Murguía's wife, Sally, who is also a lawyer, agreed to move to his neighborhood. The couple had two children, Ramón Miguel and Amalia, whom they raised within the Kansas City public school system—a decision that Murguía says brought them criticism, but which he firmly stands behind. In 2021, Ramón Miguel and Amalia had both completed their four-year college degrees.

> *"I try to keep close to the stories of our community, even today. I don't want to separate myself from those lives and those stories, because I think it would not give me the context to speak up."*

Murguía defies the prototypical "rags to riches" narrative that defines success in part by the amount of money one can make and the distance between an individual's start and finish lines over the course of a lifetime. For him, his home community is not something to be overcome. "I try to keep close to the stories of our community, even today," he said. "I don't want to separate myself from those lives and those stories, because I think it would not give me the context to speak up at these Board meetings."

He is inspired by a law school classmate, Bryan Stevenson, who says "There is power in proximity. Get close to people and communities who are at risk—and stay close."

Looking Forward: Working toward justice requires more than "diversity"

In recent years, the language of diversity, equity, and inclusion has gained greater traction in nearly every segment of civil society—from the emergence of social movements such as Black Lives

Matter in 2015, to the ongoing push to diversify corporations and politics.

In the case of philanthropy, an increasing awareness of diversity, equity, and inclusion has led to a growing number of articles, presentations, and studies that try to break it down to a science and prescribe antidotes for philanthropy's seemingly intractable Whiteness and exclusivity.

While it is critically important to continue diversifying foundation Boards and grantees around the country, Murguía believes funders should not lose sight of justice as the ultimate destination, which is separate from and goes beyond the value of diversity. Overemphasizing diversity alone can lead us to get caught up in a numbers game, or a question of how many people of each given category (based on race, ethnicity, sexuality, etc.) can be brought into a room together. He challenges foundations to find creative and effective ways to redirect capital to communities that have historically been left out, discriminated against, and under-invested in. The solution is not as simple as adding a few voices from people of color.

Murguía well knows what people can achieve when they have a say and receive investments in their communities, when they feel a sense of belonging, and when they have access to the resources necessary to pursue their dreams. He envisions a future where all children have the opportunity to go to college, like he and his siblings did, and rise to positions of influence no matter their background. Philanthropy has a role to play in achieving this vision, but it takes hard work, self-reflection from those on the inside, and a true commitment to justice.

2 ADVOCACY
HOW 2020 ALTERED THE ELECTORAL SYSTEM

MARKOS MOULITSAS ZÚNIGA

It was June 16, 2015. Reality television star Donald Trump announced his candidacy for President. Everything about his declaration communicated gilded elite: the announcement took place at his ritzy Trump Tower as he descended a golden escalator and boasted of a $10 billion net worth. Yet, while his gaudy displays of personal wealth might scream elite Republican, his campaign, from the beginning, was anything but business as usual.

"When Mexico sends its people, they're not sending their best," Trump said in his announcement. "They're sending people that have lots of problems, and they're bringing those problems with us [sic]. They're bringing drugs, they're bringing crime, they're rapists. And some, I assume, are good people." Trump would, from the very beginning, say what few would say out loud, eschewing veiled appeals to racism, so-called dog whistles, for overt out-and-out racism. He may be gone from office, but the genie of demagoguery is not yet back in the bottle and part of his legacy will undoubtedly be the importance of messaging—about people of color, the Deep State, his economic record, and his capacity to deliver on his promises. But let's focus on his messaging about Latino immigrants and Blacks.

His first television ad of the campaign warned of hordes of brown-skinned immigrants invading our Southern border, with the narrator saying, "He'll stop illegal immigration by building a wall on our Southern border that Mexico will pay for." It didn't matter that the images were actually from the other side of the globe, showing Moroccans crossing the border into the Spanish

enclave of Melilla in 2014. (Spain has two tiny cities on the African continent.) Trump didn't need to traffic in reality; he used
whatever tools he had at his disposal to amplify racial fear and
resentment.

Unfortunately, it was the right message for far too many people,
giving Trump his narrow presidential victory in just a handful of
key states and leaving much of the nation in shock. How could this
huckster, two-bit, idiotic bigot con this many people? How could
we go, overnight, from having twice elected our nation's first Black
president, to choosing someone who explicitly ran against our
nation's diversity? Indeed, Trump has twice proven himself capable of drawing a new kind of voter to the polls. Trump's 63 million
in 2016 was bad enough, but that number was *74 million* in 2020.
(For context, Republican Mitt Romney received 61 million in the
2012 presidential election, before the GOP lost the educated sub-
urbs, and Republicans got 51 million votes in the 2018 midterm
elections.)

The appeal to which they responded and the reason why former
Vice President Joe Biden also drew millions of new voters to the
polls offer an important lesson for the future: really engage voters
and power high turnouts.

Imagine a White person living in rural America in the coming years, locked out of the prosperity enjoyed by the urban and
liberal elite, unable to buy into their economic and educational
opportunities. The youth are abandoning this person's town for
greener pastures, leaving them alone, bitter, angry at their losses.
They are aging, further adding to their isolation, as their children
move away and focus on their own children. Democrats talk about
making college more affordable, or even of forgiving college debt,
but that does nothing for them. In fact, they believe their taxes
are now paying for *others* to have better educational opportunities
than they or their families have. Their manufacturing jobs have
disappeared, their family farms have been driven to extinction
by automation and consolidation, and the coal mines where they
might have worked have been shut down by do-gooder environ-

mentalists. Whatever hope Trump gave them of a manufacturing and coal-mining revival is now dead. Alcoholism and drug addiction are rampant. These people have nothing left to lose, so their attitude? "Fuck them all."

Regardless of Trumpism's aspirations, the disaffected rural and unemployed voters can only be ignored at the peril of their falling under the trance of future demagoguery. The parties must deliver on the promise of a bright post-pandemic future for them, too, and continue to replace fear-mongering with real policies and honest answers that engage and mobilize voters.

Trump's secret power was his ability to whisper directly to their id, using fear, hatred, and anger to draft them into service. Conservative media amplified that message, spreading the word far and wide. And, as Trump solidified his hold on the Republican Party, it was no surprise to see his party double down on the divisive, bigoted rhetoric during the 2018 midterm elections. Leaning heavily on anti-Latino sentiment, Republicans ran on two major narratives: hyperventilating hysteria about a caravan of Honduran migrants making its way to the Mexico–U.S. border, and the pervasive presence of menacing-looking Salvadoran MS-13 gang members in Republican advertising.

The reality of the caravan was tragically pathetic—four thousand ragtag refugees fleeing violence and economic devastation in their own land, desperate for any hope of a better life. The trip, by foot, was slow and treacherous. They had no papers and thus no real hope to cross the border. They certainly weren't going to slip through unnoticed. Trump couldn't contain his glee, writing dozens of tweets attacking the caravan, such as, "Many Gang Members and some very bad people are mixed into the Caravan heading to our Southern Border. Please go back, you will not be admitted into the United States. . . . This is an invasion of our Country and our Military is waiting for you!" and "I am watching the Democrat Party led (because they want Open Borders and existing weak laws) assault on our country by Guatemala, Honduras and El Salvador, whose leaders are doing little to stop this large flow of people, INCLUDING MANY CRIMINALS" and "Anybody entering the United States illegally will be arrested and detained, prior to being sent back to their country!"

At one point, afraid that perhaps he hadn't ramped up the fear factor high enough, Trump even tweeted that "Criminals and unknown Middle Easterners are mixed in [the caravan]." (They weren't.) The Thursday before the general election, Trump actually called a press conference to declare that he was mobilizing the U.S. military to secure the border, a $200 million deployment without any practical application—other than helping support Trump's narrative of a nation under siege. The day before the election, Trump declared at a campaign rally in Ft. Wayne, Indiana, "Democrats are inviting caravan after caravan of illegal aliens to pour into our country, overwhelming your schools, your hospitals, and your communities. If you want more caravans, if you want more crime, vote Democrat tomorrow. . . . If you want strong borders and safe communities, no drugs, no caravans, vote Republican."

Of course, it was all ridiculous posturing, but Trump's base ate it up. Finally, someone was standing up to the "illegal" hordes. And Fox News happily fanned the flames. From mid-October to Election Day, the channel featured a "FOX NEWS ALERT" daily on the caravan. "The migrant caravan in Central America is growing," announced *Fox & Friends* co-host Steve Doocy breathlessly after one such alert. On another episode, guest co-host Pete Hegseth said, "When you see a lot of young men carrying the flag of their country to your country to break your laws, it looks a lot more like an invasion than anything else."

Still, as Republicans spread fear about the caravan, they realized that the narrative had a fatal flaw—those Brown people were *really far away*. While the story appealed to conservative voters' desire to "protect America," it didn't really hit them *at home*. So Republicans had a parallel story to sell—that of terrifying Salvadoran MS-13 gang members *IN YOUR BACKYARD!*

As far as gangs are concerned, MS-13 are bit players in the

United States, a mere street gang having neither the resources nor the clout of the Mexican cartels, the Italian mafia, or Russian and even Kosovan gangs. According to FBI statistics, there are eight thousand to ten thousand MS-13 gang members in the United States, or less than 1 percent of all gang members. José Miguel Cruz, Research Director at the Florida International University Latin American and Caribbean Center, called the gang's presence in the United States "a federation of teenage barrio cliques that share the MS-13 brand" with no national or transnational leadership to corral them together. Their efforts to traffic narcotics across the U.S. border have proven comically inept. *InSight Crime*, a publication tracking organized crime, even had a story titled, "5 Times the MS13 Tried—and Failed—to Become Drug Traffickers."

Still, if a ragtag crowd of desperate refugees was fodder for conservative fearmongering, MS-13 provided even better material. Their motto is "Kill, Rape, Control," and prison photos of MS-13 gang members covered in elaborate demonic-looking tattoos are genuinely terrifying. If they were too inept to forge international drug routes, who cared?

Most important, unlike Albanian, Italian, or Russian gang members, MS-13 are conveniently Latino, thus making it easier to equate immigration with death, violence, and fear. It was Republican catnip. Trump certainly couldn't resist, saying about the gang, "They have transformed peaceful parks and beautiful quiet neighborhoods into bloodstained killing fields." A study by the Wesleyan Media Project found that *one-quarter* of all television ads run by Republican candidates warning against immigrant violence heavily featured imagery of MS-13 gang members.

Republicans had one more anti-immigrant argument up their sleeve: the economic one. You see, in the Republican telling, those "illegal" immigrants were stealing American jobs, bankrupting the government, and taking advantage of American hospitality. A reporter for the *New York Times*, talking to diners in Mahoning County, Ohio, wrote: "In a county that is 89 percent white and less than 2 percent Hispanic, they spoke of undocumented immigrants bankrupting Sun Belt hospitals, dragging down wages and burdening taxpayers." That kind of logic is ridiculous, of course, but it sent a brutally effective message in rural America. In 2012, President Barack Obama carried Mahoning by over 28 points. Hillary Clinton won it by only three points in 2016. Trump flipped it in 2020, winning it by two.

Still, while the GOP's anti-immigrant rhetoric proved effective in rural districts and states, suburban America—particularly its White, college-educated women—was utterly repulsed by that rhetoric. "They view this literally as a crisis. The Trump presidency is a crisis to democracy, our values, our morality," Christine Matthews, a Republican pollster, told *Vox*. "It is making women physically sick. That is the word they use all the time—the word is 'nauseous.'"

Without Trump on the 2018 ballot, Republicans were utterly decimated outside of their rural strongholds. Democrats picked up forty-one seats in the U.S. House, thirty-eight of them in suburban districts. It seemed for a moment that perhaps Trump's election was merely a historical aberration, that America didn't truly feel as hateful toward Latines as it had seemed. Furthermore, Latine turnout in the midterms was up almost 50 percent from the 2014 midterm election, to 40.4 percent. And, while that number was still less than the White (57.5 percent) and Black (51.4 percent) turnouts, the gap was narrowing.

Since 2010, the Latine share of the U.S. population has steadily grown at a yearly rate of 0.2 to 0.3 percent, according to the U.S. Census Bureau, moving from 16.4 percent a decade ago to 18.5 percent in 2019. Latinos make up at least a quarter of the population in six states: New Mexico (48.8 percent), Texas (39.4 percent), California (39.1 percent), Arizona (31.4 percent), Nevada (28.8 percent), and Florida (25.6 percent). California, a state so large and economically powerful that it would be the world's fifth-largest economy if it were an independent country, is the bedrock of any Democratic presidential map. All of the other states on that list, except for New Mexico, are critical presidential battlegrounds.

For example, in 2016, Texas had 10.4 million Latines, a little over 4.8 million of them eligible to vote. Yet, according to the U.S. census, only 40.5 percent of eligible Latinos voted in that year's presidential contest. Among Whites, that number was around 63 percent. If Texas Latinos had voted at that same 63 percent rate, they would have cast nearly 1.1 million more votes. Hillary Clinton lost the state by 807,179 votes. The larger Latino vote still wouldn't have been enough to give her the victory, but it would have cut Trump's margin of victory by over 300,000 votes—the difference between winning the state by nine points and winning it by five. And that's at that sorry 63 percent turnout rate. In comparison, 68 percent of eligible California Latinos voted in 2016.

To be fair, Latines are both an immigrant and a young community. Both green-card holders and undocumented immigrants are unable to vote. The median age of a U.S.-born Latine (81 percent of all Latinos in the country were born here) is twenty-eight, and Latinos have remained the youngest of any racial and ethnic group since at least the 1980s, according to the Pew Research Center. (The median age for Whites is 43 years.) Prior to the 2020 census, 32 percent of U.S.-born Latinos were under the age of eighteen, unable to vote, while another 26 percent were eighteen- to thirty-three-year-old millennials—the lowest performing voting age group. Even Trump's explicitly anti-immigrant 2016 campaign didn't boost Latino turnout more than a point here or there.

However, 2020 looked a lot different. Joe Biden drew *16 million new voters*, almost entirely from among people of color. What was unexpected, and a gut punch to so many, was that Trump got *11 million more votes* than in 2016, helping Republicans win critical down-ballot races. The 2018 midterms had given Democrats hope that the American electorate was swinging in their direction. The election in 2020 told us that it had been a pipe dream, and that the message of bigotry, xenophobia, and division didn't just have strong political appeal—it had one of the *strongest* political appeals.

Trump and the GOP's 2020 rhetoric doubled down on the Black

Lives Matter protests and calls to "defund the police" that swept the nation after the murder of George Floyd by Minneapolis police. Just like the Honduran caravan, this was a ready-made moment for both Trump and his state media at Fox News, personified by Mark and Patricia McCloskey—the a-hole millionaires in a walled-off corner of St. Louis, Missouri, waving their guns as peaceful Black Lives Matter protesters walked by, minding their own business. Trump couldn't have invented a better bogeyman to stoke fear among conservatives. "The more chaos and anarchy and vandalism and violence reigns, the better it is for the very clear choice on who's best on public safety, and law and order," said former Trump Senior Advisor Kellyanne Conway, who had been one of his 2016 campaign managers.

Did the Trump campaign's racist messaging drive conservatives to the polls in those shocking numbers? Undoubtedly, but the impact of the Black Lives Matter movement wasn't one-sided. A record turnout from core Democratic constituencies contributed to Joe Biden's 16 million new votes. Among eighteen- to twenty-nine-year-olds, 25 million voted, or about 53 percent—an all-time record. This age group, disproportionately Asian, Black, and Latino, voted for Biden by a nearly 2-to-1 margin. Black voters over the age of sixty-five favored Biden with 95 percent of their vote, as did 90 percent of Black women, 84 percent of Black men, 70 percent of Asians and Pacific Islanders, 69 percent of Latina women, and 59 percent of Latino men. White voters? Biden only got support at the polls from 44 percent of White women and 39 percent of White men voters.

Yet Biden's seven-million-strong national popular-vote victory and 306-vote Electoral College victory (compared with Trump's 232 votes) masked just how close we were to a second Trump term. In 2016, Trump's victory hinged on 77,744 votes in just three states: Michigan, Pennsylvania, and Wisconsin. Biden's hinged on just 76,514 votes in Arizona (where he won by 10,457), Georgia (11,779), Nevada (33,596), and Wisconsin (20,682). Flip those four states, and Trump would have won the Electoral College 275 to 263.

In Arizona, Trump got four hundred thousand more votes in 2020 than he did in 2016, when he won the state by 3.5 points—a 25 percent increase in votes. Joe Biden got five hundred thousand more votes than Hillary Clinton received, a mind-boggling *43 percent increase*, just enough to squeeze out a 10,457-vote victory. Latines were a big part of that story, increasing their share of the voting population from 15 percent in 2016 to 19 percent— from roughly 362,000 votes in 2016, to around 643,000 in 2020, a whopping 281,000 increase. Biden won Latines 61 percent to 37 percent, according to exit polls, netting 154,349 critically important votes.

In Georgia, where Latinos make up 9 percent of the population, they were 4 percent of the vote both in 2016 and 2020. But, given that nearly one million more votes were cast in the state in 2020, that meant Latino turnout increased by around 20 percent, or around forty thousand. Per the exit polls, Biden won Latines 67–20, giving him 65,148 votes net in a state he only won by 11,770 votes. What's more, Biden netted 14,000 votes from those new Latino voters alone, without which he would've lost the state.

In Pennsylvania, Biden received around 129,000 votes from Latinos, who made up around 5 percent of the voter poll. He won the state by just 80,555 votes. In Nevada, Biden garnered around 51,000 votes from Latinos, in a state he won by 33,596. Wisconsin is the only one of these four "tipping point" states in which Latinos didn't, by themselves, provide Biden's winning margin. He got around 16,000 critically important votes from Latinos in a state he won by 20,682.

Of course, Latines aren't a monolithic group. Republicans successfully won back Miami Cubans (and likely Venezuelans and Nicaraguans), who had defected in 2016. The GOP claimed Democrats were socialists, a powerful message among people who had fled their homelands because of *real* tyrannical socialism. Trump's message also reached previously non-voting Latinos in the Rio Grande Valley counties along the Texas–Mexico border. Many of them work in immigration enforcement jobs, while others fear human- and drug-trafficking activity.

In fact, just like Trump managed to turn out non-voting Whites in large numbers, he did the same with Latines, increasing his numbers among those voters from roughly 4.3 million in 2016 to around 6.4 million in 2020! Of course, Democrats also increased their numbers, from around 11 million to around 14.7 million. Thus, Democrats gained a 600,000-vote net advantage from Latino voters nationwide. But Democratic strategists are certainly nervous about what that might portend for the future. Few people expected Trump's share of the Latino vote to increase, from 28 percent in 2016 to 32 percent in 2020, given his bigoted track record. No one knows if those are anomalous results based on Trump's bizarre and unconventional appeal to certain segments of the electorate, or if it hints at real shifts in the electorate. One election is never enough to discern long-term trends. But if Democrats want to lock down Arizona and make Texas truly competitive, they'll need to bolster their margins with Latino voters.

The 2018 elections gave us hope that Trump's successful appeal to bigotry had been an accident; 2020 proved otherwise. There is an American constituency that is receptive to racial, ethnic, and religious hate and division, one that is otherwise disengaged from mainstream American society and institutions.

That overt appeal to bigotry and racism significantly boosted Latine turnout in several key states and, in particular, the four tipping-point states that could have given the victory to Trump. Although the Latino turnout still lags behind that of Black and White voters, the very shape of our nation's politics will continue to be heavily influenced by the extent to which they wake up and exert the power that is theirs for the taking.

But perhaps 2020's greatest lesson was that boosting Latino

turnout doesn't automatically mean Democrats gain the advantage. It is clear that the Latino community can be as ideologically diverse as any other. That might convince Republican lawmakers that repressing and suppressing the Latino vote doesn't automatically give them an electoral edge, and it should certainly convince Democrats that they can't assume Latines are with them without a concerted and sustained effort to woo them directly, talking about the issues of most importance to their community. In other words, they cannot be taken for granted.

And ultimately, in a world in which White voters are increasingly Republican, and Black voters are solidly Democratic, Latinos may end up being the ultimate swing constituency—a great place to be once both parties figure this out.

3 COMMUNITY ORGANIZING
POWERING CIVIC ENGAGEMENT

MATT NELSON

Our democracy is in peril. Money rules the most influential law-makers, major political parties, and the entire electoral system. The few who hold enormous wealth decide who gets to vote, run for office, and have power—power even to poison our air and water! True, this form of power can take a person far in U.S. politics. But organizing, when done well, can build a countervailing force for underfunded candidates and issues by working at the speed of trust, cooperation, and leadership.

In response to these rapidly evolving times, diverse, dynamic Latine communities are building an innovative and transforma-tive kind of politics that is interpersonal, community oriented, transracial, transnational, and powerful, despite a lack of finan-cial resources or adequate investments in our communities. This country has much to learn from U.S. Latines about surviving and thriving in the midst of life-threatening conditions.

Let's consider an overview of Latinx voters and their priorities before we offer new strategies and share goals to transform U.S. democracy and make it more inclusive and representative—today, tomorrow, and for decades to come.

From the Ground Up

Two weeks prior to Election Day 2020, NBC Correspondent Nicole Acevedo reported on some of the grassroots efforts young Latine organizers were undertaking.[1]

In Pennsylvania, one of the crucial battleground states where Donald Trump had claimed victory in 2016, Maegan Llerena, the twenty-seven-year-old Executive Director of Make the Road Action PA, was at the helm of reaching young Latine voters in her home state. "Our families and our neighbors and our community are literally dying," she said in the broadcast. "People will not make it with another four years of Trump."

For many Latinxs, especially young first-time voters, their support for Joe Biden was not only a direct response to Trump's calamitous COVID-19 pronouncements. Their votes were also against the racism that was on full display when Trump launched his campaign in 2015, spewing White supremacist rhetoric targeting Mexicans, and indeed throughout his presidency. Almost two-thirds of Latinxs (62 percent) surveyed in the Election Eve Poll reported that racism and discrimination toward Latinxs had increased during Trump's term.[2] Voters were demanding an end to what he and other elites continue to perpetuate: profits over people and White supremacy over racial equity. We took to the streets and polling places to declare "*¡Ya basta!*"

This national outcry against racism was not lost on Yumaira Saavedra, a young Mexican American first-time voter in Pennsylvania, who was also interviewed by NBC's team for Acevedo's report. Saavedra's vote for Biden was solidified once her first choice, Bernie Sanders (endearingly nicknamed "Tío Bernie"), dropped out of the presidential race. Saavedra recalls being shocked and disgusted when, early in Trump's 2015 campaign, she first heard him referring to her loved ones as "rapists" and "criminals." It left her wondering: "Wow, this is really what [Trump] thinks of us?"[3]

Saavedra was among the 89 percent of Latines who supported the national racial justice protests in the summer of 2020 in defense of Black lives.[4] On systemic police violence, she said it had been sad to see that "it had to come to a man who died from police brutality to realize that we need to change now."

Immediate change is what Saavedra and the estimated 13.6 million Latinxs who voted for Biden were seeking.[5] But change, as we all know, can take on very different meanings, depending on whom you ask and in what part of the country.

Growing Numbers and Mighty Forces

In notable ways, the general election season was different for organizers. COVID-19 forced us to switch from dependence on in-person efforts to get out the vote, to scaling up our digital technologies to connect with registered and prospective voters. We relied on a full suite of voter outreach SMS tools to register voters and to get them to sign up to vote by mail, return their ballots on time, and verify their vote had been counted. And our efforts paid off. We witnessed record participation in early voting, with over 100 million people casting ballots early.[6] Of the entire cohort of early voters, about seven million were Latine—many of them first-time voters who were the likely targets of such digital campaigns.[7]

According to journalist Juan González, Latinx voter turnout in 2020 reached a historic high, with 64 percent of the Latinx eligible voting population casting ballots.[8] If this election was any indication of what is to come in future elections (which, arguably, it is!), Latinx voter rates appear to be comparable to those of Blacks and Whites.[9]

In addition to the historic turnout and the transformations we made to remain connected to voters, we observed the growth of seeds that had been planted and nourished by organizers and grassroots leaders long before 2020.

We saw Georgia flip from red to blue, thanks in large part to the massive efforts Stacey Abrams doubled down on after narrowly losing her gubernatorial race in 2018; the movement that she and a coalition of organizers and activists built recognized the value of every single Black and Brown voter in the state and prioritized their consistent engagement over time. We trust that the organizing drives in support of the fiercely contested U.S. Senate campaigns will inform efforts to keep the state blue in the future.

In a similar way, Biden seized marginal victories in Arizona and Wisconsin, which were catalyzed by Latine and Native American turnout, notwithstanding a long history of Native voter suppres-

sion and the devastation wreaked on the Navajos and other First Nations by the coronavirus.

Pennsylvania, spurred by pre-election activism, also turned blue. With an estimated three hundred thousand new Latinx voters in the 2020 election—many of them Puerto Ricans who were forced to leave the island after Hurricane Maria hit in 2017—grassroots leaders warned of the state-level dangers of another Trump presidency.[10]

And, after going red in 2016, Michigan also went to Biden in 2020, thanks to the crucial backing of Black voters and voters under age thirty, demographics that Biden knew he would have to win over if he hoped to pave a path to the White House.

In each of these states, BIPOC (Black, Indigenous, and People of Color) voters residing in metropolitan areas—Atlanta, Phoenix, Tucson, Milwaukee, and Philadelphia—understood what was on the line in this election, for both themselves and their loved ones, and they turned out to be the most pivotal forces in Biden's clinching the national victory. There's no doubt Latine power helped to usher in a new political era.[11] And we won't—we must not—let those who hold institutional power forget that.

Latinx Voters Are Anything but Average

While it's true that the "average Latine voter" is more likely to have been born in the United States;[12] be a millennial;[13] reside in California, Florida, or Texas;[14] and lean Democratic[15] (especially on issues related to the economy, education, and healthcare[16]), there's much more to the story. The reality of votership and voting behavior among Latines is much more complex. To think beyond the myth of the Latine voter is to consider other factual but less-discussed details about who has made up and continues to make up the Latinx electorate.

It requires us to understand that the majority of Latines say religion plays a critical role in their lives (ergo their politics), with over half of Latines nationwide identifying as Catholic, and an

ever-expanding base of 11.5 million Latinx Christians identifying as born-again Evangelical Protestants.[17] While the majority
of Catholics and mainline Protestants historically vote in favor
of Democratic candidates, Evangelicals tend to be more undecid-
ed in their support for candidates. Referring back to the last two
presidential elections, Trump was able to elicit slightly more support from Latinx Evangelicals than were the Democratic candidates, likely through the persona he created for himself as pro-life
and a defender of religious liberty (for some).

In addition to religious identity, economic issues, immigration
experience, family ties, and concerns about totalitarianism and
socialism also come into play for different Latinx communities,
as does party affiliation. Roughly 32 percent of Latinx voters followed party lines and supported Trump in the 2020 election.[18]
After all, almost 30 percent of Latinx registered voters identify as
Republican, and, for the past few decades, about that proportion
of the Latinx electorate has consistently voted for the Republican
presidential candidate, except in 2004, when George W. Bush
secured 44 percent of Latinx votes.[19]

After much speculation that 2020 would finally be the year
Latine voters would help turn Texas and Florida blue, both states
delivered for Trump due to the longstanding loyalty the state
Republican parties have cultivated from *tejanos* of Mexican
descent and Cuban (and more recently Venezuelan) immigrants,
respectively.

When we acknowledge facts such as these, our political identity
comes into clearer focus, as do the identities of our family members, friends, neighbors, colleagues, and fellow church members.
It's at this point that we can more easily and accurately investigate
the culture we individually and collectively embody, as well as the
ways in which we can contribute to change it.

The Power of Culture

At every moment of every day, we are shaping culture and culture
is shaping us, whether we realize it or not, whether we consent to

its whims or not. Culture—commonly defined as a set of values, belief systems, norms, practices, and behaviors—permeates everything we do. We all live and breathe culture and constantly participate in its reproduction; it's expressed in the clothes we wear, food we eat, places we frequent, recreational activities we enjoy, interactions we have, political figures we support, ways we spend our dollars, how we identify ourselves, and so on. No one is exempt from culture.

If culture is so fundamental to our everyday existence, it must also be recognized as fundamental to our civic life. To acknowledge the power of culture is to understand how it can be leveraged in movement organizing to create narratives and a "new normal." Perhaps that new normal can even amount to a new democracy ruled by genuine relationships and people, rather than by money, empty promises, and backdoor deals.

If there is a single trait that connects Latinx communities—and those of other people of color as well—it is *familismo*. Familism places the needs of family, including the extended family and wider community, over individual pursuits. This cultural trait, long observed and studied by social scientists, distinguishes the Latinx community from the dominant White American culture, which more commonly tends to emphasize the nuclear family above a wider community, extreme individuality above collectivity, and competition above cooperation.[20]

When former Democratic state representative Amy Mercado spoke to an audience at the 2018 Netroots Nation political convention, she referred to familism as a cultural cornerstone: "My grandmother fed everybody in the neighborhood." Mercado, a mother of six children who was also caring for ailing grandparents, joked, "My grandmother has always adopted all of my kids' friends. I ended up with more children than I actually birthed! There's a reason for that. It's that village mentality that you take care of all."

In Latine households all across the country, reciprocity and social cohesion are prized above all else. The highest earners support family members at home and abroad in the form of cash remittances. Pretty much everything in the home is shared, including food, clothing, chores, jobs, faith practices, legal advice, interpretation—literally, *everything*.

And, like everything in the world around us today, the concept of familism is subject to change too. As young Latines come of age and grow close to their friends in local communities and on digital platforms, as well as at school and work, they broaden the familist umbrella. So blood, or family ties, is not the only factor for building solidarity. Shared struggle and shared circumstances also take center stage for Latinx youths, as evidenced by the Trail of Dreams in 2010 (a walk from Miami to Washington, DC, in support of the passage of the proposed DREAM Act) and the increasing multiracial coalitions that formed across the nation a decade later to root out systemic racism.

Undoubtedly, our reliance on this rich, evolving cultural trait must be leveraged if we are to multiply the power of Black and Brown unity across the country, to overcome the egregious lack of political investment in Latinx communities, and to counter the rampant voter suppression that undermines democracy. Mutual purpose will help provide the cohesion necessary for future elections.

Overcoming the Status Quo

We need to set the record straight on Latine turnout: Latines vote. We vote even when odds are intentionally stacked against us. We vote even when a global pandemic threatens to deter us from the polls. Look no further than Trump's two presidential election cycles to understand this point.

In 2016, a record-breaking 12.7 million Latinx voters cast a ballot, with about one in five ballots representing a first-time voter.[21] In 2020, a few months shy of the general election, the National Association of Latino Elected and Appointed Officials (NALEO) predicted that more than 14.6 million voters would head to the polls, a 15 percent increase in turnout from 2016.[22] But by December, turnout stood at 20.6 million, a whopping 62 percent increase from 2016![23]

While this turnout is indeed reason to celebrate and rejoice, we can't ignore another reality: if 20.6 million (about 63 percent of registered Latinx voters) turned out, that means about 12 million Latines who were eligible to vote did not. There are myriad reasons why, including apathy, which comes from having so often been overlooked or viewed as unreliable.

Attorney Sonja Diaz, co-founder of the Latino Policy & Politics Initiative at the University of California, Los Angeles, rightly summed up the frustration around a lack of political investment in BIPOC communities:

> We've seen again and again that voters of color are second-tier in the minds of political strategists who favor persuading likely voters. There is not sound data on these voters, making them more costly in the eyes of political operatives. It's a failure of American electoral politics. And both parties are to blame.

If eligible Latines are already voting in high numbers, imagine if non-registered or non-voting Latines were actually contacted by canvassers. According to polling outfit Latino Decisions, three months ahead of the 2020 election, slightly over a third (35 percent) of Latine adults had been contacted by the Democratic or Republican Party, or any nonpartisan civic group, to encourage them to register or to vote.[24] (Statistically, Latinxs who are contacted by a campaign or candidate are nearly twice as likely to vote early, according to Latino Decisions.)

In September 2020, the Biden campaign got its wake-up call when polls showed Biden was lagging among Latine voters in Florida. They scrambled to save face and some votes, according to Fernand Amandi, a Florida Democratic pollster and strategist. "To their credit, they turned around the engagement. It went from zero to eighty overnight. But they were trying to do in six weeks what the Republicans have been doing for five years." Over the years, Amandi has had a consistent "I told you so" message to Democrats: You need to be on the ground and in the community with Latinx voters . . . and not just when it's convenient for you. That same month, according to the Biden campaign, they increased their spending on paid media to at least $10 million for Spanish-language ads as part of the overall $280 million in ad buys across TV, digital, and radio.[25]

But here's the problem: even when you track the flow of money and see who it's going to (or not going to), we know the investment isn't genuine. We know it's out of touch. And we know it's ineffective.

The lack of sincere investment in the Latine voting bloc—on both sides of the political aisle—needs to be overcome. So, too, does the widespread strategic voter suppression enabled by (primarily) Republican politicians and strategists, who have learned how much non-White voting blocs, especially Latine, are growing forces (in their minds) to be reckoned with and controlled.

We've seen it. We know it all too well. Gerrymandering. The purging of registered voters from state rosters. Reducing the window of time for early voting. Denial of voting rights to former felons or people currently imprisoned. Shockingly long wait times at in-person polling places. The consolidation or shuttering of polling locations. Mandating the presentation of photo ID at polling places. English-only ballots. Closures of drop-off ballot sites for mail-in voters. Restricting mail-in voting eligibility during a global pandemic. Rejecting mail-in ballots for alleged signature discrepancies. Efforts to "Stop the Count." The list goes on . . .

Since the establishment of our democracy, voter suppression and election fraud have been mainstays of our political process, only to accelerate in the aftermath of 2013, when the Supreme Court, in *Shelby County v. Holder*, voted to abandon key voting protections established under Section 5 of the Voting Rights Act of 1965. And we know who's disproportionately affected by this decision: Black, Asian, Native American, and Latine voters.

Leading the Charge

As historic as political abandonment, voter suppression, and election fraud are, so too is the resistance to them. That fight continues today. Latinx grassroots organizations have consistently powered voter outreach, even when they didn't have the financial or logistical backing from campaigns. Joseph Garcia, Executive Director of Arizona-based Chicanos Por La Causa, expressed surprise when the Biden campaign and Democratic Party neglected to reach out to the nonprofit to support voter outreach efforts for 2020. Chicanos Por La Causa, a large southwestern direct-services provider, took matters into its own hands. "If Latinos are going to wait for the Democratic Party to save them, they'll be waiting a long time," Garcia told the *Washington Post*.[26]

Likewise, the Culinary Union in Nevada took a proactive approach. About 50 percent of the influential union is Latinx, and its members have been among those hardest hit by COVID-19 and its economic effects. Even so, at the beginning of August 2020, about five hundred hospitality workers began canvassing, mobilizing voters, and working phone banks in Reno and Las Vegas to get out the vote for the Biden-Harris ticket. And, on a larger scale, Voto Latino, led by CEO María Teresa Kumar, registered more than six hundred thousand voters for the 2020 election cycle, 73 percent of whom were between the ages of eighteen and thirty-nine.[27]

If turning out the vote is a crucial piece of the puzzle, so is preserving the integrity of each ballot.

Since 2004, a coalition of democracy, civil rights, and peace groups have united to circulate a "No Stolen Elections!" Pledge of Action to ensure a fair and just election—a non-negotiable necessity for true democracy.[28] A core component of No Stolen

Elections! was the establishment of voter assemblies, self-organized community spaces where ordinary people come together to discuss reports of fraud and voter suppression that threaten the integrity of an election, and, if necessary, to take action to prevent elections from being rigged. By bringing thousands of voters and activists together to meet face-to-face, voter assemblies create an independent avenue to speak and act collectively against election fraud, sidestepping mainstream media narratives and political spin to connect lawyers and election experts with people in these communities who are concerned about fair elections.

Immediately after the general elections, Presente, where I serve as Executive Director, joined several progressive organizations to hold pro-democracy #CountEveryVote events in big cities and small towns across the country. This multi-city national demonstration of our confidence in American democracy demanded, as I said at the time, "that every vote be counted and that a government of, by, and for the people is sworn in."

Presente will continue to help lay out the infrastructure for a new level of organizing and power building for Latinx and immigrant communities in the United States. Our vision is to help prepare and support people to build and strengthen movements that do not yet exist. We have combined efforts with Alianza Americas, a network of more than fifty migrant justice organizations serving the Americas. By connecting those groups with Presente's membership, hundreds of thousands of Latine-led activists stand ready to act. We continue to attract and connect seasoned organizers, as well as a wider audience of community members who don't yet see themselves as activists. In this way, we are ensuring the movement grows meaningfully. It's our hope that as more people are encouraged to tell their own stories, they'll be connected to the work and each other on a deeper level, forging a movement dedicated to justice and predicated on personal relationships.

As we persist in our work, we will serve as a resource for organizers and activists who go beyond transactional interactions and social media discussions to gain a better understanding of the importance of political theory, the power of narrative, and knowledge of social movements.

Envisioning a New Democracy

We've seen the evidence that organized people can beat organized money. Now, just imagine if we lived in a country where both parties recognized BIPOC communities as an important voting bloc and truly invested in the recruitment, training, and promotion of grassroots candidates and their campaigns.

We are encouraged by continued Democratic efforts to pass federal legislation to strengthen protections to ensure eligible voters can easily register and participate in elections; keep purges from wiping eligible voters off the rolls; automatically register young people to vote when they turn eighteen, along with all newly sworn-in citizens; and restore the voting rights of people who completed requirements of a felony conviction.

What would it be like to live in an America that made it easier for voters to cast their ballots through secure electronic voting systems that had been individually vetted beforehand to assure their ease of use and resistance to tampering, if the Federal Elections Commission were overhauled to support these efforts and funded a public information campaign targeting voters ahead of each national election?

How glorious would it be if national elections were declared a federal holiday, a festive occasion of people coming together to talk, eat, dance, laugh, and, most important, celebrate that all their voices were heard, that they mattered?

How to Leverage Latine Power to Transform Democracy

So, how can Latinx culture and power be leveraged to overhaul our democracy so that it is more inclusive and more just?

Foster relationships. We must nurture our relationships, old and new alike. We must create a culture built on trust and

humanity, a point former state representative Mercado highlighted at the Netroots Convention: "We are trying to really talk
to these people one person at a time," she said about connecting with Puerto Ricans who had recently arrived in her Florida
district—whether displaced due to economic factors or climate
disasters. "It's not only about, 'Hey, you need to register to vote!'
It's, 'Hey! Welcome to Florida! How can we help you? What are
the services that you need? How can we assist in those needs?'"
Once settled with their basic needs met, those who are eligible to
vote are much more likely to be ready and eager to engage in the
electoral process.

Promote voting. We should make sure that every single member of our families, our closest friends, our social media circles,
and our neighbors is registered to vote, if eligible. More important, we should make sure they understand the electoral process
and any potential issues. If our relationships are rooted in trust,
anyone who does not understand how to vote or how to interpret
the ballot will be forthcoming and even reach out. We must know
that, as a family-oriented people, Latines are more receptive to
political messaging from a family member or other loved one who
is politically engaged; we tend to align our vote with that of our
closest loved ones.

Follow up. We must stay in touch—even when there is no election or formal "ask." For example, reach out to people in online
communities—such as closed Facebook groups—to take action
and share information on their social media accounts or via text
messaging.

Gain ground. Every space should be viewed as an opportunity
to contest entrenched power. This means having a presence on every local committee and every level of government. This means
discussing politics at the dinner table, in classrooms, at church, at
work, and at youth soccer potlucks. Spreading the word on candidates and issues and having a vocal presence in each forum serve
to influence fellow voters as well as policies that affect local communities.

Get creative. We must get creative and know our audiences. While in-person interactions, relationship building, familism, and culture change are the building blocks of Latine organizing, tech tools are essential to scaling that power, as we learned in 2020. Digital tools, including the ability to reach millions of people through text messaging, are important for educating future generations of voters. Not only are young people today less likely to have access to civics courses in underfunded public schools, but they are also the most likely to socialize in virtual venues, such as the Twitch gaming platform. In October 2020, U.S. Representatives Alexandria Ocasio-Cortez (D-New York City) and Ilhan Omar (D-Minneapolis) decided to take part in the online game *Among Us* because they knew it was a way to reach young voters and draw them to the polls.

In addition, we must hold in our collective memory the summer of 2020, when—amid a global pandemic, violent assaults on Black lives and everyone who stood in defense of racial justice, an unprecedented hurricane season, and devastating wildfires across the western part of the country—we showed up in record numbers. We took care of one another when we were sick. We grieved unimaginable individual and collective losses together. And through our participation in a historic election, we made it known that we, the people, hold the power and will determine our political destiny.

PROFILE: HERMAN GALLEGOS

A pioneering civil rights activist and one of the first Latinos to sit on U.S. corporate Boards or serve as a trustee of a national foundation, Herman Gallegos has dedicated his long career to creating a more just and equitable society.

His was a long journey from the barrio to the boardroom. He was born in the hardscrabble mining town of Aguilar, Colorado, and learned later in life of the Ludlow Massacre that took place in Ludlow, Colorado, in 1914, just a few miles from his hometown.

The massacre was part of a violent clash between striking workers at Colorado Fuel and Iron Co. and the state militia. John D. Rockefeller Jr., who was the majority shareholder of the steel conglomerate, was widely believed to be responsible for the killings. His philanthropic endeavors through The Rockefeller Foundation, which had launched the previous year, helped to rehabilitate his image.

"Little did I realize that someday there would be a connection between this history in Colorado and my life's work helping philanthropy become a true catalyst for positive social change in American society," Gallegos said in an interview for this profile. In 1979, he was among the first Latinos to join the Board of The Rockefeller Foundation.

Gallegos attended San Francisco public schools, graduated from San Jose State University, and earned a master's degree in social work from the University of California, Berkeley. Later in life, he was awarded an honorary doctorate from the University of San Francisco.

He has served on the Boards of many foundations and corporations. Together with Luz Vega-Marquis and Elisa Arévalo, he
co-founded Hispanics in Philanthropy in the 1980s. He continues
to advocate for civil rights and for increased diversity in philanthropy and in corporate boardrooms. He would like to see philanthropy reformed to emphasize serving the public interest.

Leadership Lesson #1: Seek out help and mentorship

Gallegos's family moved to San Francisco during the Great
Depression when he was still a child. Like many others, for a time
they relied on government assistance, including food. When Gallegos was nine, he lost a leg in a train accident. Because his family
could not afford $116 for a prosthetic leg, his elementary school
principal referred them to a nonprofit agency then known as
the Crippled Children's Society. The agency bought him his first
artificial leg.

"This experience helped shape my lifelong perspective about the
importance of the public and private sectors' being there to help
those in need get back on their feet, and in my case, literally—on
my feet."

He counts several people as crucial mentors who guided him
through his younger years, including a man with whom he cor-
responded for fifteen years. He turned out to be a landscape
engineer for the famed Hearst family, which was known for developing what was at the time the nation's largest newspaper chain
and media company. Years later, when Gallegos was working in
San Francisco, he became friends with Randolph Hearst, a scion
of the Hearst empire.

Another mentor was Amelia Anderson, Executive Director
of the Potrero Hill settlement house in San Francisco, where, in
his teenage years, Gallegos worked part time as a janitor during
World War II.

From these mentors, he learned that "despite the hurts and
obstacles that poor people and those from minority backgrounds

often experience, there are persons ready to find effective ways to help those less fortunate to change and improve the conditions of their lives, and other challenges tied to the adversity they may face."

Much later in his career, after many years of activism, Gallegos continued to seek out advice from people he respected. In his efforts to figure out in what direction he should take his career, he separately invited three older, successful, and well-known people to lunch to pick their brains. One of them suggested he consider joining a few corporate Boards as an outside director. Another advised, "Don't take the first position offered to you. Take the best," which he did.

Thanks to Ruth Chance, then Executive Director of The Rosenberg Foundation, he was elected in 1972 to the foundation's Board of Trustees and became one of the few Latinos in the country to serve on a foundation Board.

It started a new stage in his career, in which he sat on a number of foundation and corporate Boards, in many instances as their first Latino Director. They included, among others, The Rockefeller Foundation, the San Francisco Foundation, The California Endowment, The Dole Foundation, The Hogg Foundation, and the National Campaign for Human Development, as well as Union Bank, SBC Communications, and, by presidential appointment, the Student Loan Marketing Association. He also served as a U.S. Public Delegate to the 49th United Nations General Assembly, which started in 1994.

Leadership Lesson #2: A little bit of yeast leavens the whole dough

Gallegos's career as a social justice and civil rights activist began in 1952, when he began training under famed community organizers Saul Alinsky and Fred Ross Sr., who also trained labor leaders César Chávez, Gilbert Padilla, and Dolores Huerta. Ross used his famous "one-on-one" method of organizing, meeting with individuals one at a time to build trust and get to know each person on a personal level. This would be followed by small gatherings at people's homes, where they could talk about issues facing the community.

A new generation of community-based leaders began to organize Latinos in the barrios and colonias of California. In these areas, their impact is plainly visible today in the streetlights, paved streets, sidewalks, recreation centers, and robust business sectors—infrastructure that wasn't there in the early 1950s. But more important were the hundreds of community-based leaders, including Gallegos, who were trained and ready to take responsibility.

Gallegos was the first President, with Chávez as Vice President, of a social justice group that became the first chapter of the Los Angeles-based Community Service Organization (CSO), where Ross had worked a few years before. The new chapter was located in the East San Jose neighborhood known as Sal Si Puedes, which means "Get Out If You Can" in Spanish.

> *"By building trust and giving ordinary people the tools and training to get started, real movements organized for long-term power can go on to fight for responsible social change."*

With forty chapters statewide, CSO became a key player in passing civil rights legislation, fighting racial profiling by police, and carrying out unprecedented voter registration and get-out-the-vote campaigns among the rapidly increasing Mexican American and other Latino populations in California. In 1960, under Gallegos and Chávez's leadership and with the support of many other organizers, over 160,000 Latinos became first-time registered voters.

"By building trust and giving ordinary people the tools and training to get started, real movements organized for long-term power can go on to fight for responsible social change," Gallegos said. "A little bit of yeast leavens the whole dough."

Gallegos again put his community organizing experience to

good use when, in 1965, he was invited by the late Dr. Paul Ylvisaker, a prominent urban planner, to serve as a consultant to the Ford Foundation to make the case for supporting the rapidly growing Latino population in the United States, beginning with the Mexican and Mexican American populations in the Southwest. He was joined by labor activist Dr. Ernesto Galarza and scholar Dr. Julian Samora, the Latino Studies pioneer.

Their report to Ford led to an initial $638,000 grant to launch the Southwest Council of La Raza, which later expanded to become the National Council of La Raza and is now known as UnidosUS. During his three-year consultancy with Ford, Gallegos organized the new council and served as its founding Executive Director. For more than fifty years, the organization has supported Latino communities by promoting their economic, political, and social advancement through a network of nearly three hundred affiliated community organizations throughout the United States.

With support from the Ford Foundation, many important Latino institutions have been created, such as the Mexican American Legal Defense and Educational Fund (MALDEF), the preeminent Latino legal civil rights organization. The foundation not only gave generous financial support, but also greatly encouraged other foundations to open their doors to Latino causes.

Leadership Lesson #3: Be open to reconciliation

Early in his career, Gallegos learned the importance not only of calling out injustice, but also of being compassionate and open to reconciliation and dialogue.

When Gallegos was a child, his teenage brother was insulted by an employee of the local grocery store for his imperfect English. Their mother organized a boycott of the store and made them walk farther to buy their daily groceries elsewhere. After a year of carrying groceries up the hill and right past the front of their former store, the owner gave in. "She came over and cried and apologized, and they subsequently gave my brother a job," he said.

This lesson stayed with him: "As an organizer I've learned

that there's no such thing as a permanent enemy or a permanent friend." He also learned the power of nonviolent protest.

Years later, in 1974, he was elected to the Board of Directors of Pacific Telephone and Telegraph Company, which later merged with SBC Communications and eventually became AT&T. When Gallegos joined the Board, he found one Director, once heavily invested in corporate agribusiness and a powerful opponent of farmworker organizing, who refused to welcome him or even to shake his hand.

That Director knew of Gallegos's close association with farmworker activists, such as Galarza and Chávez, and likely perceived him as a firebrand, a radical, militant Chicano. The Director seemed to resent serving on a Board with someone regarded as "the enemy." But as they got to know each other through their work on various committees and at Board retreats, they began to see each other in a different light. They shared their insights regarding agribusiness and labor issues. They didn't change their respective positions, but they came to respect each other's right to disagree. From this experience, Gallegos learned that effective leadership is possible even where differences persist.

Serving on the Boards of large publicly traded corporations, such as SBC, was not without its challenges. Gallegos remained deeply rooted in the community from which he sprang, but he had a strong sense of duty to the corporate interests he was elected to serve. Some questioned his credentials, implying that he was there purely due to affirmative action and not on his own merits. Some employees initially thought he should act as a "Hispanic Director," there to solve the problems of Latino workers. "I didn't want to be pigeonholed as a constituent Director," Gallegos said. "I was there to do the same job as every other trustee," to represent the best interests of the company.

While he didn't hesitate to speak up on minority-group issues, he made it clear he expected others to do so as well. In time, he went on to enjoy strong support from Latino employees, as well as from other staff and officers at the corporations where he served.

At foundations, too, he experienced some challenges, though

for the most part he enjoyed great relationships with other trustees, with staff, and with other members of the leadership. Two CEOs made it clear that his questions were not welcome. They were looking only for someone to rubber stamp their ideas and policies. By that point, Gallegos had a great deal of experience as a Board member. He understood his role and responsibilities. "My response to each was, 'If there is a problem, it is not your job to jawbone a trustee.'" And he told both to take up any issue with the Chair, who could then communicate with him.

To others interested in Board service, he offered the words of the Rev. Martin Luther King Jr.: "There comes a time when one must take a position that is neither safe nor politic or popular, but he must take it because his conscience tells him it is right."

On the occasion of Gallegos's retirement from the SBC Board after thirty years, his fellow Director Carlos Slim called Gallegos the Cal Ripken Jr. of the Boardroom, after the Baltimore Orioles baseball player nicknamed "The Iron Man" who played in 2,632 consecutive games over twenty-one seasons, ending in September 1998. In his thirty years as Director, Gallegos never missed a Board or committee meeting.

Looking Forward: The Challenge to Reform Philanthropy

Gallegos encourages the philanthropic sector to turn its gaze inward and commit to meaningful change.

"Will foundations adopt transformational policies, or go back to the status quo and business as usual?"

Foundations "have an essentially elitist mechanism for accumulating and distributing tax-protected funds for the 'collective good,'" he said. "Will foundations adopt transformational policies, or go back to the status quo and business as usual?" Among the policies he hopes to see are increased transparency and accountability to the communities that are served, and for foundations to follow the wisdom of Ford Foundation President Darren Walker, who advises his colleagues "to go after inequality, not just its effects."

He suggests working with the Council on Foundations, progressive foundations, and community-based affinity groups to develop a framework for what real reform would look like. He said that his experience has shown that national commissions and incremental changes have not been sufficient. But the philanthropic sector needs to address what serving the public interest actually means; how Boards can become more responsive to grantees; and how to lessen the sense of ownership that foundation donors have been known to retain, to the detriment of its mission.

Gallegos notes that many organizations are leading the way for these changes, including Hispanics in Philanthropy, where he continues to serve as Emeritus Board Director, as well as the Council on Foundations, the Center for Effective Philanthropy, and networks representing other communities of color, such as the Association of Black Foundation Executives, Asian Americans/Pacific Islanders in Philanthropy, and Native Americans in Philanthropy. These organizations provide advocacy as well as on-ramps for communities to engage directly with philanthropy through mechanisms, such as giving circles and online giving communities. They make it easier for individuals to support their own communities and interests, rather than just relying on philanthropy.

He hopes that foundations will become more adventurous in their giving patterns, diversify their Boards and staff, and become more proactive in identifying and supporting grantees that represent diverse communities.

There's more work to be done, but foundations have an opportunity, Gallegos mused, to finally live up to their promise of serving as powerful catalysts for positive social change and to help solve the nation's ongoing struggle to become a more just, inclusive, equitable, multiracial, and multiethnic society.

4 IDENTITY
A FAMILY OF DIVERSE COMMUNITIES

HECTOR MUJICA

My personal story will resonate with many who have come into a Latino identity in the United States, although perhaps not for the most common reasons. I was born in Caracas, the capital of a country plagued by corruption, mismanagement, and a complete disregard for democratic principles. But if you backtracked thirty years, you would see that Venezuela was once one of the most prosperous South American nations.

Unlike so many Latin American immigrants, I got off to a very good start, having the privilege of coming from an upper middle-class Caucasian (read: White-passing) family in Venezuela. My parents, both college educated, enjoyed a status and degree of privilege that ultimately facilitated their transition to the United States. My dad had the foresight to study computer engineering at Universidad Simón Bolívar, one of the best universities in Venezuela. After hard work and a flourishing career in Caracas, he landed a senior management role in a U.S.-based tech company. That led to my family's eventual immigration to Miami, thanks to a visa acquired with the backing of his Fortune 500 employer. Our move happened right in the nick of time, just before Hugo Chávez was elected president of Venezuela in 1998. My mom, on the other hand, dedicated herself full time to raising three kids. Never underestimate the privilege of having a parent by your side while growing up, particularly to help you navigate the nuances of a new culture, new language, and the many wonders of a new home. These were a set of privileges not many Latinos or immigrant families have, and one that set us on a path toward opportunity.

In the United States, my parents had a network of friends who helped orient them upon arrival, which led us to move to an enclave that was half Latin America and half the United States: a city just under an hour north of Miami called Weston. It is endearingly known as "Westonzuela" because of the high density of the Venezuelan American community there. Moving at a young age and growing up in Weston gave me a highly unusual experience. I got to attend an elementary school where more than two out of every three students were Latin American.[1] My entire community, peer group, and family group were Spanish speakers who had a similar origin story to mine.

Although I was among people who looked like me and came from a similar place, I still had to deal with self- and societally induced pressures to assimilate. I wanted to quickly learn English and felt an urgency to minimize my accent and adapt to the new social norms. These included what to wear, which music to listen to, and what hobbies to pursue. I recall even asking my mom to stop including *arepas* in my lunch. Instead, I opted for Lunchables and Capri-Sun to fit in with my new peers.

Assimilation is a powerful concept. It sets the bar high, usually positioning White, Eurocentric culture as the standard to aspire to. Integration is key to belonging to the dominant culture. This process brings many benefits, such as "fitting in," but also comes at great cost, such as risking the loss of your cultural authenticity.

It wasn't until much later in life that I had the opportunity to reflect on those days and how hard it is to belong when you are different. And, when it's hard to belong, you'll do anything within your power to do just that. I had to constantly navigate this new context and make judgment calls about which spaces were safe to be my authentic self in, and in which spaces I had to camouflage myself, according to how I was expected to show up. I had to straddle two worlds: a familial one, and the one that expected me to be something I did not yet understand—all while being one of the more fortunate U.S. immigrants, one who got to grow up in a Latin American enclave. My process of adapting would have been considerably more difficult had my dad's new job been in a state like Alabama, instead of South Florida.

The extent of my assimilation was curtailed through my undergraduate days, which were spent surrounded by people who were largely similar to me and in places comfortable to me. I attended Florida International University (FIU), which had a student population that was 64 percent Latino.[2] In many ways, my surroundings positioned me to believe I was living in a post-racial America. But this would shortly change.

After FIU, I landed a job at Google, and I moved to Northern California in late 2011. I ended up in one of the few coveted roles at Google.org, being a rare Latino voice at the tech giant's multimillion-dollar philanthropic arm. There, I had the opportunity to look after our work in Latin America, as well as help kick-start efforts more focused on U.S. Latinos. This presented a peculiar view into understanding the Latin American and U.S. Latino context and brought me close to the narratives and experiences of the most marginalized.

It wasn't until I left Florida that I started to realize that I had been living in a trance, unaware of what other Latino experiences were like. I went from my privileged South Florida paradigm, with a certain type of Latinos more often coming from South America and the Caribbean, to the Bay Area, where the majority of Latinos are of Mexican and Central American descent. Their story was different from mine. They had experienced discrimination and exclusion—and these were the Latinos who had landed a job at Google and made up less than 4 percent of its workforce.[3]

Although we shared the same ethnic brand, we had very different definitions and understandings of what the Latino community was or should be. I was at a crossroads: was I a Caucasian Venezuelan American, and by extension Latino, as I had seen myself in Florida, or a Brown Latino, as people were seeing me in California?

This identity crisis happens quite often in the Latino community, whether it be light-skinned Latinos who are not Brown enough, or Latinos who are not fluent enough in Spanish, or who don't play soccer or don't dance salsa enough. It became a real-world lesson on the nuances of belonging and othering.

It forced me to expand my definition of "we," creating room for people whose belonging experiences had been much more complicated and significantly less welcoming than mine. Over time, I became familiar with the story of the West Coast Latino community. In doing so, I became more deeply intimate with the legacy of activist icons, such as labor stalwart César Chávez and the farmworkers movement, cultural icons, such as Frida Kahlo and Selena, and programs like the Braceros (a controversial 1942–1964 U.S. government-supported Mexican farmworker program that led to labor abuses). I began to more intimately grasp the depth of the Latino experience and the richness of our collective history, which expanded beyond the East Coast realities that were often influenced by Caribbean or South American origins. I also became aware of and increasingly empathetic toward the plight that Mexicans and Central Americans faced in their migration stories.

These were narratives that had always been a continent away from the comforts of my ethnic-majority bubbles in South Florida. These experiences also guided me to understand the Latino community through the lens that I view it today.

Latino Identity Unpacked

The Latino identity is one that is adopted by new immigrants and handed down to generations of Americans. It is also an identity that is based on ethnic background and physical appearance. It is hard to imagine that millions of people coming from dozens of unique and distinct countries, with intersecting identities, such as race, gender, and others, would quickly adopt a new identity and behave and reason as a unified community. In fact, when you expect Latinos to be politically aligned and share perspectives with every other Spanish-speaking country, you reduce millions of unique people to the identity of one European colonizer. Whether one uses Latino, U.S. Hispanic, Latinx, or Latine, it is a broad-stroked term of convenience that lacks depth. Even so, the Latino identity is a way for "people to find commonality," as Dr. Manuel Pastor, professor of sociology and American studies and ethnicity at the University of Southern California, described it for me. Although fragmentation offers a challenge, Hispanic communities have more in common than they have differences, and these commonalities will help strengthen America moving forward.

First, let's look at a snapshot of Hispanic-origin people from 2019 Pew Research Center reports, which were based on the U.S. Census 2017 American Community Surveys:

- 70 percent over five years old are proficient in English, while Spanish use is slowly declining. Spaniards, Panamanians, and Puerto Ricans have the highest English proficiency rates.
- 79 percent were born in this country.
- 18.3 percent were living in poverty in 2017, compared with 13 percent for all Americans.

Although U.S. Latinos may not be one homogeneous, monolithic group, it is important for all of the United States that our strengths and assets, as well as our needs, be understood. That is why it is so important that we understand the layers of fragmentation in these varied communities.

I've come to understand that those who identify with these Latino labels tend to be fragmented primarily along three dimensions: race (including societal hierarchy), country of origin, and assimilation. I believe that each of the dimensions, once layered together, influences the lens through which we view our Latino identity and the way we interact with the realities of the United States.

RACE is often ignored but is incredibly relevant. *Americas Quarterly* estimated in 2015 that 40 percent of Latin America's population is Indigenous or Afro-descendant.[4] Latin America has not adequately grappled with a troubling, unjust past; one that involves a perverse history of colonization, slavery, and exploitation of both Afro-descendants and the Indigenous peoples of the Americas. Spanish colonists instituted a caste system across the region based on classification by racial purity. A nomenclature developed that included now-familiar terms, including *Mulatto*, to refer to people born of a White parent and a Black parent (a mixed-race person generally), and *Mestizo*, which traditionally referred to a person of European and Amerindian descent, as well as people with generally mixed ancestries. Sociologists at the University of California noted that this may have played out differently across the Latin American region. In some countries, the less than completely Black or Indigenous combination represented by Mestizaje was embraced to lessen racial divides, but in most, it was almost entirely rejected.[5]

"The widespread denial of systematic disadvantage suffered by racial and ethnic minorities is [an] important mechanism through which ... Mestizaje retarded ethnoracial mobilization and antiracism policy [in Latin America]," the UC researchers said.[6] These realities have prevented the reckoning in Latin America that would be comparable to that seen in the United States, starting in the 1950s with the civil rights movement and with today's Black Lives Matter movement.

This racial structure has also created a socioeconomic divide that is reflected in the class structures of the region. In most Latin American countries, economic inequality often breaks along ethnic and racial lines. According to the World Bank, Afro-descendants account for about one-quarter of Latin America's population, are overrepresented among the poor in every country in the region and are two-and-a-half times more likely to live in chronic poverty than are Whites or Mestizos.[7] This feeds into racialized identities in the region and the norms that accompany them. In Latin American culture, for example, it is socially acceptable in many places to resort to generalizations in referring to anyone of Afro descent as "El Negro" (the Black one), people of any Asian origin as "El Chino" (the Chinese), and so on.

My Caucasian family in Venezuela benefited—unconsciously—from a measure of privilege resulting from living in a society with an unspoken racial hierarchy, similar to if not more explicit than that with which the United States is still wrestling. My family was White passing, and in a Venezuelan context, my family was considered to be White. In these hierarchies, the most fair-skinned, tallest, most European-apparent Latin Americans often dominate the highest ranks of society, and the Afro-descendants—or, even lower in the hierarchy, the Indigenous descendants—often are relegated to the ranks of the most marginalized. This privileging of light skin over dark is at the root of an evil known as colorism. These dynamics spill over into the United States through immigration and reinforce racist norms evident within some sectors of the Latino identity.

Dr. Carmen Rojas, a Latina and colleague in philanthropy, reflected on how this reality has shown up in her life. "White supremacy is a sickness that has affected us all. It has infected everyone," said Rojas, who is the President and CEO of the Marguerite Casey Foundation. "The way it shows up for Latinos is as a desire to increase proximity towards Whiteness and against Blackness. Against Indigeneity." She talked about how her father used to always share that his great-great-great-grandparents hailed from Spain, a claim that light-skinned people of Latino origin sometimes use to secure some of that European whiteness.

We need to get better about talking about race and racial justice in our community," she added. "We think, because we are Latino, we are exempt from this conversation, and the truth is: We are not."

In a U.S. context, the lighter-skinned Latinos often break with the darker-skinned Latinos, narrowing the "us" and creating a "them." A light-skinned Latino, accustomed to perching higher in the social hierarchy in the country of origin, may take a demotion when migrating from an upper-class life in Latin America to a middle-class life as a U.S. Latino. Individuals in this category often benchmark their livelihoods against upper-middle-class White Americans and adopt an "I don't have it as good as White people" mentality. However, previously marginalized Latino immigrants (read: darker-skinned Latinos) may come to the United States with an "I have it so much better here than back where I come from" mentality. These paradigms inform perceptions, and those perceptions create reality.

The murder of George Floyd catapulted the United States into a racial reckoning that has forced the establishment to confront inconvenient realities about the state of inequality and the systems of perpetual oppression that exist in our status quo. In many ways, this is also a time for the Latino communities to reflect on our actions and inactions toward others in and out of our own area, whether in explicit or complicit behaviors.

"Our reckoning is with ourselves, with our own cultures, with our own identities," Mary Skelton Roberts, a philanthropy peer and Afro Latina, said when sharing perspectives about oppression in the Latino community. "We must stand in solidarity because we've also been the perpetrators of oppression." This truth, that as an identity group we are both responsible for the systems of oppression as well as among the oppressed, is one that needs to be acknowledged before we can continue to move forward.

The **COUNTRY OF ORIGIN** also becomes a hindrance in collective belonging and identity. The larger Caucasian populations in some South American countries, such as Chile, Argentina, and Uruguay, often have greater access to opportunity and generally stronger economies. In contrast, El Salvador, Honduras, Nicaragua, and Panama are majority Mestizo, and a large portion of Central America's population is Indigenous or Mestizo. These smaller countries tend to have fewer opportunities and weaker economies. This is not to say that race is the only relevant factor in socioeconomic outcomes, but it would be naive to say it plays no role.

Latinos originate from over thirty countries, each with its

own accents, customs, role models, and nuanced contexts. About 62 percent of Latinos in the United States are of Mexican descent, and more than half of the Mexican American population lives in Texas and California.

When speaking about her identity, Skelton Roberts—Senior Vice President of Programs at the Energy Foundation and Chair of Hispanics in Philanthropy—shared that she is "first and foremost *cubana*," or American Cuban, and that her Black identity, not to mention Latino identity, did not come into play until she went through a deeper self-reckoning over time. "*'Latino' inicialmente para mí no significaba cubana. Era para los mexicanos y los latinoamericanos*," she said, based on the history of the term, which was initially and predominantly used by Mexican Americans in referring to people in the United States, as well as Latin Americans generally. Dr. Pastor also reflected on a similar experience, having been born in New York to working-class Cuban parents and growing up among Mexican Americans in Los Angeles. He recalled that, at first, he had a hard time fitting in, since the dominant definition of Latino in Southern California was Chicano, and he was an outsider to that specific experience. Now, as an adult and an academic, he challenged me in our conversations with a frequent question: "What is a Latino, anyway?"

Perspectives such as these are not isolated. According to the Pew Research Center, 51 percent of Latinos preferred to identify with their families' country of origin, while only 24 percent preferred the term *Hispanic* or *Latino*.[8] This leads to drastically different lived experiences that can completely alter our understanding of each other's realities and even our ability to empathize with alternate journeys, again creating a narrower "we."

Contrast that with the experience of someone like Dr. Rojas, who is half Nicaraguan, half Venezuelan, and was born and raised in California. She describes her experience in California, where "there doesn't seem to be a geographical imagination beyond Mexico." She embraced the Mexican American cultural experience, which helped her embrace the Latino identity as a whole.

Later in her life, after encountering Indigenous Latinos more closely, she began to really challenge the concept of identity.

"What are the parts of us that we leave behind because we are Latino in this country?" she wondered. "There is a spectrum of things that make us Latino, and the identity demands that we embrace all of those things. But, in reality, it's demanding that we deny our origin identity."

Another way this dimension shows up in the Latino identity and community is in political ideology. Members of my family, having seen firsthand the impact of a socialist leader succumbing to corruption and associating that with socialism, have an extremely difficult time voting for left-of-center candidates in the U.S. political system. This situation happens frequently with American families who hail from Venezuela, Cuba, and Nicaragua, among others. According to Pew, nationwide in 2012, 58 percent of registered voters of Cuban origin said they affiliated with or leaned toward the Republican Party, as opposed to around 65 percent of Latino voters (non-Cuban) who leaned Democratic. Similar trends were seen with Venezuelan American communities, indicating a country-of-origin pattern.

Lastly, we have **ASSIMILATION.** The longer Latino families have lived in the United States, the more likely their members are to disengage from their Latino identity. The closer Latinos are to their immigrant roots, the more likely they are to identify as Latino. At least one study found that, by the third and fourth generations, the self-identification diminishes significantly, and assimilation of local norms and culture dominates the remaining identity. A blanket "American" identity, rather than a Latino or country-of-origin identity, emerges with each passing generation, according to the Pew Research Center.[9]

A similar trend happens with language. A 2017 study showed this progression: 61 percent of immigrants from Latin America were Spanish dominant; 6 percent of the second generation were Spanish dominant, and none of the third generation was Spanish dominant.[10] According to the same analysis, young Latinos

born in the United States were less likely to understand and identify with their Latino heritage, compared with older individuals,
immigrants, and first-generation Americans. Dr. Pastor said that,
in his high school Spanish classes, he would go back and mark a
few exam answers wrong because he didn't want to "be the one
to get all the answers right because I had Spanish from home.
There was lots of internalized racism pushing me toward greater language assimilation," he recalled. That was something I too
remember doing in my high school Spanish classes. Now, integration is not in itself a bad thing. It is part of the organic process of
adaptation. But we must be aware of these processes, which can
dilute the cultural strength of a Latino identity.

I have historically identified as a Spanish-fluent Latino and a
Venezuelan American (versus just a Latino), as White passing,
as an immigrant, as a Caucasian Latino, and as a member of the
middle class, cis male and heterosexual. All of these dimensions
build to the way that Latinos engage with their identity, and this
fragmentation makes it difficult to find cohesion and common
ground from which to move forward.

A Unifying Path

It is important for Latino groups in the United States to reconcile some of their differences, leave their dimensional silos, and
embrace common goals. We can achieve so much more politically,
educationally, and socioeconomically not only for Latino communities but the United States as a whole. To a large extent, by
sheer numbers, we are the future, and it will be up to us to power
the United States ahead.

To get to a place of common ground, we must acknowledge
some truths. I've come to understand three truths about Latinos
that are important to evaluate, particularly if we hope to change
the national narrative and stereotypical perceptions about American Latinos.

All Latinos are not created equal. This is actually a half-truth.

I agree with the U.S. Declaration of Independence's statement that "all men are created equal." But I mean that not all Latinos can be lumped into mass generalizations and equal sets of expectations. Latino lived experience shapes the lens through which we see the world, and there are dimensions that often shape the bend of that lens. If you've come from a socialist-leaning country, say Kirchner's Argentina, Chávez's Venezuela, or Castro's Cuba, your lived experience may make you apprehensive toward anything on the left side of the political spectrum. If you are of Afro descent, your experience with identity, power, and belonging is vastly different from those of people perceived to be White.

Whether from an upper-class neighborhood like Weston, a middle-class community like Washington Heights, New York, or a working-class barrio in East Los Angeles, no Latino experience should be dismissed. Experience molds Latinos to have different outlooks and perspectives. Keeping in mind others' backgrounds is imperative. Without it, we have a tendency to paint people with too broad a stroke. Generalizations are often inaccurate and divisive.

Latino, whether you want it or not. Regardless of the status held in one's country of origin, your racial heritage, your societal pedigree, and your family's immigration story, in the United States you are a Latino, with all the baggage and stereotypes that this classification carries, as well as all the power, strength, and grit this label personifies. Like it or not, we are viewed as one collective Latino community. And when we, as a community, view ourselves as the complex, unique individuals that we are, we can start to own this reality and fully flex into it. This is not to imply Latinos should not have pride in their country of origin. I am a proud Venezuelan American, but I am a Latino first.

In the book *The Righteous Mind: Why Good People Are Divided by Politics and Religion*, social psychologist Jonathan Haidt speaks about this innate concept of community building: "[The] ethic of community is based on the idea that people are, first and foremost, members of larger entities such as families, teams, armies, companies, tribes, and nations," he wrote. "These larger entities are more than the sum of the people who compose them; they are real, they matter, and they must be protected." That, of course, includes ethnic groups such as the Latino community. But these groupings don't come for free.

"People have an obligation to play their assigned roles in these entities. Many societies therefore develop moral concepts such as duty, hierarchy, respect, reputation, and patriotism," Haidt added. I would argue everyone coming from a Latin American background should, as a result, play a role in advancing the community and helping to rewrite the existing narrative so that it is inclusive of the diversity of the whole.

The Latino identity is an asset, not a liability. The Latino identity brings immense value to American society. Latinos are invested in their families, often with financial obligations to serve as supplemental breadwinners to their extended families, both domestically and in their country of origin through remittances. Latinos keep the pulse of their country of origin while engaging with the realities of their current home. It is a dual identity, a transnational identity. Embracing the duality of our belonging positions us to be cultural diplomats, enabling us to bridge cultural divides and helping us deal with our day-to-day lives.

Latinos, like many other multicultural groups, possess the ability to become expert navigators of difference and retain an innate ability to switch between worlds. This code-and-decode process helps us develop a cognitive advantage, an advantage that must be celebrated.

More can unite us than separates us, if we let it. Understanding how we are different and embracing those traits is how we stop othering from happening; we must start to see individual groups of Latinos as uniquely valuable, rather than intimidating or different. The Latino identity, with all of its nuances, has ample space for common ground, such as recognizing shared lived experience, acknowledging common cultural ties, and creating pathways toward unity through empathy.

Latinos only stand to benefit from strength in numbers to build true power, whether economic, political, and improved community, national, and transnational well-being. Leaning into the reality of our nuanced identities, viewing ourselves as part of a collective, and acknowledging the strengths we bring to the table will facilitate our strategies moving forward.

The High Road Is More Inclusive

If we could unlock a nuanced approach toward unifying Latinos, the implications would be tremendous. A majority of the Latino population in the United States is concentrated in the West and Southwest, with Mexicans making up some of the largest populations of Latinos in California, Arizona, New Mexico, and Texas, followed by the Northeast, with its concentrations of Puerto Ricans and Dominicans, and South Florida, with its mix of Andean and Caribbean populations. The regional reach, combined with the growing national economic activity of the community—estimated in a 2015 Congressional report at a combined $1.3 trillion[11]—shows promise for greater influence and participation.

Let's examine a few tactics that I recommend:

Increase belonging. A 2018 Pew Research Center study found that about half (49 percent) of Latinos expressed serious concerns about their place in America, with the number increasing if we look at just foreign-born Latinos (57 percent).[12] This sense of belonging was alarmingly low, and the proportion of those with serious concerns about their place in America was higher (41 percent) than reported by Latinos who had been surveyed eighteen months earlier, in January 2017, prior to the Trump administration's taking office.

Shifting the narrative to celebrate the diversity of the community, rather than oversimplifying the U.S. Latino experience, is imperative. There is no such thing as the "Latino culture" or the "Latino vote." *Latino* represents a diverse group racially, culturally, socioeconomically, and by origin. By acknowledging Latino diversity, one can avoid the erroneous assumption of equitable starting points, which encourages a mentality of: "If I could do it, you should be able to do it, too."

Through bridging we create space for belonging, as we are reminded by professor john a. powell, who leads the University of California, Berkeley, Othering & Belonging Institute. We need more bridges within the Latino community, which will by extension create a greater sense of belonging.

Get close. Our elected officials, whether they are Latino or not, need to show up for the community in tangible and meaningful ways. At the end of the day, Latinos, just like everyone else, are pursuing dignity and opportunity. They appreciate the authenticity of people who work for the common good and show an interest in their personal welfare. As Venezuelan Americans, people in my family equate the destructive work of the post-millennium Venezuelan government with socialism, and socialism, in turn, with Democrats. However, my family members consistently vote for the former National Democratic Committee Chair, U.S. Representative Debbie Wasserman Schultz. They are pleased to help send her back to Congress every two years. They do so because of a personal connection: I spent two years working with her and came to understand that she genuinely cares for the Venezuelan American community.

Technology as a tool to unify. In his 2015 book, *Geek Heresy: Rescuing Social Change from the Cult of Technology*, Kentaro Toyama speaks about technology as not being a solution in and of itself, but an amplifier. Amplifying tools can amplify bad practices, as well as good solutions. I am optimistic about technology. In today's Digital Age, two-thirds of Latinos are on social media, and 74 percent of Latinos said they regularly use the internet in some capacity.[13] The use of technology in the community helps to build bridges with countries of origin, keeping Latinos engaged and actively straddling both worlds. In my family's case, being able to remain connected with Venezuela has been essential for their peace of mind and also for their ability to organize, share resources, and ensure a level of accountability.

Domestically, technology also plays a community-building role. The reach of digital platforms across Latino communities presents an opportunity to leverage tech to build empathy, understanding, and connection. Technology can be used not only as a medium to understand one another and the nuances of our journeys, but also as a practical tool to help share narratives that shift perceptions and increase belonging. We have started to see trends through video platforms. They have allowed content creators to share their stories, elevating, acknowledging, and celebrating cultural nuances across Latino enclaves, all in an effort to increase cultural understanding. These tools also help amplify the birth of movements, such as the spotlight put on the separation of families and detention of children by the U.S. Border Patrol through the hashtag #nokidsincages.

Be ruthlessly pragmatic. Seeing people and situations up close can break even the strongest bias. But, beyond proximity, I believe that it is critical to appeal to issues that matter to all Latinos, not just segments of Latinos. This requires a certain level of pragmatism and objectivity, while having a deep understanding of the tradeoffs.

This also requires elevating the conversation to find commonalities that the collective community can stand behind, such as ensuring dignity and respect for all Latinos, seeking pathways to opportunity, and instituting sensible and fair immigration practices. If we are pragmatic in our collaboration and keep collective power building in mind, we can attain our immediate goals and more.

This exercise should create space for dissenting ideas, resolutions through dialogue, and eventual power through institutional coalition building. Latinos must focus on building institutional power that can transcend liberal and conservative points of view.

Understand that we all have a role to play. The solution to the lack of Latino cohesion and community starts with each person who identifies as Latino, but it doesn't end there. By making conditions better for Latinos, you are lifting up all racial minorities that identify as Latino, as well as those who don't. This is also not a turn-key solution. The solution is as complex and multifaceted as Latinos are.

It is time for the Latino community to place collective action ahead of partisan politics. Commonly shared Latino values could be and should be essential in the design of public policy, in the planning of communities, in the development of an educational curriculum that celebrates and dignifies Latino contributions, in health systems that optimize addressing Latino needs and health challenges, and in creating economic opportunity systems that provide the right pathways and safety nets to meet the community where it is.

Looking Ahead

It is a given that key U.S. Latino values include family, opportunity, culture, and identification with multiple groups. Furthermore, findings from a late 2019 marketing survey[14] of 1,069 U.S. Latinos also reinforce some of these and other values that I have been discussing:

Identity. Of respondents, 84 percent described their culture as a mixture of Hispanic and American cultures. (Pew Research results showed 54 percent of Latinos surveyed[15] said that traditions, celebrations, and holidays make them feel connected to Hispanic culture.)

Family connections. Almost two-thirds (64 percent) of respondents use social media to maintain ties with family and friends.

Belonging. Two-thirds (66 percent) pay attention to bilingual ad campaigns that reflect Latine experience.[16] Acknowledging these values can help create a roadmap of opportunities that are more responsive to the broad needs of Latinos and, by extension, peer communities with like-minded, broad, and nonpartisan values.

As Latinos, we have a responsibility to help shape and develop a world that is responsive to our needs, yet we often fall short. One example would be the two separate legislative caucuses in Congress. The older and larger Congressional Hispanic Caucus serves exclusively Democrats, while the Congressional Hispanic Conference serves exclusively Republicans. Their separation leaves little room for collaboration or the development of bipartisan ideas; it creates an ideological echo chamber, leaving no room for practical, pragmatic solutions. Failing to see anything good on the other side makes dialogue impossible.

I am optimistic that we'll see increasing numbers of Latino candidates in future elections, and that they will lean into platforms centered on the nuanced Latino experience. They will include candidates who can bridge and help straddle dual realities and talk foreign policy to both Cuban Americans seeking regime change back home and Mexican Americans and Central Americans seeking stability and peace, rather than drug cartel power plays and violence. I envision a future where Latinos—as well as all groups that make up the mosaic of America—are proportionately represented, and everyone enjoys the same rights. In this future, children are not placed in cages, Latin American foreign policy is a keystone, not an afterthought, and all Latinos have equitable access to upward mobility and opportunity.

This future is possible. As a community, we have made strides. Just as people from many different Latin American roots have adopted the Latino identity, I am confident that the future holds a better-represented, more understood, and more prosperous Latino community. To advance, we must appeal to that very sense of collective community and shared humanity—as Latinos and Americans. We all must employ strategies that allow us to understand and respect one another, while also having the resolve and dignity to seek common ground and collective action.

"You need to be cautious about the past being a predictor of the future," Dr. Pastor warned me. "Would we have predicted thirty years ago that there would be coherence around a Latino

identity? That so many groups could feel included and represented
in it? Would we have predicted that Latin culture would be mainstream? That Latino identity would show up in unexpected ways
in how we define ourselves? Probably not, but here we are." This
reaffirmed in me that change is possible, and not only possible but
within reach.

Having been exposed to many of the realities and lived experiences of my fellow Latinos, I now fully embrace my Latino identity as an integral part of who I am. I have grown to understand
the value in my own unique experience and my heritage, and I
have striven to retain my authenticity and take pride in it.

Latinos are diverse, with different trajectories and backgrounds,
different political ideologies, and a full spectrum of socioeconomic realities. But there are points of commonality, obvious ones like
a shared language, culture, and heritage, and the more subtle,
such as shared grit, hustle, entrepreneurial ability, and tendency
to favor the collective, whether it be one's family and extended
family or one's larger community.

I am not intending to only suggest how the Latino community
can achieve unity; it is also a formula for broader society to engage
with Latinos. Having a nuanced understanding will help with
how our community is addressed, portrayed, and perceived, and
with how brands, politicians, and individuals interact with us. It
can take what is an often misunderstood and stereotyped group
and make it a more fully understood part of American society.

Latinos have long been portrayed as a sleeping giant. Such a
giant is a myth. The Latino community is made up of many individual parts, with histories that have been molded by time, by
assumptions, and by a colorful and at times tragic past. Solidarity,
respectful disagreement, and collective endurance—traits integral to the idea of community—are possible for Latinos. As long
as our focus is on our differences, we will struggle to find collective power. If we instead place more emphasis on our similarities,
the possibilities are endless.

The events of the coronavirus pandemic reminded us that we

belong to each other and are interconnected and interdependent. Just like so many other Americans, we are nearly all descendants of pioneers, of migrants who took risks and traveled to make a new home in a new place. Latinos are a group that thinks globally, understands intersectionality, has an entrepreneurial spirit, and is constantly finding ways to progress. If we work toward greater understanding of this complex identity, we can, perhaps, unlock our collective voice and together lift ourselves and this country.

PART II

WOMEN'S ISSUES ARE OUR FUTURE

5 DOMESTIC VIOLENCE
AGAINST ABUSE IN LATIN AMERICA AND IN THE UNITED STATES

ANJANETTE DELGADO

They were everywhere, the women. A multicolored throng of flesh dressed in pink tank tops, leopard-printed bike shorts, and strappy red sundresses, the hues themselves defiant, the protesters unconcerned with showing skin—a message to the patriarchy that there is no garment or behavior that makes a woman culpable for abuse perpetrated against *her*. The only uniform? A piece of black gauze. A makeshift blindfold to wear while chanting, squatting, and shuffling from side to side in formation. A line dance of a protest for women everywhere. From Paris and Berlin to Mexico City and Buenos Aires, and from New York City to Istanbul, where repression of the protesters was all but assured, the women chanted, loudly, row after row pointing straight ahead and denouncing:

El violador eres tú (The rapist is you), followed by:
Son los pacos . . .
   It's the cops . . .
Los jueces . . .
   The judges . . .
El Sistema . . .
   The system . . .
El presidente . . .
   The president . . .

And later,
El estado opresor es un macho violador
   The oppressive state is a rapist *macho.*

"Un violador en tu camino" ("A Rapist in Your Path") was sung for the first time during a flash mob in Valparaiso, Chile, on November 20, 2019. By the end of 2020, millions of women in over two hundred cities had performed the feminist anthem against gender violence created by the Chilean collective Las Tesis and based on the work of Argentine and Brazilian feminist anthropologist Rita Laura Segato, perhaps best known for her research on the relationship between gender violence, racism, and colonialism. And though the song is clearly decrying all violence against women, and rape in particular, those verses apply to no other form of gender violence as much as they do to the domestic kind, where the government's complicity is clear, brazen, and often institutionalized in ways big, small, and always breathtaking. Which government, you ask? Every last damn one of them, is the only possible answer.

Because it is that precision, that nuance, that is *the* skill used to infuse public messaging with patriarchal codes of behavior in every context of our lives that counts. It is in this nuanced way of appearing to help, but not really, that "the system" (another word for the uneven partnership between government and civil society) walks the tightropes of public opinion (playing them like Yo-Yo Ma plays a Montagnana cello), acting as if it were effectively condemning intimate-partner violence while allowing it to continue unchecked. Even worse, it can be weakly checked—left safe as the law of the global land year after year and decade after decade, all of it made worse since the onset of the COVID-19 pandemic, which has reversed the many years of gains made by antiviolence activists worldwide.

Yes, the system is powerful and slow to change. But we, individually and collectively, can turn it around. We can take action to transform our societies until domestic abuse becomes an exceedingly rare aberration.

And you may ask, "Well, isn't that what has been done?" Yes, and no. A good job has been done publicizing the horrifying numbers and making them available to those who want to help.

THE U.S. BY THE NUMBERS[1]

24 people per minute, on average, are physically abused by an intimate partner in this country alone. In the course of one year, this equates to more than 10 million women and men.

1 in 7 victims/survivors who contacted the two national hotlines in 2014 and 2015 were Latinas.

1 in 4 women and 1 in 9 men experience severe intimate-partner physical violence, intimate-partner sexual violence, and/or intimate-partner stalking.

1 in 3 women and 1 in 4 men have experienced some form of physical violence by an intimate partner. This includes a range of behaviors (e.g., slapping, shoving, pushing) that may or may not be considered "domestic violence."

1 in 7 women and 1 in 25 men have been injured by an intimate partner.

1 in 10 women have been raped by an intimate partner. Data is unavailable on male victims.

1 in 4 women and 1 in 7 men have been victims of severe physical violence (e.g., beating, burning, strangling) by an intimate partner in their lifetime.

1 in 7 women and 1 in 18 men have been stalked by an intimate partner during their lifetime to the point where they felt very fearful or believed that they or someone close to them would be harmed or killed.

More than 20,000 phone calls are placed to domestic violence hotlines nationwide on a typical day.

15 percent of all violent crime involves intimate-partner violence.

72 percent of all murder-suicides involve an intimate partner; 94 percent of the victims of these murder-suicides are female.

1 in 15 children are exposed to intimate-partner violence each year, and 90 percent of these children are eyewitnesses to this violence.

Decades have passed since a World Health Organization (WHO) report found intimate partners visiting sexual violence on nearly one in four women.[2] This includes 23 percent in Guadalajara, Mexico, 22.5 percent in Lima, Peru, and 23 percent in Leon, Nicaragua. When data were available, WHO researchers found, "sexual assault by an intimate partner is neither rare nor unique to any particular region of the world."

How is this possible? How do we live in advanced, rich, educated societies in which women and girls are brutalized at a rate higher than that at which they die of illnesses, such as diabetes, heart disease, and even cancer? How are we capable of systematically turning our backs on behavior defined to encompass "wife abuse, sexual assault, dowry-related murder, marital rape, selective malnourishment of female children, forced prostitution, female genital mutilation, and sexual abuse of female children," as well as "any act of verbal or physical force, coercion or life-threatening deprivation, directed at an individual woman or girl that causes physical or psychological harm, humiliation, or arbitrary deprivation of liberty and that perpetuates female subordination" in the Cadernos de Saúde Pública published since 1985 by the Sergio Arauca National School of Public Health and the Oswaldo Cruz Foundation in Río de Janeiro, Brazil?

To complete the full picture of what we are dealing with, I would add sexual harassment at work to the degree to which workplaces strive to become a familial home of sorts, with "team player" responsibilities, parental figures (bosses) we obey and trust and need for our survival, as well as peer relationships that extend outside the workplace and play an important role in women's health, quality of life, and self-esteem.

Intimate partners killed 78 percent of the women murdered in U.S. workplaces by a personal relation between 2003 and 2008, according to a National Institutes of Health study.[3] Homicides by personal relations ranked second only to robberies and similar crimes for women's workplace homicides.[4]

Now, maybe, it is complete, this picture of intimate part-

ner plague that kills a third of the women who were intentionally murdered everywhere in the world in 2017, according to the
United Nations Office on Drugs and Crime.[5] This is the story of
violence that belongs to all of us, one as pervasive, severe, and
insanely, obscenely, varied as it is resilient. Resilient beyond belief.

And why? What set of factors protects it, ensures its perpetuity
and deep, awful reach in the world

> *Son los pacos . . .*
>> It's the cops . . .
> *Los jueces . . .*
>> The judges . . .
> *El Sistema . . .*
>> The system . . .
> *El presidente . . .*
>> The president . . .

This is gender violence's not-so-secret weapon: the government's
decades-long (centuries-long, even?) star turn as an agent of the
patriarchy working to ensure that domestic violence—a term so
ubiquitous and euphemistic that the crime is often shrugged off
as unsolvable—accomplishes the most Machiavellian harm in
the spectrum of gender violence, being domestic (and thus, private?) oppression: consistent, multi-layered betrayal from within
the home and from the outside, by the system that fails to ensure
safety.

And does the system accomplish this by force? Oh, no. No. It
doesn't need to. For this, the right tool has always been a silken
tongue.

Governments' Magic Trick

In May 2020, as the COVID-19 pandemic raged across the world
and signs of its fatal consequences in Mexico became public, President Andrés Manuel López Obrador was unequivocal: 90 percent of all domestic violence calls for help to the country's 911

emergency assistance system were fake; exaggerations by women that amounted to little more than a collective prank. "It's been proven," he said—wearing his green, red, and white presidential sash—as he denied that quarantine had wreaked havoc in families whose foundations were built on the patriarchal "tradition" of entitled violence as a means to coerce submission.

He did not reveal what evidence he had for saying this, instead letting Mexicans believe that he must know something they didn't. After all, he was the president. But the only thing that was proven is that women across Mexico made more than 115,000 calls reporting violence to 911 in March 2020, when the quarantine was decreed, up 22 percent from that pre-quarantine February, according to the Spotlight Initiative. That number is, sadly, wholly credible.

The president chose to use the power of the government behind him to declare his view of life in Mexico under quarantine as the truth, a view not much different than pre-COVID life when, according to him, "there has always been harmonious cohabitation."

"The Mexican family is different from families in Europe and the United States; Mexicans are used to living together, being together," he added. "I'm not saying that there is not this confrontation in Mexico, of course there are differences in all families."

If you were an abused woman in Mexico when your president said that, you could be forgiven for thinking violence was normal, was accepted, and that you were wrong for "complaining" about the (one-sided) "confrontations" that tended to end with a man's fist crushing your face. Of course, by this reasoning, you're unfair for crying out against those "differences" within *your* family that could too easily land you in the hospital. The government tool used here? I call it patriarchal demagogy, psychological and cultural pressure from an overpowering source that shames less powerful citizens by accusing them, in most cases, of not telling the truth—portraying them as little more than children staging hurtful, unseemly pranks just to get attention.

El presidente . . .
The president . . .

Often-barbaric treatment had been normalized. The Women's Liberation Movement in no way "influenced" or created the "the issue," and it didn't have a hand in making it be seen as anything other than what it was: a damn shame.

When it comes to the government's response to domestic violence, messaging is often ignored in favor of solutions to concrete problems, such as lack of resources, policy, and laws, and maybe rightly so. But many countries have stringent laws against intimate-partner violence on the books. Little do they matter if, day in and day out, our children are exposed not only to the impunity and the messaging but to the violence. And they are.

Yet messaging is, indeed, as important for the husbands and wives of tomorrow as it is for those who would protect the abused, among others. We can help others realize what women, male allies, transgender, and other activists have long broadcast: tolerance for gender violence hurts us all. We can then inspire more writers, celebrities, and social media influencers, as well as public health authorities, to join the effort and add to the message's power. Imagine if victims of intimate-partner violence had the benefit of a multilingual National Ad Council campaign against the gender violence and domestic abuse that scars whole families, whether small or multigenerational, and models bad behavior for today's youngsters? What if we could rouse the talented creators of successful national campaigns like "Buzzed Driving Is Drunk Driving" and "Flu Vaccination" to help us open more eyes to this insidiously "private" problem, finally changing prevalent male attitudes of dominance

There are other things that most of us can do, despite societal pressures. Over time, notions harden. They become our reality. We become those people who believe it is wrong to come between a man and *his* wife, to meddle with the sacred privacy of a family, or, God forbid, get caught not minding our own business. And the abused woman (overwhelmingly, we are talking about women here) knows she will not be supported by the state. She knows there are laws, shelters, policemen. But are they there for her? Will

One of the reasons López Obrador's public comments were powerful was that they appeared spontaneous—not thought or intentional, making it harder to assign evil motives or strate intent to them. Things did not work out as well for the governm in Malaysia.

There, they introduced an ill-conceived plan: a series of onl posters advising the nation's women to help the country surv its COVID crisis by not nagging their husbands and refrain from "sarcasm" when asking for help with household chores. F tunately, because it was planned and public, their motives w undeniable, and the public backlash was swift when the dome violence numbers kept going up.

El Sistema . . .
      The system . . .

In the United States, we do not fare much better. Not only we elevate a predator to the highest elected office, but the fed government can still treat domestic violence outrageously w our tax dollars. The National Criminal Justice Reference Serv (NCJRS) has, since 1972, offered criminal justice and drug-rela information to "support research, policy, and program devel ment worldwide."

Before its content and services were moved in February 2 to the Office of Justice Programs website, the NCJRS "explain that domestic violence began to be understood as a criminal through the influence of the 1960s and 1970s Women's Liberat Movement.

This was blatantly enabling for prospective abusers and th who would ignore their duty to investigate, prosecute, and pro the victims. It is also misleading messaging that our taxes pay In the United States. In the country where, according to the *J nal of the American Medical Association*, "Women . . . are m likely to be assaulted and injured, raped or killed by a curren ex-male partner than all other assailants combined."

The NCJRS site ignored that, prior to feminism, women girls were subject to sexual abuse throughout recorded hist they protect her? If so, for how long? How effective can they be against an enemy who knows her intimately? Will they keep her in the life of her children if she files a complaint that she's unable to pursue against very bitter odds?

If the messaging a victim hears cannot convince her of that protection, she will, rightly, be unable to believe it herself. When the abuser strikes again, she will figure that she can manage it alone. She will "return to him." But does she really? Or does she choose the option that will kill her slowly, that will let her feed her children? The option that limits the risk to one source of danger, rather than face the unknowns of a system she doesn't understand?

Meanwhile, her "decision" convinces others in society (her friends, if she still has any, her family, strangers tempted to be good Samaritans) to "leave it be." After all, "if the woman will not leave when she has a chance, why should I put myself at risk to confront her abuser?"

That quote is taken from an account of the urban legend that exists in every culture. You know the one. The innocent bystander intercedes to defend a woman from a man who is beating her, only to be attacked by the woman herself, in defense of "her man." There must be thousands of variations of that story around the world. The subtext is that it is okay to not help a woman in this situation. After all, not only does she allow it, but she protects her aggressor.

These stories never recount the bystander interceding to save a child from an adult, stepping in to stop a human being three to five times bigger than a child from assaulting her in public, often under the guise of discipline.

This is how victims of abuse become isolated. The woman is betrayed by her culture, and by her government, by law enforcement, and by pop culture, then by the lover or husband, and finally, by her own friends and family. Ultimately, she doesn't see a reason not to betray herself. Where would she go? Where would she be safe? This is how abused women are coerced and enlisted to function as a co-enforcer, informant, middle manager, ally, and, sometimes, mediator on behalf of the oppressor and against their own self-interest.

Of course, once in a while, an institution gets it right. In April 2020, the United Nations called for urgent action to combat the worldwide surge in domestic violence. "I urge all governments to put women's safety first as they respond to the pandemic," Secretary-General António Guterres wrote on Twitter, putting the onus on governments, where it belongs—not on women, not on the pandemic. This, unfortunately, has not been a common occurrence.

The Beatles recorded "Run for Your Life," a Lennon-McCartney hit, in 1965, at the height of the Women's Liberation Movement, recognized all over the world as feminism's second wave.

"You never heard it?" I ask my mother, incredulous.

She smiles dolefully. "*No, mija. Es que eran otros tiempos.*"

It dawns on me later that what she means is that times were different for her. That she was only nineteen and pregnant with me. My father would beat her if she forgot to dust, wouldn't allow her to answer the door when someone knocked, or pick up the phone when it rang. He was a man who punched and kicked her down a steep stairway in her seventh month of pregnancy.

Later, we lived in Villa Carolina, Puerto Rico, a small *urbanización* with every house exactly the same that, more often than not, each housed a mother, a father, a couple of children. Now I know our house was different. In it, the radio was always turned off; the television turned low on mornings when my father slept; my sister and I always quiet. The only memorable soundtrack was my mother's pleas for him to stop hitting her, which filtered through the door of our bedroom at night. Sometimes all night. Ours was then a life of tension that knew relief only when he mercifully left the house for work. (Even on short errands, he took us along, keeping his eye on us at all times.)

It's why, while everyone rightly celebrated each new pandemic stay-at-home order, I shuddered, my childhood coming back to me like music wafting in from someone else's open window. Every time, it left me breathless, making me imagine every horror that could befall a woman like my mother, a child like me, or anyone else trapped with their violent tormentors for more than a couple of days at a time "for the foreseeable future," bereft of their one escape valve: their aggressor having to go to work, or leaving the house to blow off his (very rarely, her) never-ending steam.

I was right to worry. Within days of the first shelter-in-place pandemic orders, which made running for your life less of an option for millions of victims, the headlines all over the world were staggering:

"Women are using code words at pharmacies to escape domestic violence during lockdown"

(CNN, April 6, 2020, about measures taken
in Europe)

"Some cities see jumps in domestic violence during the pandemic"

(KPTV, Fox-12 in Oregon and CNN, April 4, 2020)

"Self-Quarantine Amid Coronavirus Pandemic Will Likely Lead to Increase in Domestic Violence, WHO Warns"

(CBS News, April 3, 2020)

"Aumentan casos de violencia de género durante cuarentena por el coronavirus"

(Univision, March 24, 2020, report from Puerto Rico)

"Coronavirus: Fourteen women murdered in Turkish homes since lockdown"

(Middle East Eye, April 2, 2020)

"Coronavirus Is Leaving Michigan's Domestic Violence
Survivors Alone with Their Abusers"

(The 'Gander, April 6, 2020)

Of course, abuse would have a universal language. Of course, governments would enable abusers everywhere by enabling them. Abusers took advantage of the quarantine, which allowed them to exert more control over their victims when there was a stigma to ignoring the call to "Stay the Fuck at Home."

Even those who would help were hampered by the pandemic. Mothers might have hesitated to go to a shelter for fear of putting their children at risk of the virus, especially when a recession had left so many without jobs and made it impossible to secretly stash away money to leave. And even fewer donations to organizations that help domestic violence survivors meant fewer resources for those seeking help, never mind the fear of becoming sick and leaving your children at the mercy of their abuser. All of those headlines were not the result of coronavirus. They were about things that happened in reaction to stories, both the ones we have been taught to tell ourselves, and the ones our governments are ever so adept at telling us.

Messaging or not, there are things we can and must do to change the story.

Make the laws we do have more effective, and the ones we don't have easier to achieve. Advocate for much needed public service campaigns to help victims stop their victimization and protect their children. Otherwise, all the laws in the world will not change a thing. And nothing will change. Not for us. Not for our children. Not for our grandkids.

Let's not leave it all up to the activists and advocates in and out of government, either. We can also help as individuals.

Let's provide timely information that can save their lives. Let's offer shelter, money, or food. Let's check in on friends we suspect might be facing violence at home. Let's not look the other way. Let's call, let's text, and, when we know the abuser is not around, let's send information, such as lists of shelters open in every state.

FREE AND CONFIDENTIAL RESOURCES
AGAINST INTIMATE-PARTNER VIOLENCE

Visit domesticshelters.org and input your zip code to start your search. Offers information in Spanish and eleven other languages.

Call the National Domestic Violence Hotline (TheHotline.org) at 1-800-799-SAFE (7233). Help is offered in English, Spanish, and almost any language.

Live chat feature in English, Spanish, and over two hundred languages is offered 24/7.

- Deaf or hard of hearing (TheHotline.org/get-help/deaf-services) may call TTY 1-800-787-3224, or access advocates who are deaf 24/7 through the National Deaf Hotline by video phone at 1-855-812-1001, Instant Messenger (DeafHotline), and email (nationaldeafhotline@adwas.org).
- Information on Creating a Safe Plan in English and Spanish: Staying Safe During COVID-19 (thehotline.org/resources/staying-safe-during-covid-19)
- Advice for LGBTQ and transgender victims of domestic violence (thehotline.org/resources/abuse-in-lgbtq-communities) and the people who want to support them.

Love Is Respect (loveisrespect.org) at 1-866-331-9474 serves teens and young adults. Telephone, live chat, and texting services available 24/7 in English and two hundred languages, including Spanish.

Safe Horizon (safehorizon.org) helps with crisis counseling and safety planning and assists in finding shelters in English and Spanish. Call 1 (800) 621-HOPE (4673). It also operates a confidential chat feature.

The National Sexual Assault Hotline (rainn.org) operates 24/7 and is confidential. Available in English and Spanish. Call 1-800-656-HOPE (4673) or contact via chat (hotline.rainn.org).

The StrongHearts Native Helpline (strongheartshelpline.org) for domestic/sexual violence is available from 6 a.m. to 9 p.m. EST. It's confidential and specifically for Native communities: 1-844-762-8483.

Let them know that hotlines and other resources have been more active than ever; that choosing a friend or relative with whom to create a safe plan can be the best safety measure under the circumstances, and that maybe we can be that friend or relative.

But let's also tell some new stories, like one about the woman who was able to leave her abuser behind and now has her own business. And the one about another woman, the one with children, who created a childcare co-op and secured a grant to provide security to the premises of the new community venture. And the other one who wrote a book about this. And the one who recorded her abuse and locked her abuser away for life. What if we could all become storytellers, secret agents for peaceful homes? Wouldn't it be great to create that story together?

Remember that sometimes the best messaging is a caring friend who checks in on you. If you suspect someone is at risk, call often, drop by, let them know there is help available and, if you can, do some messaging of your own: tell them a good story.

6 GENDER RIGHTS
BODILY AUTONOMY AND DEMOCRACY

CARMEN BARROSO AND DANIEL PARNETTI

The year is 2030. The place is Chimaltenango, Guatemala. Xmucane, a seventeen-year-old K'iche' girl, will soon graduate from high school. She has a boyfriend, and they have been teaching each other the joys of sex, but she has never been pregnant. Her science teacher gave a class on safe sex, and she is able to get free condoms and pills at a nearby clinic, where the nurse gave her good advice without judgment.

Her older sister recently returned from the United States and bought a small farm on which to grow organic avocados. She now has no need to flee from the gangs that previously ravaged her community. Most gangs have disbanded, having taken advantage of the productive jobs created by socially conscious investments and the fair-trade agreements that the country signed a couple of years ago.

Xmucane's sister purchased the farm with money she saved from her salary at a well-paid tech job in California. Her employer followed the law that prohibits discrimination against women and developed a special program to recruit a diverse and skilled workforce. She had an unwanted pregnancy but was able to have a safe and legal abortion.

Both sisters are free from the fear of being beaten or raped by their partners. The men in their lives have become comfortable with the idea of strong and independent women. They have learned to respect and love them. A sexuality education campaign through social media reinforces a growing societal recognition that gender equality is beneficial for all.

After the COVID-19 pandemic, a major social campaign on the importance of universal healthcare was promoted, and the government invested in strengthening the public health system and in training a qualified health workforce. Their mother took advantage of the new opportunities and became a nurse, helping the community stay safe and preventing the outbreak of new diseases.

Xmucane's sister and her mother are productive workers who contribute to the economy of their country. The three women will not be held back by the need to care for a large family, by discrimination in hiring practices, or by sexist attitudes that stigmatize women. They are educated citizens who make informed political choices, the importance of which they learned when they joined the women's movement and the Latine movement, both of which warmly welcome Indigenous collaboration and have now fully incorporated a gender-equity perspective.

An Impossible Dream?

The racial justice movement over decades has eroded complacency about structural racism. The movement exploded after the killing of George Floyd in Minneapolis in May 2020. We have a new awareness of the different ways that systemic injustices intersect and how they affect the most vulnerable members of our society, including women. Yet, widespread injustices remain, and huge social transformations are still needed.

Similarly, even though we have seen significant positive changes in the past decades all over the world, an alarming global wave of authoritarianism—mostly on the right but also on the left—threatens to wipe out past achievements and undo recent democratization. Fortunately, there are social movements that can counter these regressive forces, especially if people are willing to learn from the past.

The fate of young women like Xmucane and the future of democracy are closely tied together because democracy cannot survive, let alone flourish, without a shared sense of prosperity, as well as opportunities for all citizens to reach their full potential. Authoritarian movements in Latin America have risen to power thanks to the demagogic manipulations that have caused people to fear social change.

The links between gender equality and democracy are strong, both in the United States and in Latin America. Probably more than anywhere else, politicians in Latin America have used gender equality as a scapegoat to distract attention from the real causes of extremely unhealthy concentrations of wealth and power. Donald Trump's 2016 election to the U.S. presidency both benefited from and energized the wave of authoritarianism worldwide. It certainly turned around the initially unpromising candidacy of Jair Bolsonaro in Brazil in 2018. Both countries' candidates gathered the support of an astounding number of voters, a large proportion of whom were women. The women may have discounted both candidates' misogyny because these voters had a greater fear of political and social instability, real or imagined.

Achieving gender equality and empowering women are now goals in a large number of international agreements. Based on a wealth of evidence, initially gathered by feminist researchers, there is a growing understanding of their importance for sustainable development and for the well-being and human rights of all. Recent studies have shown that, in countries with higher gender equality, men also live longer and are less prone to self-destructive behaviors. Even the rates of suicide are lower.[1]

Activists for gender equality would be well advised to learn from past experience and tie their efforts to nonviolent movements for social justice and democracy. Latin American gender relations have evolved and women's movements have promoted change, especially in the areas of reproductive rights and gender-based violence, which are key to achieving justice for half of the human species. Still much more progress is needed to bring about equity.

Unequal and Incomplete Progress

Women today truly have seen changes that are broader in scope than ever before, and in many circles, women have equal social standing with men. But the societal changes that have opened doors for some have not reached all women. Conflicts between work and family are still widespread in the United States and

Latin America. Women in poverty, women of color, young women, women with disabilities, lesbians, transwomen, Indigenous women, and others still face oppression.[2] The gaps between the gains of more privileged women and those of Black and Brown women also have become more evident with the economic downturn caused by the pandemic.[3] However, the mainstream women's movement has yet to fully incorporate the issues that disproportionately affect poorer women, such as low wages and access to healthcare and childcare.

Although systemic racial injustice was rightly exposed in 2020, systemic gender injustice has not yet received the attention it deserves. The spotlight may now be on the lack of opportunities for people of color, although gender divisions in labor are still ignored. Policies and budgets have been painfully slow in acknowledging that women are still the majority of essential workers. Furthermore, the work of educating children—whether at school or at home—has continued to be largely done by women, without recognition and support. The pandemic lockdowns have also exacerbated the vulnerability of women to domestic violence, but this has yet to prompt any government policies or budgets for prevention and treatment.

The lives of most women are probably better than those of previous generations, yet this is a far cry from real justice. In order for people similar to Xmucane, her sister, and their loved ones to have a future like the one we have envisioned, we must overcome formidable barriers by challenging violence against women; ensuring reproductive rights, including access to abortion, for all women; and broadening the ranks of women leaders in all walks of life.

To get to that future in Latin America, we need to address the economic and social disparities that have fed the wave of authoritarianism and that are tearing societies apart.

A Growing Movement Opposes Violence Against Women

Gender-based violence is still pervasive in Latin America. A report for the Global Partnership for Sustainable Development

Data shows that the region has the worst indicators for women's physical safety in the world.[4]

The #MeToo movement was started in 2006 in the United States but didn't really take off until 2017. In the interim, women's movements throughout Latin America organized to protest misogynistic violence and femicide. The first massive protest took place in Argentina in 2015, with the slogan "Ni Una Menos" (Not One Less). It was triggered by the killing of fourteen-year-old Chiara Páez by her boyfriend. The protest, organized by a group of journalists, writers, and activists, brought together both women and men, as well as opposing political parties, student organizations, trade unions, and even conservative religious groups to demand social change.

These rallies quickly transcended Argentina's borders. Women's groups called for international solidarity via social media platforms, sparking a transnational response. Similar demonstrations were soon ignited in Chile, Bolivia, Colombia, Mexico, Paraguay, and Uruguay, even crossing the Atlantic to Spain and elsewhere. In each country, the protests were triggered by local cases of gender-based violence, but they all converged around the Ni Una Menos theme.

The movement represented a turning point that helped make gender inequality and violence against women more visible, putting a spotlight on an often-concealed social problem and sparking intense debates in the mainstream media, in schools, and within families.

Even before Ni Una Menos, the women's movement had started achieving significant victories in the struggle against gender-based violence in Latin America. Due in part to these widespread and well-organized social mobilization efforts, several countries adopted legislation that criminalized violence against women. First, laws against domestic violence were adopted in almost all countries in Latin America, and about half of the countries in Latin America and the Caribbean have adapted their penal codes to criminalize femicide.[5] But progressive legislation often does not extend beyond being in the legal code. Even the victims of the crimes these laws would penalize were scarcely aware of their rights.

The results were more positive in some countries than in others. Due to a massive communications campaign, Brazil's law against domestic violence—also known as Lei Maria da Penha after a women's rights activist who was left paraplegic by her violent husband—quickly became part of everyday discourse, countering the prevailing perception of domestic violence as a private affair.

Yet millions of Latin American women continue to be neglected by their countries' legal systems, and as many as 98 percent of cases of femicide and violence against girls and women go unpunished in the region every year.[6] Laws alone are insufficient to change this reality, and more will have to be done to educate the public and change culture.

Unequal Access to Sexual and Reproductive Healthcare

Most women in Latin America's thirty-three countries no longer want to have large families, as their mothers did. They are, by and large, having two or three children at most. Nonetheless, an estimated 24 million Latin American women[7] and girls who do not want to have children lack access to modern contraception, and many have to rely on abortions to interrupt unwanted pregnancies. The vast majority of Latin American women live in countries that severely limit access to legal abortion. They have to rely on clandestine abortions, which, especially for poor and younger women, are usually unsafe and can cause severe health problems—even death.

The region is home to unenviable statistics regarding unintended pregnancies (about 50 percent of all pregnancies are unwanted, one of the highest rates in the world). A high number of them end in abortions. Some progress in providing access to information and contraception has brought about a decrease in the number of abortions, but at a much slower pace than in most of the countries where abortion is legal and safe.[8]

The high rate of adolescent motherhood, second only to Sub-Saharan Africa, puts the region in the hall of shame.[9] Early motherhood negatively affects not only the adolescents but also their children, their families, and society as a whole, according to numerous health and economic studies.[10]

Uruguay and Mexico City, and, to a lesser degree, Argentina, Colombia, and Chile, have adopted more liberal reproductive laws in recent years, but many countries still have draconian laws against abortion. Women's organizations from Guatemala, Nicaragua, and Ecuador have filed a case before the UN Human Rights Council challenging the laws in their countries for not giving abortion access to adolescents who were victims of rape.[11] They were empowered to do so by the Program of Action adopted in 1994 at the UN Conference on Population and Development in Cairo, with support from Brazilian and other regional women's groups. That Program of Action informs today's reproductive health policies and programs, including access to contraception.

Another significant step forward occurred in 2015, when the United Nations General Assembly adopted seventeen Sustainable Development Goals. The fifth of these goals is to *achieve gender equality and empower all women and girls*, with one of its targets to ensure universal access to sexual and reproductive health and reproductive rights. To help measure compliance with this commitment by 2030, the United Nations subsequently adopted three important indicators: women's access to contraceptives; the rate of adolescent motherhood; and laws that guarantee access to sexual and reproductive healthcare, information, and education.

Key Philanthropic Investments

During the twentieth century, private foundations made some investments in the nascent women's movements in Latin America. As relatively small as those investments were, they produced huge returns. The Ford Foundation was a pioneer in the early 1970s, followed by the John D. and Catherine T. MacArthur Foundation and smaller foundations in the 1990s.

NURTURING THE SEEDS OF SOCIAL CHANGE

I came to the United States from Brazil in the early 1970s to study for a PhD in social psychology. I was on a scholarship from The Ford Foundation, part of its program to support the Fundação Carlos Chagas (Carlos Chagas Foundation) in establishing an objective method for selection of students for a consortium of universities. While immersed in the study of statistical methods, I squeezed out some time to learn about the gains of the women's movements here in the United States. I was so impressed that I wrote to a senior researcher in Brazil suggesting that she launch a movement that I could join when I got back. We were close friends, but she responded with deep scorn, an attitude she and others maintained throughout the years after I returned and established the first women's studies center in Brazil within the Chagas Foundation, where we both worked. Feminist ideas were considered irrelevant to Brazilian society, a concern of bourgeois women, who were "mal-amadas" (unable to get a man to love them). In spite of the opposition of my colleagues, a small cadre of feminist researchers was formed and was able to not only shed light on a range of gender issues but also help to build a critical mass of feminist thinkers around Brazil through a nationwide grant competition that Chagas managed. Today, gender studies attract thousands of scholars, established in universities and research centers all over the country, and most of it closely interacts with a broad and diverse women's movement. The seeds planted by The Ford Foundation's strategic grants, renewed for more than two decades, fell into fertile soil of a nascent women's movement eager to link its demands to solid evidence.

Ford's support in Brazil also was a lifeline for progressive intellectuals persecuted by the 1964–1985 military dictatorship. But it was complicated—both a blessing and a curse. On the left, from which feminists would have naturally drawn support, there was deep suspicion of Ford's historical links to the CIA. At the same time, in the simplified version of Marxism widely embraced by the Brazilian intelligentsia, the only conflict deserving attention was the basic antagonism between capital and labor. Women's issues were no more than a distraction for most of them. Into this space stepped the women's movement, with support from foundations and like-minded international organizations. That backing allowed feminist scholars to gradually assume leadership positions.

Support from foundations led to the launch of a number of research programs in Brazil. Academics and activists benefitted from and better supported each other. Meanwhile, women from grassroots movements marched to protest violence against women, or in favor of daycare centers for the children of working mothers. Activists started to receive considerable attention from a media eager to cover news that would not be targeted for censorship by the military regime.

It is clear that U.S. foundations played a crucial role. They would be wise to renew and deepen their commitments to the future of the region and to the women's movement, seeding and providing long-term support, not just for research but also for programs that advance civic engagement and human rights.

Moving Forward

The limited progress toward gender equality so far brings exasperation and hope—exasperation because of a new awareness of huge, ever-growing inequality, and hope because of the possibility of imagining a world where gender equality will prevail. At the same time, this uneven progress also has given birth to stronger, more sophisticated attempts to "keep women in their place." In Brazil and other countries in Latin America, so-called gender ideology has become a target for right-wing propaganda. A coalition of conservative politicians, Evangelicals, and the Roman Catholic Church claim with straight faces that efforts to promote gender equality will end up feminizing boys, turning girls into lesbians, and ultimately destroying the family. This view has informed many of the policies of authoritarian governments in Latin America, which were initially both inspired and strengthened by the Trump White House. On the other hand, the women's movement in Latin America and the Latine movements in the United States can reinforce each other's resilience, especially now that Latine voters in the United States have a pivotal role in U.S. politics. It is an opportune time for collaboration, as feminist Latinas increasingly move Latine movements and the Democratic Party in a more progressive direction.

Lessons from the United States

Trump's defeat in his bid for reelection was a source of hope for many, amid concern that supporters of his domestic and foreign policies might continue blocking progress in key areas. The 2020 election reflected an extraordinary shift, with public opinion favoring more progressive policies in the United States. For instance, *New York Times* columnist Nicholas Kristof cited a poll showing 89 percent of the population sampled during the 2020 political primary season supported higher taxes on wealthy individuals to reduce poverty.[12]

Politics in the United States and in our countries of origin throughout Latin America are deeply interlaced, not only by the bonds of Diaspora but by hemispheric cultural and political ties. People all over the world watched the U.S. election as if their lives depended on it—and they actually did. What happens in the United States profoundly affects more than the economy of other countries around the world. Now even more than ever, the United States is seen as the country at the forefront of what is possible. Activists everywhere feel encouraged by the positive results here, just as native authoritarians felt strengthened by having a fellow authoritarian occupy the White House.

Nationwide, a higher proportion of Latinas than Latinos supported former Vice President Joe Biden over incumbent President Donald Trump. It is quite plausible that part of this gap—like similar gender gaps in other groups of the population—might be the result of men's slower progress toward embracing gender equality. Even though there have been significant improvements, institutional sexism still prevails, while gross violations and abuse of women remain widespread and largely ignored. Social movements should look for ways of denouncing sexism as strongly as they do racism. The multiple benefits of gender equality for both men and women need to be high on the agenda of any movement in defense of democracy.

The variations among states in Latine support for Biden invites a look at additional layers. Our identities, and therefore our motivations, are countless. Movements need to deal with this multiplicity, putting "an emphasis on pluralism and respecting what is unique across race, ethnicity, language and the many places Latinos call home," as Marisa Franco, the co-founder and Director of Mijente,[13] wrote in the *New York Times*. In particular, we need to face the legacy of racism still prevailing in our countries of origin, not in an accusatory mode, but in a constructive spirit of healing the deep wounds of our societies and our cultures, and building a new, nonracial world. The women's movements in the United States and in Latin America are increasingly multiethnic, and young women of color are assuming leadership roles everywhere.

The ability to exercise sexual and reproductive rights and to be free of gender-based violence are highly linked to other social and economic rights. This is the moment for the gender equality and sexual and reproductive rights movements in the United States—especially its Latinx groups—to join forces with movements fighting for immigration reform, for a better school system, for universal healthcare, and for labor rights, among other pressing issues. The pandemic particularly exacerbated the inequities suffered by Latinx women and exposed the interconnectedness of rights. Twenty-nine percent of White women surveyed reported delaying or canceling a sexual and reproductive health visit to a medical provider or trouble obtaining birth control, compared with almost half of Latine women (45 percent).[14] The intersecting issues that affected the country's most vulnerable populations could only be redressed by better social and economic policies for problems faced by essential workers, such as job insecurity, low pay, and health risks, which were compounded, as we saw, by their greater exposure during the pandemic.

Lessons from Latin America

For the women's movements in the United States and Latin America, many important lessons can be drawn from Ni Una Menos. The first one, key to its success, is that it moved beyond the "preaching to the converted" mentality, opening the coalition to nontraditional allies that helped augment the movement with widespread support. It highlighted gender solidarity, and men from all walks of life became actively involved in the campaign, eliminating the traditional confrontation between genders that left empathetic men on the sidelines. This helped build a partnership that uplifted both women and men.

The second lesson comes from the intensive use of social media as a tool to give visibility to neglected social problems. Ni Una Menos was born on social media, when journalist and social activist Marcela Ojeda posted the now-historic tweet, "They are killing us: Aren't we going to do anything?" in reaction to yet another woman's murder. The tweet sparked mobilizations all over Argentina. Social media created national and transnational solidarity and allowed for women's groups to coordinate simultaneous rallies, helping to grow the movement beyond Argentina.

The Ni Una Menos movement has evolved, broadening the interpretation of violence against women and starting a historic debate on the decriminalization of abortion, a key issue for Latin America, where as late as 2020, 97 percent of all women lived in countries with restrictive abortion laws.[15] In 2018, a bill to legalize abortion was approved by the lower chamber of Argentina's Congress but narrowly lost in the Senate. The debate energized thousands of women and men from different generations across Argentina, helped create an informal cross-party coalition of female legislators, and further inspired the women's rights movement. With support from Argentine President Alberto Fernández,

Latin America's fourth most populous country enacted a law in December 2020 allowing elective abortions up to fourteen weeks of pregnancy, and later in cases of rape and when the woman's health is at risk.

Ni Una Menos and other women's rights movements have shown that dialogue with groups that hold different views is essential if we want to win the battle for democracy and build a more inclusive and just world. Movement leaders need to make a conscientious effort to understand the reasons why others support retrograde policies or elect leaders who undermine democracy. Based on lessons learned from the recent past, it is crucial that leaders defend their political independence and autonomy. This includes being wary of left-leaning political parties that might be perceived as natural allies but have either betrayed or diluted their promises to support the movement's demands. Movement leaders must stay alert and demand accountability from all governments, irrespective of their political leaning.

Despite the turns to the right and to authoritarianism, the ripple effect from the U.S. election offers new hope. Both in Latin America and the United States, progressive movements are increasingly committed to joining forces across a wide range of interconnected issues. Gender equality can blossom in the fertile soil of a more empathetic and democratic society.

Women activists concerned with gender equality and sexual and reproductive rights must also support comprehensive measures against racism and other democracy-enhancing causes. In doing so, we can create a world where a Xmucane and her loved ones can thrive, and where democracy can flourish for the benefit of all.

PART III

LATINE PERSPECTIVES

7 HEALTH
THE WAY BEATRIZ SOLIS SAW IT

ROBERT K. ROSS, MD

"Raise your words and knowledge, not your voice . . . it is rain that grows flowers, not thunder."

—*Rumi*

In August 2015, I was invited to participate in a memorable meeting at St. Joseph's University in Philadelphia. A group of a dozen faith, nonprofit, and philanthropic leaders was assembled to meet with members of Pope Francis' advance team, including one of the Pope's top aides. The purpose of the meeting was to collect insights from our group about where the Pope might spend some of his time during his first visit to the United States—aside from the obligatory state and political encounters.

I do recall with precision, however, how the Pope's top aide greeted our group. He said the following: "The Pope appreciates your work and leadership in America, because he believes that communism provides for equality without freedom, and capitalism provides for freedom without equality."

There is a proverb that goes something like, "A guest sees more in an hour than the host in a lifetime." And, from my perspective, the Pope's representative really nailed it regarding the meaningful role of our philanthropic sector. Our mission is more than "charitable"—it is fundamentally about change. And the change we seek is to address—and help fix—the realities of structural inequality in America, where the combination of runaway capitalism and racial injustice results in savage inequities for the poor,

people of color, and immigrant communities. Infusing some sem-
blance of inclusion, fairness, and equity into America's civic landscape is what the work of foundations must be about. Housing the
homeless, for example, is fine work—but getting at the root of why
so many are homeless is about policy and structural change.

More than six years after the Pope's visit, structural inequality and racial injustice have been blatantly exposed for all to see
across America, as COVID-19 unmasked all manner of health
and economic disparities—in particular those faced by Black and
Brown communities. The role and purpose of the field of philanthropy is now an existential question before us.

So, with this broader question in mind, it is appropriate to
assess and assert the impact of Latinx professionals in the foundation world. My thesis is that, since structural and racial inequality occur by human hands and human action, it stands to reason
that human action can fix them. The civil rights movement and
the farmworker movement are evidence of this, with grassroots
activism by impacted communities leading the way. Those of us
who are privileged to labor in the world of private foundations
are familiar with "theories of change," "logic models," and other
forms of analytic rigor to shape the impact we seek. But I submit
that our field suffers from a lack of moral and spiritual resolve. It
is of critical importance, therefore, that we in philanthropy feel as
much as we think. We must feel the pain of injustice, marginalization, and stigmatization experienced by communities; we must
feel the values of Belonging and Inclusion; we must believe in the
agency of those directly impacted by the adverse conditions.

As an Afro Latino executive in philanthropy, I see the moral
and spiritual dimensions of our work now growing in importance. It requires us, as Black and Brown people, not to check our
cultural and spiritual ancestry at the door of philanthropy, but to
rediscover it and assert it in our work. How then, as an Afro Latino CEO, do I channel my *abuela*'s kitchen-table love and soul into
my leadership in philanthropy? This is the unique and powerful
contribution of the Latine professional in our field. Our nation's

civic soul is in crisis as a result of racism, divisiveness, and a sheer lack of inclusion and belonging.

Rather than theorize at some lofty level about the vital role of the Latine professional in the foundation world, let's get concrete about the impact that such a professional can have when the moral and spiritual dimensions of our work are applied. Some of us are called upon to speak for others who cannot. I'm here to share the story and the vision of a beloved colleague who shaped a health-equity agenda, a legacy that many of us honor and celebrate.

Her name is Dr. Beatriz Solis, though we lovingly called her Bea, and she passed away on March 20, 2020, at the age of fifty-eight. If Bea were with us today, she would be calling us to action. She would say the following:

- Use this moment of racial awakening to invest in coalitions across Black and Brown communities.
- Become an activator, a connector, a strategic builder of collaborations.
- Health and justice are inseparable. If some are excluded, our collective health is diminished.
- People hold the power to change. Start by strengthening and empowering community and its leaders.

Bea served as the Director of Healthy Communities South Region for The California Endowment (TCE) for thirteen years. Born to immigrant parents from Mexico and Nicaragua and raised with six other siblings, she understood the value of giving back from a young age. Her father was a union shop worker, and her mother was a United Rubber worker. They embodied sacrifice and working hard for the good of the family and others.

Grounded in her roots, Bea studied Latin American studies and anthropology at UCLA, her dream school. As a student, she was involved with organizations that were fighting for justice at a contentious time when war and violence were prevalent in various parts of the globe, including Central America. She then went on to earn her master's and PhD in public health from UCLA and eventually joined the TCE family.

Her work at The Endowment became a legacy—leaving a foundational blueprint for how our institution engages in "the work," and has arguably influenced the field of philanthropy beyond the walls of TCE. For Bea, the spirit of giving back went deeper than the philanthropic transaction of a grant. She understood our mission and work through the lens of a social movement, a social justice construct where impacted communities are at the forefront of needed change.

As a proud Latina, Beatriz took on issues of community inclusion and power, gender justice and womxn's leadership, and Latine issues, such as immigrant rights, the only way she knew—with soul. "Soul" emanates from a place of love—and Bea had an endless love for community. In this case, *community* is defined as everyday, marginalized people: womxn, LGBTQIA, young people, Indigenous communities, people of color, immigrants, and others who have been historically disenfranchised. As Aurea Montes-Rodriguez of the South Los Angeles Community Coalition noted, "It was really important for her to center conversations around everyday people, and she had this real clear belief that, in addition to lifting up their stories and voices . . . [the work was] also about shifting the power equation."

Beatriz operated on the belief that those directly impacted by social injustices are ideally suited solution makers. Grants that she made were anchored in meaningful inclusion of authentic community voices, experience, and engagement. If community came knocking at her TCE door, Bea would open her door, heart, and ears. But for Beatriz, this was simply not enough; making grants in this manner was one thing—but elevating these themes into the core of TCE's overall grant strategy was transformational for our foundation.

The California Endowment's Senior Vice President, Dr. Tony Iton, observed, "Bea helped us translate love into justice. She took the passionate feelings of those communities vulnerable to racism and discrimination, helping turn those feelings into strategy to build power—holding systems accountable to get the outcomes communities deserve."

Community power-building as our core grantmaking strategy needed to become the focal point, our North Star. So, for Bea, creating transformative and sustainable change meant supporting and building social, political, and economic power in historically marginalized communities. It meant getting at root causes. It meant building community leaders. It meant changing institutions from the inside out. It meant people power. Through her bold leadership in our Building Healthy Communities (BHC) California statewide initiative, Beatriz championed health-equity campaigns to address gender justice issues, extend healthcare to immigrants, and build up statewide civic engagement and voting power, to name a few. She was an activator, a connector, a strategic builder of cross-sectional collaboration between existing partners and organizations—all in the name of fighting the good fight.

But emanating from Bea's heart was the gender justice and womxn's empowerment work. By 2014, The Endowment had embarked on boys and men-of-color work, but it was Bea who insisted that focused attention was also needed on girls and young women of color—incarceration rates and school suspension rates among them were unacceptably high as well. Bea also affirmed the urgency for healing and power-building within our LGBTQIA, cisgender/transgender women, and nonconforming community. In response, Bea pioneered the Sisterhood Rising Leadership Retreats and the Grassroots Womxn Rising Conference for girls and womxn to not only bond and heal, but also to inherit tools and resources for building movements for leaders in their home communities.

Behind the scenes, Beatriz was convening and supporting women in leadership, mentoring young women, and hosting sisterhood gatherings for women of color. "Bea was very proud to be a *mujer*—a fierce, strong *mujer*, and was unapologetic about that," Maria Brenes of Los Angeles's Inner City Struggle said. "She just carried herself with dignity and grace and affirmation about who she was, and who she was representing in her work."

As a daughter of Latine immigrants, Beatriz understood that health and justice for all also happens when no one is excluded, regardless of status or income. So, after the passage of the Affordable Care Act in 2010, when our undocumented community faced continued barriers to accessing healthcare, she rose to the occasion. Bea was instrumental in supporting our #Health4All campaign, uplifting the narrative and experiences of undocumented Californians who contribute billions in tax revenues to our economy, yet are marginalized from services. Statewide organizing and mobilizing led by young "Dreamers" then strengthened the health safety net at countywide and statewide levels. Through this movement, the stage was set for a Health4All bill to be introduced and later passed in the state legislature, winning the expansion of Medi-Cal (California's Medicaid program) benefits for undocumented children across the state.

Beatriz understood community power and voice as the key social determinant of health. One of the ways that marginalized communities can exert power and effect change is by voting—voting is at the heart of a well-grounded, functioning democracy. With key grantee leaders working in concert with Bea, we began to support Integrated Voter Engagement (IVE) work in a coalition-building, alliance-building framework with grassroots organizations across the state; the #VOTA campaign was one such example of civic power-building for healthier communities. The IVE and #VOTA campaign work were stellar examples of how Bea strategically channeled the wisdom of grassroots organizers into grantmaking strategies for our foundation. For Tara Westman at The California Endowment, the IVE work was an example of how Bea "encouraged us to stretch ourselves beyond what we think is possible, and put those aspirations into everyday practice."

Within the space of philanthropy, Beatriz was undoubtedly a community organizer herself. She served on the Boards of both Hispanics in Philanthropy (HIP) and Southern California Grantmakers (SCG), extolling the virtues of community voice, power, and engagement with colleagues. "I would say that for Bea, centering equity as the premise for the field of philanthropy, as the lens to view our work through, was her biggest contribution," is how Chris Essel of Southern California Grantmakers put it.

Bea continuously challenged our philanthropic culture to not only give marginalized voices a seat at the table, but to hold the microphone as well. For example, when Bea authored a report about the *promotoras de salud* (Community Health Promoters) program, she invited the *promotora* leaders to our staff meetings so that we could hear directly from them. With time, The California Endowment would become one of the largest funders in the nation of community-based *promotora* programs.

Community-driven immigration policy was also a key theme of Bea's work with us. Working in partnership with leader-colleagues, such as Antonia Hernández at the California Community Foundation, Bea pushed our foundation to engage in work to support inclusive and complete counts of the federal census. She advocated inside our foundation for supporting the inspiring work of Dolores Huerta and others pushing on behalf of California's farmworkers, and she personally challenged me to use our foundation's brand and reputational capital in advocating for unaccompanied minors several years ago. Bea's advocacy to support the voices of farmworkers and community *promotoras* affirmed this observation from co-worker Sandra Witt: "She absolutely believed in people and people's ability to change the world and make it better."

Bea was a key "disruptive" leader for us within the walls of our foundation. In our earlier years as a foundation, we ascribed to an all-too-common, traditional approach to the development of grantmaking strategies, which can be reduced to 1) gather the research and data about a problem, 2) cook up our own solution, and 3) expect communities to rally behind our cause. This is the intellectually convenient—but morally lazy—approach that still plagues too much of our field. But Bea was a key thinker-doer behind the lessons of our ten-year Building Healthy Communities work, where we learned how health equity is advanced and driven by community voice and power. We now call the theory of change "ABC":

Agency + Belonging = Change

"Agency," of course, represents the matter of people power to drive change; "Belonging" represents the ethos of Dr. Martin Luther King Jr.'s "beloved community" of inclusion, brotherhood, and sisterhood; and "Change" represents the results of policy and systemic change to promote health and racial equity. Our foundation's Theory of Change to advance our mission is, indeed, data and research supported. But it is also chiefly anchored in the heart and soul and experience of community. Bea played a key role for us in how our thinking became transformed.

At The California Endowment, Bea reported to me and Dr. Iton—so technically, Tony and I were her bosses. But in reality, we looked to her for values-anchored wisdom, guidance, and strategy more than the other way around. In this incredibly difficult, divisive, and pivotal moment in our nation's history, Bea would advise me in this manner about how we as a foundation should respond: "Stay true to our values, listen to those communities who are hurting and are most impacted, trust the people, and invest in their voice, agency, and power." Bea was a strong believer in cross-racial, cross-ethnic alliance building—and I suspect that, during this moment of racial injustice and racial awakening in our nation, she would advise more thoughtful investments in coalition building across Black and Brown communities.

Looking forward, our foundation will wind down a decade of Building Healthy Communities work to embark on the next ten years of investments in pursuit of our mission. Our Board of Directors has approved a ten-year framework anchored in community and grassroots power building. Bea's fingerprints are indeed on this ten-year investment strategy; working with Drs. Manuel Pastor and Jennifer Ito at USC's PERE Center on Equity,

she commissioned what we believe is the first-ever extensive "power building" mapping project for California. As of this writing, Dr. Ito has mapped the community power-building work of more than seven hundred organizations across our state, and Bea was savvy enough to help marry the rigor of academic research with the heart-and-soul magic of grassroots organizations across the state—organizations that engage in what civil rights legend John Lewis referred to as "Good Trouble." The next billion dollars of our grantmaking will be focused on investing in this "power-building landscape" to advance health equity, racial equity, and wellness in marginalized communities.

"Her mission in her life, for home and in society, drew from her core philosophical belief in the virtue of positive thoughts and good deeds," her loving husband and life partner, Mohammad Pasebani said. "By example, she instilled this in her family, as well as the community. She embodied the belief that, with the power of love, real change is possible."

Her sons, Avi and Aydin, recalled lessons from Bea's passions.

"There is a saying that 'it is what it is,'" Avi said. "But you must dare to scratch the surface deep enough to discover there is much more there."

Aydin recalled that Bea was an admirer of thirteenth-century theologian and poet Molana Rumi: "Raise your words and knowledge, not your voice . . . it is rain that grows flowers, not thunder."

Los Angeles County Supervisor Hilda Solis, Secretary of Labor in the Obama administration, summarized:

> My sister Bea was a full-time, wholly dedicated giver and lover of humanity—both inside of our loving family, and in her civic pursuits. Her number one priority was lifting up the struggles and experiences of the most marginalized and disenfranchised among us. She consistently placed their voices and their issues front and center in her life's work.

This, my friends, is the story of the impact that a single Latina had on the spirit and work of our foundation, and on our field. Dr. Beatriz Solis, who passed away from cancer in 2020, would not in any way consider herself a hero or superhero. She simply brought her heart, her soul, and her love of community to the work—in the same manner that an *abuela* in a kitchen pours love into the preparation of a meal *para la familia*.

If our field of philanthropy is to have a meaningful, durable impact in addressing structural and racial inequality across our nation, we must have and demonstrate soul—we must have *alma*.

8 EDUCATION
ACCESS TO COLLEGE DEGREES

MÓNICA LOZANO

Higher education, long the key to social mobility and economic growth, has become more essential than ever. In an increasingly global, high-tech economy, workers with a college degree are more likely to land a higher-wage job and improve the quality of life for themselves and their families. During tough economic times, they—and their communities—face less instability and hardship and can recover more quickly. We have learned that even against a pandemic, higher education can bolster workers' resilience and increase job seekers' chances of finding employment.

Latinos have enthusiastically embraced the pursuit of higher education, though many may come from families that tradition-ally have been hindered from accessing such opportunities. Now, more Latinos are graduating from high school than ever before and enrolling in college at a rate that has grown to be slightly high-er than that of our White peers.[1] Whether we are first-generation undocumented immigrants from South America, or can trace our roots through many generations to Mexico, our desire and ability to succeed are evident.

But, while the number of Latinos in college has been rising, the barriers to completing a degree have been growing. State funding for public higher education has declined steadily over the years, with sharp cuts made during recessions and never fully restored.[2] Our students bear more of the financial burden, paying higher tuition and fees while receiving fewer services. Moreover, the cost of going to college encompasses ever-higher living expenses, such as housing, food, transportation, technology, childcare, and healthcare. Even students from middle-class families are struggling to afford full-time college attendance and must balance work and other responsibilities, resulting in a longer, more circuitous journey to a degree.

For Latino students, the hurdles are even higher. Most are first-generation students from low-income families, and many are also undocumented. They need resources, experience, and confidence to navigate the complex higher-education system, and help from the institutions is often unavailable or inaccessible. To newcomers, the climate on campuses that are still dominated by White administrators, faculty, and students can feel indifferent at best, or hostile at worst. With these compound challenges, is it surprising then that the completion rate for Latinos has fallen further behind that for Whites?[3]

Our country cannot afford to squander so much potential. Throughout its history, the United States has benefited by expanding higher-education opportunities to more people. The sale of federal lands in the 1860s established state universities that specialized in agriculture and engineering so the country could compete in an industrialized world. To lay the groundwork for post-war prosperity, the GI Bill paid tuition and expenses for millions of World War II veterans. The Great Society programs in the 1960s, aimed at fighting poverty and racial injustice, included increased federal support for higher education and established scholarships and low-interest loans for students.

Another seismic shift is overdue. Our system of higher education is not adequately welcoming and serving a large segment of our student population, one that is critical to our country's future economic prosperity. By 2050, Latinos are projected to make up 30 percent of the country's workforce, compared with about 18 percent today. The share of non-Hispanic Whites in the workforce is expected to shrink to less than half.[4]

However, the urgent need for change faces tough resistance. Colleges and universities are competing with many other priorities for funding and attention at a time when public commitment to higher education has been diminishing. Even more difficult are the social challenges. Restructuring higher education to better serve today's much more diverse student population will involve a serious examination of systemic racism. How are higher-education institutions failing to address students' inequitable experiences, which contribute to inequitable student outcomes? And what must institutions, and the individuals who lead and work within them, do to bring about change?

Despite the challenges, I am confident that broader and deeper changes can happen, and soon. The crises of 2020—the pandemic, recession, and police violence—have exposed the impact of racial bias and institutionalized racism in our country and are propelling a reckoning in all sectors, including higher education. More Latinos are in the positions of power and influence needed to push for meaningful progress. And in recent years, innovative strategies have moved more Latinos and other underrepresented students to graduation, showing the potential that can be realized when barriers are removed. Next, we must champion even more Latino leaders into top higher-education roles and scale proven strategies. Our vision, for all students to have the opportunity to attend college and earn a degree, is attainable. For this generation and those to come—and for the benefit of our whole society—we can and must push forward.

Building the Movement

Of all issues important to Latinos, increasing educational access and success is my biggest passion. One of the most cherished stories passed down in my family tells of my grandfather's visit in the early 1900s to Dolores Hidalgo, the birthplace of Mexican independence. There, he was stunned by the lack of schools. After he returned home to San Antonio, where he had emigrated from Mexico, he wrote an editorial for his newspaper, *La Prensa*, lamenting that without opportunities for education, the country of his birth could never advance. So, he started a campaign to build a public school in Dolores Hidalgo, which is in the north-central Guana-juato state. Readers donated, sending in envelopes of pennies, and their names were published in the paper with the amount they gave. Within eight months they raised $36,000, and three years later two schools were built: one for girls and one for boys. Togeth-er, they formed Mexico's highest-capacity primary school com-plex. During my childhood, our family made several visits to the schools, and one hundred years after they were built, the schools are still open. The original investment—achieved through small individual donations from many—has long since been returned through the achievements of thousands of graduates.

When I was publisher of *La Opinión*, based in Los Angeles, I saw that same dedication to education from the Latino community, and that same focus on opportunities for future generations. Poll after poll showed that Latinos of all backgrounds, more than any other ethnicity, believed that a college education could help their children obtain a higher quality of life. But many of them, par-ticularly first-generation immigrants, did not know how to help their children access or navigate the unfamiliar system of higher education. *La Opinión* published articles explaining the education system and how parents could support students in choosing high school classes, applying to colleges, and filing for financial aid. We also partnered with nonprofits, developing programs to take fam-ilies on campus visits and creating networks of feeder high schools to nearby campuses. It was at an education event where a nonprof-it leader introduced me to Governor Gray Davis; that encounter led to my appointment to the California State Board of Education in 1999 and, two years later, to the UC Board of Regents.

My connection with Governor Davis and seat on the Board of Regents, one of the most influential positions in California higher education, were the result of growing Latino political power. So many of us had been galvanized by the anti-Latino, anti-immigrant climate that had gripped the state during the 1990s. As the population had become dramatically more diverse, some political leaders had blamed immigrants and their descendants for the state's economic problems. In 1994, voters passed Proposition 187 to bar undocumented immigrants from schools, hospitals, and other public services. Two years later, voters passed Proposition 209, banning the use of affirmative action in higher-education admissions. This was followed by the passage of Proposition 227 in 1998, which effectively eliminated bilingual education in the state.

Latinos fought back, leveraging the very tool that was used against our community—the ballot box. Record numbers of Latinos became citizens and registered to vote; more Latinos ran for public office. Their organizing and engagement helped Davis, as a candidate who had campaigned against Proposition 187, to become the state's first Democratic governor in sixteen years. Proposition 187 was never implemented, and the courts eventually declared it unconstitutional.

The affirmative action ban, however, remained. A growing number of us on the Board of Regents questioned how the university system could truly serve California if its student body did not reflect the state's demographics. Proposition 209 was a part of the legal framework, but the University of California also operates under a public service mission. As more education advocates and researchers have questioned the bias and value of standardized tests, the Regents have supported changes that made the admissions process more holistic, factoring in a student's high school, household income, and family education history. After data showed that the number of out-of-state students, most of them White and higher income, was dramatically rising, the Regents capped their admission. A study of transfer students resulted in the University of California system's reducing barriers so that students had a clear pathway from all, not just a select few, of the state's community colleges. The rate of admissions of Black and Latino students is still less than optimal, but our efforts have helped create more equitable processes that improved access.

I have stepped down from the Board of Regents, but many of my former colleagues on today's Board continue to advocate for Latinos and other underserved students and to evaluate and implement ways to effectively recruit and enroll students from diverse backgrounds. In 2020, the Regents unanimously voted to repudiate the ban on affirmative action that their predecessors had helped create. Although California voters did not pass the repeal of Proposition 209, the power of the affirmative action ban is declining.

In 2017, I became President and CEO of College Futures Foundation, a philanthropic organization working in partnership with leaders and groups around California to ensure low-income students and students of color have equitable higher-education access and outcomes. We know that educational attainment leads to socioeconomic mobility and a better life. Ensuring the college success of students facing the most formidable barriers will help all of us thrive—our families, communities, economy, and society.

The work of College Futures and our partners is ambitious. We seek nothing less than to catalyze systemic changes in higher education for hundreds of thousands of diverse, talented students in a massive state with a boom-bust economy and the world's largest college and university systems.

The way we do it is together with strategic partners and dedicated leaders; it requires concerted effort and the will to adapt and innovate. For example, we support cross-sector and cross-segment partnerships between K-12, higher education, and business in regions where coordinating and connecting degree pathways to higher-paying job opportunities will mean the most for students and for the local economy. We work with higher-education faculty, researchers, and advocates to reform remedial education and to make it easier for students to transfer into a four-year university in a reasonable amount of time without overwhelming debt. We fund research that helps policy makers and higher-education leaders understand which financial and informational barriers are most insurmountable for students right now and why. We support the leaders of higher-education institutions to focus on equity in ways that translate to improved policy, practice, culture, and decision making.

Catalyzing systemic change in our state and nation requires many champions. But the coordinated efforts of many do matter—even in the most challenging circumstances, and often *because* of the challenging circumstances. Many contributions make a movement.

A generation after trying to close doors on immigrants, California now serves as a model for others in creating opportunities, particularly for undocumented students. After it became the first state to allow undocumented students to be eligible for in-state tuition and financial aid, others followed. The "sanctuary" movement spread from California campuses, to cities, to the state, and across the country, with local authorities refusing to help federal agencies arrest undocumented immigrants. California was on the forefront of rejecting the Trump administration's attempts to scapegoat and exclude immigrants. When, for example, the U.S. Department of Education declared that undocumented students were ineligible for receiving pandemic relief aid, California Community Colleges sued and won.

Our movement, forged against Proposition 187 and in favor of an inclusive society, lives on. There is important work for us to do together.

Diversity at the Top

We cannot and should not have to wait for another generation to make more progress. We also know we need to go beyond winning incremental improvements. We need a restructuring of our educational system that puts students at the center and supports them from admission to completion.

The crises of 2020, exacerbated by the callous rhetoric of the Trump administration, revealed not only the pervasiveness of racial bias, but also how racism is built into the foundation of our country's key institutions—healthcare, education, and law enforcement. The pandemic, recession, and police brutality made it painfully clear that Blacks and Latinos were more likely to get sick, lose their jobs, drop out of school, suffer injustice, and die. Support for overhauling institutions is growing, but to be truly serious about making change, we need to start at the top. Change will come faster and go further with more leaders who are people of color. In higher education, when administrators and faculty leaders look like and understand the experiences of the students they are serving, campuses immediately feel more welcoming and inclusive. Latino leaders are more likely to have the expertise in how to increase success for students because they themselves have experienced structural barriers. They are also likely to make equity *the* priority, rather than one of many goals.

Yet even as higher education has seen extraordinary growth in the number of Latino students, the ethnic background of leaders has remained overwhelmingly White. Just 4 percent of college or university presidents were Latino in 2016, the same percentage as in 2001, according to the latest data available from the American Council on Education.[5] Across the leadership tier—executives, division and department heads, deans, and associate deans—a mere 3 percent were Latino, according to the College and University Professional Association for Human Resources.[6]

The Latino talent for these positions is ready and available. But implicit biases are embedded in most hiring and advancement processes. Governing Boards and executive search firms need to become more diverse and expand their networks. The characteristics and skillsets that colleges and universities prize in leaders also need to evolve. For example, performance metrics should value the ability to improve student access and success just as much as, if not more than, fundraising prowess or political savvy.

Félix Matos Rodríguez has shown the impact of being intentional about diversifying campus decision makers and influencers. The Puerto Rican-born scholar of Black and Latino studies became the first Latino president of Queens College in New York in 2014 and chose people of color for nearly half of his Cabinet positions. Under his Presidential Hiring Initiative, 48 percent of faculty hires during his five-year tenure were from underrepresented groups, compared with 25 percent previously. Student success also increased, and Queens College ranks in the top 1 percent of schools nationwide for socioeconomic mobility, moving students from the bottom 20 percent to the top 20 percent.

In 2019, Dr. Matos Rodríguez became the first person of color to be appointed Chancellor of the City University of New York, the country's largest urban university system. Within his first year, he leveraged his position to install diverse leaders. Out of his Cabinet of thirteen Vice Chancellors, four were Latino and four were Black. Six of the nine hires to lead CUNY's campuses have been people of color, including the system's first two Asian American Presidents.

"I think Latinos have a responsibility to lead in a way that is equitable—you don't replicate some of the exclusions that you critique others for doing," Dr. Matos Rodríguez, who was one of several people interviewed for this chapter, said. "We're really interested in the benefit of the Latino community, but look at all these other communities that also got to be celebrated, got to be included. We were able to use the talent from that community in building a better university and a better New York City."

Fortunately, the momentum from 2020's racial reckoning is accelerating change. In California, the year brought two milestones in higher education. Joseph I. Castro, a first-generation college graduate, was named President of the California State University, the largest four-year public university system in the United States; he is the first Mexican American in this role. Michael V. Drake—a former University of California, Irvine, Chancellor and Ohio State University President who nevertheless has experienced police stops due to "driving while Black"—became the first person of color to lead the University of California system. Their counterpart at the California Community Colleges is Eloy Ortiz Oakley, who four years earlier became the first Latino to lead the country's largest community college system.

It is unbelievable that in the country's most diverse state, so many generations had to pass before higher-education leaders of color were elevated to the top. But even as we shake our heads, we can and must leverage this moment for our movement. In higher-education institutions throughout the state, equity has moved front and center, according to Ortiz Oakley, a first-generation college graduate who initially dropped out of school because he lacked a reliable way to commute. Administrators and faculty of color no longer feel they need to downplay their experience with structural barriers; they are speaking out and taking action. And with more public awareness and recognition of structural racism, they are gaining allies and supporters.

Under Chancellor Ortiz Oakley's direction, the California Community Colleges system has taken the boldest and swiftest steps among public higher-education systems to address structural racism. Within two weeks of the beginning of protests over the May 2020 murder of George Floyd by police, Ortiz Oakley issued a "Call to Action." Priorities in the six-part agenda include a system-wide review of law enforcement and first responder training and curriculum, and the creation of inclusive classrooms and anti-racism curriculum for all campuses. The system is fast-tracking its five-year diversity, equity, and inclusion plan, and requiring leaders to hold open dialogues and address campus-climate issues.

"More people feel comfortable speaking out than I've ever seen before," Ortiz Oakley said. "And the more we're willing to question and recognize that we inherited a system that was designed to deny access, the more we start to find answers to how we can improve. Once we open up the bottle and let that genie out, it's very difficult to put it back in." The public attention on racial reckoning may ebb and flow as other news grabs headlines. But, with dedicated Latino leaders and other leaders of color at the top, equity will remain a priority and efforts for change will be sustained. If such leaders work together, making progress will become easier.

Focus on Students

In addition to starting at the top, redesigning institutions will require changing how they view their purpose. For too long, higher education has not provided students with what they need to succeed. Instead, the popular narrative has been to blame students, particularly Latinos and other groups that face barriers, for the failures of institutions to raise graduation rates. These students are accused of being too poor, not speaking English well enough, or coming from under-resourced high schools that "didn't prepare them" for college. All too many higher-education leaders long for students they call "traditional," a euphemism for full-time, higher-income White students.

This mindset shamefully dismisses the assets inherent in the students of today and tomorrow. There is potential in every ethnicity, at every income level, and in every ZIP Code. Even when struggling with finances and other obstacles, many students are strongly motivated to advance their education. After six years as undergraduates, one in five Latino students are still enrolled and making progress toward a degree.[7] Their parents also highly value college. About 86 percent of Latino parents with children under age eighteen say that it is either extremely or very important that their children earn a college degree, compared with 67 percent of White parents.[8] The Pew Research Center has speculated that fewer Whites feel that their children need a college education to be part of the middle class because they are already ensconced there. Because a greater number of Latinos are from lower-income families, they may be more likely to link degrees with socioeconomic mobility.

To succeed for the future, colleges and universities must change the narrative about students, leverage their assets, and serve their needs with strategies that encompass three main areas:

- **How students gain access:** Schools need to re-examine how and where they recruit. Their efforts should extend beyond targeting high school seniors to developing relationships and pathways for younger high school students, as well as transfer students and returning students. Dual enrollment, in which high school students also take college courses, is a proven strategy to improve college access. College courses can be made available to students as early as ninth grade, and participation in a dual-enrollment program can accelerate students through college completion, saving them time and money. Longstanding gatekeepers, such as standardized test scores and placement exams that have disproportionately impacted Black and Latino students, need to be redesigned or scrapped altogether. Courses and program experiences need to be updated, streamlined, and clarified so that students can more effectively choose and make timely progress toward a degree.

- **How students are supported:** The types of barriers faced by students in higher education have changed, and student supports need to keep pace. Need-based financial aid programs, such as the federal Pell grant, are critical for student success. Yet, Pell grant awards have not kept up with the rate of inflation; while the maximum Pell grant covered two-thirds of the average cost of college in 1975, it now covers only 25 percent.[9] Further, financial aid should extend beyond tuition to address needs such as housing, food, transportation, technology, childcare, and healthcare. Finally, with our nation's changing demographics, schools should recognize that representation and the "who and how" of serving students matters. Faculty and staff must reflect the student population, and inclusion must be embedded into campus culture and climate.

- **How students are connected:** At key transition points— from K-12 to higher education to jobs—obstacles block or obscure the way forward. In order for our schools to graduate more students and for our workforce to grow in diversity and strength, the journey needs to be made seamless and multiple viable pathways need to be created. Businesses, K-12 districts, community colleges, and universities should work together to align education and labor needs and optimize resources. All of us need to collaborate because we have a collective stake in the success of students.

These strategies are not theoretical; they have been proven. Across the United States, colleges and universities that have leveraged these strategies to fit their particular circumstances have increased retention and graduation. Two shining examples are the University of Texas at El Paso (UTEP) and Miami-Dade College, which have long track records of incorporating strategies for access, support, and connection. Both schools welcome every student who wants to enroll, and those open doors have at the same time helped elevate their reputations for excellence. Miami-Dade College, which grants associate and bachelor's degrees, has been the training ground for many of its home city's political, business, arts, and civic leaders. UTEP produces the most Latino graduates in the country with bachelor's, master's, and doctoral degrees in science, technology, engineering, and math. Its designation as an R1 "highest research activity" campus puts it in a tier among less than 5 percent of the country's higher-education institutions. UTEP and Miami-Dade College are trailblazers, but they should no longer be unique in the higher-education landscape. We need their successes replicated everywhere.

It is not enough, however, to say that strategies alone will effect change. Commitment must be embedded into the work. We cannot expect results without making investments of time and money. Over and over, the prevailing public narrative is that students and schools have failed, without recognizing that their systems were neither designed nor given the resources to do otherwise. When Dr. Diana Natalicio began to lead UTEP in 1988, some faculty members questioned whether the university would sacrifice quality by serving more Latino students from low-income families. Dr. Natalicio aggressively sought national research grants and leveraged funding to incentivize faculty to support students. The university would back faculty members' grant proposals and match the funds—if they integrated research into the classroom and included students in their work.

"We were going to become a research university and become more selective, and those two goals were absolutely critically equal in terms of what we were trying to do. Of course, it worked out great because these students are extremely talented," said Dr. Natalicio, who retired in 2019.

Achieving results also will require consistent, concerted effort. Higher education is a complex enterprise that impacts many sectors, and all of them need to be involved to create change. Moreover, campuses and their communities face dynamic circumstances, and leaders need to have the latitude to respond accordingly. Equity in student success is "not a one-time shot," said Dr. Eduardo Padrón, who led Miami-Dade College for twenty-five years before retiring in 2019. "It takes bringing the private sector and bringing government—it takes a village. It's not this boutique program; it's not the flavor of the day. It is something that has to be consistent, and you need to go out and do it every single day."

Dr. Padrón set out to demonstrate that open access to education and academic excellence can go hand-in-hand—regardless of students' backgrounds and family income. Laying the foundation for this took years: Miami-Dade College created partnerships with various local social service agencies and legal aid groups in order to help its students and their families navigate life outside of school, and they also created a foundation to raise money from the Miami-area private sector. "It all took a concerted effort," Padrón said.

The pandemic and its resulting recession showed that higher education is capable of pivoting. Because SAT and ACT tests could not be administered in spring 2020, most universities stopped requiring them, and many may realize that better factors can be used in admissions. With campuses closed and classes and services moved online, schools had to figure out how to teach, engage, and support students in different ways. Threatened with plummeting enrollment, they focused on trying to ensure that students stayed.

"We saw institutions that claimed they could not change to serve our population transform and do so overnight," said Deborah Santiago, a co-founder and Chief Executive Officer of Excelencia in Education, which informs and organizes changes for Latinos in higher education. "It wasn't necessarily pretty or easy, but when they had to go virtual, they had to scrap all kinds of things." For too long, institutions of higher education have wasted time and energy wishing for "different" students and a return to the circumstances of another era. Our schools can do better. Collectively, we can do better. More challenges will loom, and to survive and thrive, higher education needs to be pushed toward new norms and frames. When higher-education leaders and institutions put students and their needs and perspectives at the center, colleges and universities cannot help but think and act differently. This opens up better ways to serve and support students toward their goals of graduation and their dreams of meaningful and sustaining careers.

The Future Is Here

We are witnessing a collective movement toward building a better future in this country. The challenges highlighted by 2020 did not hinder the dedicated leaders working for Latino opportunity and success; if anything, these challenges laid bare persistent, systemic barriers to equity and reminded us that the issue is urgent and the time for profound change is now.

After working for years alongside fellow advocates to increase access to higher education and improve retention and graduation rates, I see a clear link between Latinos' educational success and a growing economy, which will in turn lead to more civic engagement and stronger democratic institutions. A win-win situation.

These gains will be reciprocal. America and its institutions will benefit from an educated Latino workforce, as will the Latino communities that raised and nurtured the graduates themselves. Higher-educational attainment creates a protective shield over families and neighborhoods of color. It leads to higher income, greater employment, the ability to weather recessions, more resilient mental and physical health, access to social safety nets, and increased civic engagement. The benefits are passed on to future generations so they can keep building upon our progress.

Our public educational systems and institutions profoundly define and shape our society. They must include, serve, and lift up all of us—not only our most privileged students. If we aren't collectively living up to this public mission, we must invest in the change we want to see and be.

Educational institutions produce so many of the teachers, doctors, engineers, scientists, artists, journalists, and business and civic leaders who will shape our future. As more Latinos find support toward graduation and the necessary guidance and mentorship in their professional paths, we will see the ripple effects all around us. For example, doctors will offer a higher standard of care, including the ability to understand and effectively and sensitively treat patients of many different backgrounds, while scientists will display the kind of diversity of thought and experience we'll need to address the most challenging issues facing our nation, such as climate change and its impact on communities of color.

The private sector must do its part to continue nurturing Latinos once they enter the workforce. Even today, when it comes to the future of work and our workforce in this country, business leaders may insist on telling you, "I can't find the talent," said Ralph de la Vega, a philanthropist and former vice chairman of AT&T, Inc. However, de la Vega's own success and career show that we can build the talent pipeline by developing Latino leaders, taking young people of color and putting them in smaller markets to get them trained so they can take on bigger markets. "I think people who are not having a diverse group of people advising them and giving them their input are not going to be as successful in the future marketplace," said De la Vega, who is also former Chairman of Junior Achievement Worldwide. Latino leaders and other leaders of color who champion changes in business play an important role in opportunity and socioeconomic mobility, as do leaders in higher education. Through his philanthropy, De la Vega has built a model for how corporate leaders can become important catalyzers for educational change, too.

The process won't be easy. There will be lots of seemingly unmanageable systemic barriers to dismantle along the way. In this era of renewed calls for racial and social justice, the American public has started to recognize how institutionalized racism has historically set up too many of our students of color to fail. But the tide is shifting, along with the demographics of the United States. I want to see Latinos fundamentally valued for the contributions we have made and will continue to make. Imagine this: if we had constituted our own country in 2015, U.S. Latinos would have represented the eighth-largest economy in the world. Latinos are growing exponentially in numbers and in power. Our nation's future depends on inclusion, opportunity, and success. A different future is possible because we are already building it, with the solutions we need close within reach.

PROFILE: DOUGLAS X. PATIÑO

Today's philanthropic leaders, especially those who are Latine, stand on the shoulders of Douglas X. Patiño. His community-centered leadership helped grow investment in communities of color while diversifying Boards and decision-making roles within philanthropic organizations. Over five decades, in which he crossed numerous race and class barriers, Patiño crafted an outstanding career in philanthropy, government service, and education.

Born to a family of modest means near the U.S.–Mexico border, Patiño considers himself a "borderlander," one who easily navigates and identifies with both sides of a national border.

When he was fourteen, his family moved from Mexicali to neighboring Calexico, California, where all the authority figures he encountered were White, including police, doctors, and teachers.

"I was clear that I was *mexicano*," he said. "At times, when I felt intimidated, I didn't let racial and class barriers define me. I aimed to be thoughtful, respectful, and kind to all people."

Patiño was raised Catholic and credits his belief in a higher power for a worldview that is now more open and expansive, fueling his inner strength and helping him cope and often thrive in challenging times.

He knew from an early age that his life's purpose was to lift himself and his family from poverty, and to help others do the same, as his mother had done for him, his brother, and his sister.

Patiño started working full time in high school. After graduating in 1958, he worked evenings to earn his associate degree from Imperial Valley College, followed by a bachelor's degree in political science and a master's in education from San Diego State University. He began his career as a community organizer in the 1960s, before pursuing a doctorate in human behavior at United States International University (now Alliant International University) in San Diego. It was then that he met his future wife, Barbel Hoyer, a graceful, brown-haired, German-born student. They celebrated their fiftieth wedding anniversary in 2020. The Patiños have a son, Viktor, and two grandchildren, Lorenzo Xavier and Maya Victoria.

Patiño went on to work in government, where he was a staunch defender of workers' rights and championed college access for all students regardless of income status, before embracing a career in philanthropy.

"If you're angry about losing your job to someone, Patiño is such a good, honest guy that you have to genuinely smile as you hand him your office keys."

—*Frank Ramirez, who served with Patiño at the California Employment Development Department*

Through Board positions at major foundations and as Vice Chancellor for University Advancement of the California State University (CSU) system, Patiño has been instrumental in the investment of at least $3 billion in low-income communities, while advancing cutting-edge grantmaking practices and championing diversity initiatives at major foundations.

Leadership Lesson #1: Inspire others to advocate for themselves

Early in his career, when César Chávez and Dolores Huerta were organizing agricultural workers in California's Central Valley, Patiño was mobilizing the Mexican American community in

Sacramento. It was 1967, and there were few community-based organizations run by and for Mexican Americans in the nation when Patiño was hired as Deputy Director of Concilio, an organization in the Sacramento area. Housed in an abandoned school, Concilio created the area's first bilingual library and hosted leadership and organizing classes to magnify the community's political voice.

Patiño's people-centered approach to leadership won over his staff and the community alike. Inspired by his leadership after only one year on the job, community residents hosted a dinner to share their gratitude for his "Spirit of La Raza." In the night's program, they acknowledged his power to inspire in individuals a sense of unity and pride.

After leaving Concilio to pursue his doctorate, Patiño joined the California Employment Development Department (EDD), which serves businesses and job seekers.

Patiño replaced Frank Ramirez in leading an EDD division that prepared workers for public- and private-sector jobs. Patiño was such an inclusive leader that he diffused any tension that might have come from his succession to the position by rehiring Ramirez as his deputy and giving him more authority and opportunities for growth.

"I wanted to keep the position," Ramirez recalled in an interview. "But, if you're angry about losing your job to someone, Patiño is such a good, honest guy that you have to genuinely smile as you hand him your office keys." They went on to work together for nearly two decades.

In 1975, during California Governor Jerry Brown's first administration, Patiño was appointed Director of the EDD, becoming the first person of color to fill this post. Patiño had great success in the position, inspiring a diverse coalition of employee rights groups and major corporations to advocate for the creation of the Displaced Workers Program in California. Later touted nationally as a trend-setting initiative, it supported workers who lost their jobs in the poor economy of the late 1970s.

Governor Brown later appointed Patiño as California Health and Welfare Agency Secretary. At Patiño's recommendation, Brown hired the late Gloria Becerra as his replacement at EDD, and she became the first woman of color to head the department.

Leadership Lesson #2: When change is needed, challenge the status quo

In 1987, Patiño was chosen from a pool of 735 applicants to become the first President of the Marin Community Foundation. (Community foundations are charitable organizations dedicated to addressing local needs and supporting nonprofits in a specific geographical area.) The Marin Community Foundation, created by real estate and oil fortune heiress Beryl H. Buck, is the second-largest community foundation in the country. By 2018, its assets exceeded $2 billion.

There was great fanfare about Patiño's arrival as the first Latino leader to run a major foundation in California. But he would soon become embroiled in conflicts and power struggles.

From the beginning, he was well liked in the community. Marin residents respected his vision of using philanthropic dollars to respond to the needs voiced by the community, rather than bowing to political pressures. Internally, Patiño was criticized for building a "multi-cultural" staff valued for their color rather than their professionalism. In response to these and other concerns, the Board hired an external consultant to assess the foundation's operations. He was exonerated, and the Trustees voted to retain him as President. But just ten days after their vote of confidence in his leadership, and to everyone's surprise, Patiño announced his resignation. He knew it was time to step away from this coveted leadership position. He realized it did not fit his values. Patiño made what is often the most difficult yet critical decision any leader can make: he moved on when he knew it was time.

This experience, among others, helped prepare him for what would become his next career: transforming philanthropy from the inside out. Patiño created the New Partnership Foundation (NPF), to provide financial and technical assistance to very low-income communities that lived along the U.S.–Mexico border. By collaborating with community leaders in Mexico, NPF funded both medical supplies for families in need and educational scholarships to enable students to attend high school.

Respected for his career achievements, Patiño was appointed Trustee at Los Angeles-based The California Wellness Foundation (Cal Wellness) in 1997. He was also later appointed Trustee to two philanthropies with national reach, the Charles Stewart Mott Foundation, in Flint, Michigan, and the Marguerite Casey Foundation, based in Seattle.

Cumulatively, he was involved in making close to $3 billion in grants to nonprofits. He also influenced who benefitted from this money and how.

"With Douglas' experienced voice, we have built a model for the future of philanthropy."

—Luz Vega-Marquis, founding and former President & CEO of the Marguerite Casey Foundation

---

Most foundation trustees are White. Fewer than 15 percent are people of color. Despite the fact that 92 percent of population growth in the United States comprises people of color,[1] a mere 6.9 percent of foundation giving goes to communities of color.[2] Moreover, foundations are often extremely restrictive about how their funds can be spent by nonprofits and community leaders, often giving small amounts of money that need to be spent in a short time frame. As a result, nonprofits face challenges in planning long-term, sustainable work that is responsive to the changing needs of their communities.

Patiño's leadership is credited with helping buck these trends at Marguerite Casey and California Wellness. Nowadays, Marguerite Casey allocates 85 percent of its annual grants to social-sector organizations serving communities of color. Thanks to Patiño and other trustees, since 2002 it has also awarded sizable, multiyear grants for "general operating support," meaning each nonprofit gets to decide how the funds can best be used in service of its mission. Nearly twenty years later, these practices were being championed by many experts as smarter grantmaking practices.[3] Although they are still not widely practiced, they continue gaining momentum. Former Cal Wellness Executive Vice President Tom David describes Patiño and other influential trustees as instrumental in transforming the academic, research-focused funder into a foundation deeply committed to improving the health of the most vulnerable Californians. Patiño also had great influence in diversifying both foundation Boards. "Eighty-two percent of our trustees are people of color, and this would not have been possible if not for Douglas' leadership," said Luz Vega-Marquis, founding and former President and CEO of the Marguerite Casey Foundation. Meanwhile, thanks to Patiño and other like-minded trustees, Cal Wellness became the first foundation in the country where the majority of trustees are people of color.

Leadership Lesson #3: Forge partnerships with allies from other backgrounds and races

Early on in Patiño's organizing days, he learned the power of collaboration with those of different mindsets and identities. In the late 1960s, Latine nonprofits were largely male dominated, and it was uncommon to organize and foster leadership with women.

Patiño was heavily influenced by an upbringing surrounded by determined, goal-oriented women—his mother, grandmother, and sister. From these strong women, Patiño learned how to be emotionally intelligent, set and achieve goals, and work with others to get things done.

When he was working at Concilio, Patiño needed to evidence that there was a strong Mexican American presence in the community to be eligible for antipoverty program funds. In order to do that, he knew he needed to collaborate with women in the community, so he enlisted a group of *mexicanas* from a local Catholic Church and others to help organize. The effort helped Concilio secure a $400,000 federal grant.

Building Bridges with Black Leaders

Patiño met Wenda Weekes Moore, a trailblazing African American leader in philanthropy, in the mid-1990s. Moore became the first Black Chair of the W.K. Kellogg Foundation, one of the largest foundations in the United States. They quickly discovered their shared concerns.

"Douglas and I believed that philanthropy needed to address the new reckoning that people of color would become the majority in this country," Moore recalled. "At that time, no one wanted to say the 'R' (racism) word, nor discuss its impact on communities." Patiño and Moore began to bring together Black and Brown trustees and staffers from different foundations, creating a space for them to get acquainted, find common ground, and collaborate for greater influence in philanthropy.

The two were so respected for these bridge-building efforts that, in 2010, the Marguerite Casey Foundation partnered with the Association for Black Foundation Executives and Hispanics in Philanthropy to create the Patiño-Moore Legacy Award in their honor. The $150,000 award is presented annually to those who forge Black–Brown alliances to assist their community, organize, and fight poverty.

Looking Forward: A Leader Ahead of His Time Inspires the Next Generation

Patiño's three wishes for philanthropy for the next ten years include prioritizing support for low-income families and trusting them to identify their own needs and the solutions to those needs; dedicating long-term resources to geographic areas of greatest need; and using an equity lens in appointing diverse Board members.

"Philanthropy is here to advance justice and democracy," he said in an interview. "Those in positions of power should trust the community to drive solutions and should make investments that reflect its needs and priorities."

Patiño also encourages leaders to align their values with action and to have the strength of character to make change for themselves and their communities. And he called on Black and Brown communities to work together to break down structural barriers that impact families across the country.

"It was my choice to explore the idea that I could lift myself, my family and my community," he said. "I learned that when you give to others, you empower yourself and grow stronger."

9 CRIMINAL JUSTICE
YOUTH SYSTEM TRANSFORMATION

JULIO MARCIAL

What would you say if I told you that next year Los Angeles County plans to make a nearly $500,000 investment in the lives of individual children? Heartening, right? You may even feel relief. Such an investment would make up for the coronavirus disruptions of 2020. Rather than an investment in uplifting our kids and nurturing their growth, however, $500,000 is the amount that Los Angeles County had been planning to spend on each child it incarcerates in a county youth prison—despite the lingering dangers from coronavirus and from the even greater pandemic of structural racism.[1]

This was the "investment" that Los Angeles County actually had chosen to make in our kids—primarily our Black and Brown and Native American kids. Across the country, Black youths are five times more likely to be arrested than a White youth; for Latinos, it's almost twice as likely. Through the pandemic, when COVID-19 laid bare how truly harmful our budgeting, policies, and practices have been for low-income youth and youth of color, the most populous county in America had the largest number of incarcerated and detained youths in the nation, and their futures will surely inform the rest of the nation.[2]

What if I told you that in 2030, half the juvenile halls in this country had been converted to schools and technology or vocational training centers; that the private and public sectors had come together to provide wraparound support services for children of incarcerated parents; that schools are no longer used to criminalize misbehavior, and that community-based programs had virtually eliminated the need to arrest, detain, and incarcerate youths?

Although this may seem aspirational, the pandemic has fueled changes that we didn't expect to see for years. We're already making change. Since the pandemic hit, and the police murder of George Floyd sparked outrage across the country, activists have been pushing to move money out of law-enforcement budgets and into communities. The call for reinvestment of this nature is unprecedented and has spread across the country, from Baltimore to Portland, Oregon, and from Minneapolis to L.A.[3] My hope is that the momentum will continue, and the aspiration of schools, wrap-around support services (counseling, transportation, and other help), and expansive community-based resources quickly becomes a reality.

There are models that will make this scenario come true. How well and how fast they actually happen, however, will depend on all of us, including Latinos. And the successful strategies for implementing them can be best informed by parents and youths who have experienced incarceration.

California has been pushing ahead with its plan to virtually eliminate its Division of Juvenile Justice, with the last three prisons scheduled to close in 2023. The closures are part of a national movement away from locking up youth far from homes and are intended to promote restorative justice and rehabilitation closer to their loved ones, according to a February 15, 2021, article by *Los Angeles Times* staff writer James Rainey. Consequently, the responsibility for working with the youngsters will shift from the state to the counties. "Officials are trying to figure out what to do with teenagers convicted of murder and other serious felonies, as they simultaneously downsize juvenile halls and locked 'camps,'" the article added.

After incremental moves, L.A. County made history in November 2020, when its governing body, the Board of Supervisors, passed a resolution to transition Juvenile Probation to a new Department of Youth Development, under the county's health agency. It called for transitioning from locked juvenile facilities to home-like settings where young people would receive emotional support, counseling, and treatment. It uses a "care-first" model already working in a few places, including other big cities, such as San Francisco, New York, and Houston. It emphasizes counseling and other emotional support, as well as treatment, when needed.

"The county must resist a narrative about these young people that does not leave space for hope and healing, and insist on a structure that promotes positive youth development and rehabilitation at all costs," Supervisors Sheila Kuehl and Mark Ridley-Thomas wrote in the resolution, which passed unanimously. A projected investment of $75 million in such a department would help navigate pandemic #1: structural racism. The approach is expected to take five years.

At both the state and county levels, we must ensure that the goals are accomplished and taxpayer dollars are not wasted. We must ensure that naysayers are not allowed to use a lack of short-term positive results to waylay long-term goals.

Awakenings

Many of the more recent efforts to help youth while avoiding out-of-home placements started in the late 1980s and the 1990s with a series of studies,[4] some of which were sponsored by the federal Office of Juvenile Justice and Delinquency Program. Since then, programs informed by this research have spread at county and state levels across the country, from Hawaii to the East Coast, Kentucky to Arizona and beyond.

Some programs have already started us moving in the right direction. My friend Scott Budnick, producer of *The Hangover* film franchise, had repeatedly invited me to a creative writing class, which he was teaching as an Inside Out Writers (IOW) volunteer at the Los Angeles County Barry J. Nidorf Juvenile Hall in Sylmar, California. It is one of the largest youth detention facilities in the country. It also happens to be located near my childhood home in Pacoima, California.

When I finally went in 2008, the experience changed my life. At juvenile hall, I sat side by side with Black and Brown youths from East Los Angeles and South Central L.A., Long Beach and Pacoima, hearing tales of abuse and neglect, addicted siblings, missing fathers who had been incarcerated, and a dizzying merry-go-round of foster homes. I vividly remember that I couldn't sleep the night after my visit. I kept thinking of those boys that I met, the majority of whom looked just like me, yet they had never been afforded the same opportunities that I had. They were even more on my mind as COVID-19 swept into juvenile jails and prisons, infecting thousands of youths and staff. Given the close proximity that defines life in youth facilities, such spread was inevitable without significant reductions in population.

Despite this global health crisis and the risks involved, authorities were inexcusably very slow or remained silent about releasing data on COVID infections at many youth prisons.

There is a better way. On a typical day, roughly 70 percent of youths are held for nonviolent offenses. Youth facilities are designed to house youngsters who are suspects but have not yet been found responsible for their offenses. They consequently have high turnover rates, often with short stays serving little, if any, public safety interest.

Consider that the United States beats out much larger countries in land area—India, China, Russia—for the distinction of having the highest incarceration rate in the world, including the incarceration of children as young as seven years old within the juvenile justice system. According to a 2018 report from the Bureau of Justice Statistics (BJS), nearly 2.2 million adults were held in America's prisons and jails at the end of 2016.[5] That is more people than live in some major cities, such as Philadelphia or Dallas. Furthermore, the country incarcerates nearly fifty thousand youths[6] at the state and local levels. That means that in 2018, for every 100,000 people residing in the United States, approximately 639 of them were behind bars.[7] Many of us who have never served time know someone who has.

This issue is personal. It goes beyond my role as a senior executive in the field of philanthropy. It is true that my work has provided me an inside look into the broken criminal legal system that has harmed so many youths and people of color. But the experience of having an older brother and sister, as well as a younger niece and nephew, in and out of jail and prison also provided me with an insider's lens to the ways that systems fail our most vulnerable.

If the U.S. prison population were a city, it would be among the country's ten largest.

At the same time, the United States has by far the highest rate of criminal violence in any Western democracy or, for that matter, of any economically developed nation on Earth.

We rely on incarceration for nearly all of our social problems, which was exposed more vividly due to COVID-19. In a disaster such as that, we could no longer keep warehousing so many people. Instead, it led to early release for many, demonstrating how unfair our practices of incarceration have been.

The substantial suffering caused by excessive incarceration contributes to poverty, decreases the job and education prospects of former inmates, and in many other ways undermines human achievement.

Getting Help

I have seen firsthand the ineffectiveness and collateral consequences of the current system and the damage it causes to people caught in the broken system. One of "those people" I refer to includes my "adopted" son, James Anderson, a multiracial young man who went from prison to UCLA graduate to social entrepreneur.

My friend Scott first introduced me to James in 2012. At that time, I was a Program Director at The California Wellness Foundation (Cal Wellness), one of the largest private grantmaking foundations in California, where I was recommending $7 million annually in grants. My first meeting with James took place one month after his release. He was then twenty.

Eventually, some of Scott's Inside Out Writers students, including James, had begun trickling back home from California's notorious youth prisons, often to the same systemic conditions they had left. These include residential segregation, persistent poverty, community deterioration, alcohol and drugs, and failing schools. And when they were released, Scott always found a way to connect them to people who he thought could help.

Scott and I invited James to dinner at the famous Smoke House Restaurant in Burbank, with a long connection to the Hollywood crowd. When the original restaurant opened, you could see such stars as Bob Hope, Bing Crosby, and Frank Sinatra. Even today, Andy García and George Clooney are frequent visitors. Clooney, in fact, enjoys the restaurant so much that he named one of his companies after the business: Smokehouse Productions.

The fascinating part of meeting James at the Smoke House was that he, too, was famous—but for all the wrong reasons. James was a million-dollar kid because Los Angeles County and the State of California had spent at least that much on arresting, prosecuting, incarcerating, and supervising him. Scott had shared prior to our get-together that many people thought and continued to think that James was too angry to make it in the real world. That meant it wasn't going to be long before he made a mistake that would lead him back to prison.

The first thing I noticed when I entered the restaurant was that the inside felt like I was stepping back in time, with the red booths and old-fashioned telephone jacks at the table (in case you got an important call). There was a sense of history, which I hadn't really understood. And yet, here I was meeting a young man who had just left confinement, and I was trying to understand his path, his history, and why Scott was connecting us at that moment in time.

It had been three years since, when he was seventeen, James faced a possible sentence of thirty-five years to life in prison for participating in a gang fight that had left a man seriously injured.

He said he was lucky that he was only sentenced to seven years and one strike on his record in the juvenile court system. Consider that, with his "luck," if James at seventeen had been made to serve all seven years, by the time he was released at twenty-four he would have spent roughly a third of his life behind bars.

James grew up in the Santa Clarita Valley, one of the most conservative parts of Los Angeles County. His upbringing was defined by poverty, trauma, gang violence, and abusive parents, who were struggling through a divorce. He came home from school each day to a brother who would sometimes beat him and a father who raced past him without a glance in the evenings to lock himself in his room.

After his parents separated, James's older brother found the support and solace he craved in a local gang, whose members encouraged him to use drugs. James said his brother's addictions changed his personality and made him abusive on a daily basis. In 2006, at the age of fourteen, James joined the same gang and developed the same addiction to crystal meth. For the next three years, James was in and out of juvenile hall, until the near-fatal gang fight.

Keeping people out of harm's way and supporting efforts to prevent violence have long been my mantras, both professionally and personally. I believe that, if we can understand, deeply understand, how such violence happens in the first place, we may help our communities, our country, reduce crime and stop the school-to-prison pipeline.

I've been to more than thirty prisons across the country, and I know that it is easier to condemn violence and to warehouse people than to seek the causes and prevent them from happening in the first place. The problem is that the condemnations and warehousing mostly don't work.

Equal Justice Initiative founder and Executive Director Bryan Stevenson, who is a public interest lawyer, author, and justice advocate, has suggestions for addressing the causes. First, get "proximate."[8]

The concept of getting proximate, or close, is what Scott and I did with James, not to condemn him but rather to learn as much as we could about the systems that failed him as a child. James was completely devoted to his gang when Scott first met him in juvenile hall. But nine months later, he had changed his life and committed to helping others change as well. James and Scott are the co-founders of the Los Angeles-based Anti-Recidivism Coalition (ARC).

Founded in 2013 with grants from The California Wellness Foundation and The California Endowment, ARC has one thousand members, all formerly incarcerated men and women who have committed to reshaping their lives. They pledge to be gang free, crime free, drug free, and working, seeking employment, or in school. They commit to being of service to their community. The coalition provides resources and mentorship—even housing. ARC places its recidivism rate at just 10 percent.

It is one of the most highly regarded nonprofits in the nation, with its leadership having been invited to the White House by President Barack Obama on a number of occasions to showcase its innovative work, which has been instrumental in the transformation of the criminal justice system in California.

In the past, criminal justice advocates in California tried a heavy-handed approach, leading to the incarceration of many young people like James—deemed "too angry" and unworthy of a deeper investment. But research of youth development and youth justice shows that mental health services and community-based programs are more effective than punishment, which should be our last approach.[9] The research also shows that confinement increases the likelihood that a youth will drop out of high school and become chronically unemployed.[10]

About ten years ago, California decided to focus on rehabilitation, and the number of kids held in state facilities fell from 10,000 to approximately 680. County facilities across the state have had similar reductions. Then, in 2020, the COVID-19 pandemic hit, and California Governor Gavin Newsom decided to close state youth prisons altogether, sending kids who would have otherwise been held in those facilities back to their home counties.

Let's take it one step further to the bold idea of closing youth prisons, and focus on rehabilitation instead of cells, in every state and county. Why did it take a budget crisis and a global pandemic for us to come this far? The research is clear: separating youth from their families and communities and emphasizing punishment and retribution harms young people and their communities.[11] (A poll by The California Endowment showed overwhelming support for this move.)[12]

What About Those Very Few Who Are Too Dangerous?

The call for closing youth prisons does not mean that I believe no youth should ever be placed out of their homes. In those cases where public safety absolutely requires youths to be in out-of-home care, I believe that this should only be for the minimum time necessary to address this risk—in a warm, nurturing environment close to home, with well-trained staff that treats all children and young adults the way we would want our own children to be treated. This approach is smart policy, and it saves taxpayer dollars.

Four years ago, I joined the team at the Liberty Hill Foundation, a public foundation based in Los Angeles, to focus on a campaign to end youth incarceration as we know it. Why? Because I firmly believe that children do not belong in prison.

Reducing any youth confinement system, while ambitious, is achievable. Through restorative services, coupled with mental health treatment and educational support, community-based programs help youth recover from their past mistakes and get their lives back on the right track.

Take, for instance, the restorative justice system for youth that is administered by the Pima County Attorney's Office for the Tucson-area courts in Arizona. The three-month program refers youth who have committed minor crimes, such as graffiti or having small quantities of marijuana, to Community Justice Boards. The Boards are made up of about one hundred adult volunteers, who are supervised by four County Attorney's Coordinators. In person before March 2020 and virtually through the pandemic, they meet twice a month in teams of two with each of the youths, and sometimes their parents. In-person meetings take place at one of about a dozen sites around Pima County, which is bigger in land area than any of the smallest five states. The youths need to take responsibility for their offenses, apologize to any victims, commit to staying in school, and complete tasks required of them by their Board. Sometimes, this entails participating in a community activity, joining a sports team, and taking ACT prep or arts classes. They are also encouraged to participate in family-bonding activities, such as cooking a meal and using alone time with parents to improve communications. Mental health services and transportation to appointments are available for the youths and their families. The program, which includes expunging the offenses of the youths who satisfactorily complete it, has a 95 percent compliance rate. Although about one thousand youths are eligible to be referred to the program each year, only about three hundred were going through it prior to the pandemic due to funding limitations.

These alternatives to incarceration work. In Los Angeles County, only 11 percent of youths who participate in these diversion programs return to the juvenile justice system, compared with 33 percent of those who were confined.

The cost to taxpayers also indicates that prison should be the last resort. In Los Angeles County, it costs nearly $500,000 to incarcerate a kid for one year, versus $5,000 to put him or her through a community rehabilitation program.[13]

The resounding consensus is that the budget can reflect our values, and the values must reflect our belief in our youth. For example, the Los Angeles County Board of Supervisors unanimously approved $26 million to establish the Division of Youth Diversion and Development (YDD) in 2018, which is separate from the Department of Health Services. This division was intentionally placed in the Los Angeles County Health Agency's Office of Diversion and Reentry to emphasize the goals of keeping young people out of the justice system and connected to community alternatives.

Investing in a real future for all our country's youth is beyond smart taxpayer stewardship—it's the right thing to do. We need to learn and listen to the stories of those we continue to arrest and incarcerate, to get close to those most harmed by this system. We need to address the root causes so that all youths of color are given a fair chance to succeed, learn, and thrive, much like myself and James, who have overcome significant traumas to get to where we are right now.

For Us, It's Personal

For James and me, this issue goes beyond our roles as philanthropic and corporate leaders. One of us has experienced firsthand the juvenile justice system's traumatic and inhumane approach, and its detrimental impact on the long-term development of the youths it touches. For the other, the experience of having family members in and out of jail provided insights into the ways that systems fail our most vulnerable.

James's path through life is one riddled with great challenges and triumphs. He has come to see the challenges as opportunities to embrace the healing and growth that he believes are responsible for his successes in life. These past few years have been a journey of great reflection and transformation. He's continued to expand his horizons and dedicated himself to pre-pandemic travel in his efforts to become more intimately connected with the world around him.

In his evolution from drug addiction, gang membership, and prison to double honors UCLA graduate and meeting with then-President Obama about criminal justice reform, James felt the need to truly push past boundaries and traditional models in his efforts to create powerful change within disenfranchised communities. He realized that outside of the nonprofit model, there existed a powerful vehicle that could be used to create immense impact. He decided to transition into the corporate world and focus on helping businesses develop social impact as a core part of their identity, rather than simply as an afterthought.

James has been working at The Yerba Mate Co., the self-distributor of Guayakí Organic Brand Yerba Mate, one of the fastest trending organic beverages in the country. The Yerba Mate Co. is distributed online and across the United States to roughly six thousand businesses, primarily through organic and health-oriented grocery stores, such as Whole Foods and Sprouts.

At The Yerba Mate Co., James leads the charge on hiring ten thousand system-affected people of color worldwide as the company grows. As part of this movement, James has started looking to partner with other businesses willing to extend opportunities to those in need.

Furthermore, James's brother, Phillip, was released after serving nine years in prison, and he immediately reconciled with James after having received professional help to address his trauma and addiction. Phillip is currently working in the tech industry in the San Francisco Bay region. While in prison, the older brother earned his associate degree and learned how to code through a program called the Last Mile, which helps prepare incarcerated people for tech-industry jobs.

For me, serving as James's mentor has been one of the most rewarding experiences of my life. But I am reminded that being a mentor has nothing to do with age or experience. I say this because James is also my mentor. I have had my share of trauma for as long as I can remember.

From the start, I was traumatized by being the only member of my family to be born in the United States. My parents came to the United States to find a new home because of the lack of educational and economic opportunities in Mexico, the home-land that they loved dearly. But the pressure of living in a family where no one had documentation was terrifying. Imagine having to lie about your existence to protect your family during the most formidable years of your life?

The constant living in fear led to self-esteem and identity issues, which led to problems in school, including numerous suspensions in middle school. Studies have found that U.S.-born children of undocumented immigrants are more likely to have lower educational attainment[14] and face significant barriers to achieving higher education.[15] This research played out in my household, given that none of my siblings made it to post-secondary education.

When kids choose a profession, they tend to follow in their parents' footsteps: doctors' children often become doctors, lawyers produce lawyers, and plumbers beget plumbers. My father was a gardener and my mother cleaned houses. It was an honest living; however, living in constant poverty led to three of my siblings cutting corners, which ultimately put them into the justice system. Sadly, their kids also followed them into this broken system. Fortunately, all of them now live honest, decent lives, except one. My next older brother, Sergio—smart, artistic, and entrepreneurial—served for four years in state prison and then struggled for two decades with many of the thousands of barriers that the formerly incarcerated face. When he died in November 2020, he was just 49 years old.

I was the lucky one. My parents and siblings did whatever it took to put me (and keep me) on a pathway toward lifelong success. Although I had challenges in middle school, I was also afforded the opportunity to play sports, which helped to smooth out some of my rough spots. It meant connecting with peers from similar backgrounds and learning that resilience is a strength, not a weakness.

In addition to family support, I was fortunate to be connected at an early age to role models and mentors, who helped me navigate from the inner city to the University of California, Los Angeles, and then to a career of more than twenty years in philanthropy.

Growing Social Movement and Political Will Across the Country

In L.A. County, the home to the largest juvenile justice system in the country, nine thousand youths were either arrested or cited for crimes in fiscal year 2019. At the start of 2020, we were confining approximately one thousand youths in eight youth facilities and providing services to and supervising approximately 4,500 more through our Probation Department.

Sadly, approximately 95 percent of youths arrested and incarcerated in Los Angeles County's youth facilities are Black or Latino. Nationwide in 2017, 109,300 convicted youths were in detention, according to the National Center for Juvenile Justice. Another one hundred thousand were going through the juvenile court system. In all, the center's statistics show, out of 213,000 youths, 40 percent were Black, 35 percent White, and 22 percent Latino.

Led by a forward-thinking Board of Supervisors and a powerful base of community activists (many of whom are system-impacted young people), Los Angeles County has embarked on the Youth Diversion and Development model that connects youths with community-based services that support their development, in lieu of arrest or citation.

The model is meant to provide oversight, infrastructure, and alignment with other county efforts, such as the Department of Public Health's Trauma Prevention Initiative, to ensure that all youths in the county can connect with a continuum of services that address their needs. Its success thus far is thanks to a strong collaborative process and building of trusted relationships between county officials, advocates, law enforcement, community-based organizations, philanthropy, and youths. By fully implementing this model, Los Angeles and communities elsewhere can reduce youth arrests and equitably improve outcomes—including reduced violence.

As part of this greater effort, the Center for Strategic Partnerships, Liberty Hill Foundation, and the new county division are working to ensure philanthropic partners are at the table. We have found tremendous value in the thought partnership and expertise that local foundations have offered.

We believe the work we are doing here in L.A. County is the first of its scale across the country. With 10 million people, we are larger than at least forty states. Other U.S. jurisdictions have engaged in similar efforts, but none of this size.

Lessons Learned

Take advantage of the current political landscape and open policy window. The rate of people arrested and incarcerated nationally has been dropping for more than a decade, and this reality offers an opportunity to advance smart policy reform packages. It takes a substantial amount of in-state capacity to build support among relevant policy makers, community members, and other actors, and to change laws.

The Justice Reinvestment Initiative, over the past ten years, has worked with state government leaders to assess factors that increase incarceration rates and to craft policy reforms that are politically feasible. The "inside-game" approach has achieved an array of legislative changes by convincing political leaders that it is possible to do reforms without jeopardizing public safety or losing elections. This strategy has benefited from tens of millions of dollars of investment. It should be complemented with greater support for in-state capacity of reform advocacy groups, to hold state governments accountable for implementation and to prevent backsliding.

Change is incremental; expectations must be realistic. Based on what types of reform and systems change may be feasible within the current political landscape, even a 20 percent reduction in arrest and incarceration rates over ten years in a given state might be an impressive win.

Political will must be significantly expanded to get beyond 20 percent. For laws to change, culture must change. We must grow our appreciation for youth of all colors and incomes and expand efforts to turn away from caging people. What is politically possible cannot be achieved without support from a strong social movement pushing for criminal justice reform. Such a movement will not thrive without substantial leadership by formerly incarcerated people, their families, and others directly impacted by current criminal justice structures and policies. Two groups may be of particular interest in this regard: the organized leadership of formerly incarcerated people and crime survivors.

One hopeful movement is that of the Formerly Incarcerated and Convicted People and Families Movement. While in need of additional support, it represents an important model. Some groups of crime survivors are beginning to organize around demanding more justice from the criminal justice system, with better outcomes that truly serve their needs.

In addition to creating political pressure for change, another beneficial outcome of a social movement may be a shift in cultural norms around when, why, and how it is appropriate to use criminal justice infrastructure to solve social problems. A shift in what is considered the appropriate use of thousands of laws may sometimes achieve faster results than efforts to actually change criminal codes.

We need to create a powerful political constituency across the country that will reduce mass incarceration. Such constituencies have begun to form and have had an impact on elections, including major victories for criminal justice advocates in the 2020 elections, where U.S. voters approved sweeping measures that restored voting rights to tens of thousands of people on parole, reined in the power of several big-city police departments, and eased drug laws. For example, more than 2.1 million Los Angeles County voters approved Measure J, which will divert hundreds of millions of county dollars to social services and jail diversion and youth development programs. California also passed Proposition 17, restoring the rights of fifty thousand eligible people with a past criminal conviction, who had been permanently barred from voting.

Address issues of drug abuse, addiction, and mental health through appropriate interventions. Youths and adults suffering from these conditions should not be warehoused in jails and prisons. We need to pilot, test, and scale more-effective solutions.

An effective communications strategy must be put into place. While several national groups devote resources to communications, many groups doing criminal justice reform work at the state level lack basic communications resources. As a result, they fail to engage most effectively with the public and decision makers.

We must grow a deep bench of skilled advocates working for proactive, systemic change. The base of knowledgeable advocates and players with enthusiastic support for reform is starting to grow. But it is not yet commensurate with the size and number of reforms we're eventually hoping to achieve.

Advancing Reform: The Role of Philanthropy

Advocates, policy makers, and justice stakeholders play critical roles in promoting youth justice reform, in building public awareness, and in having the will to bring about necessary changes.

But effective and sustainable reform requires the involvement, leadership, and financial support from philanthropy.

Funders large and small have played pivotal roles in justice reform at the local, state, and national levels. Through investments in education, advocacy, programming, training, and technical assistance, as well as research, foundations have become integral partners in the reform movement. More funding partners are needed to sustain the momentum.

Roles for Funders

THOUGHT PARTNER: Encourage systems reform and seed innovation by supporting advocacy and community organizing, data collection, research, evaluation, and implementation of best and promising practices, including the promotion of public health, racial equity, and youth development frameworks.

INNOVATOR: Incubate creative, and even risky, pilot projects or initiatives with the potential for real policy and practice improvement. Two of the most transformative efforts—the Annie E. Casey Foundation's Juvenile Detention Alternatives Initiative and the MacArthur Foundation's Models for Change Initiative—have successfully used research and best practices to redefine the landscape of youth justice nationally. Smaller, targeted efforts also can change lives and offer opportunities for replication on a broader scale. These include the Sierra Health Foundation's Positive Youth Justice Initiative in California and The California Endowment's Brothers, Sons, Selves Campaign in Los Angeles.

CONVENER: Create opportunities for policy makers to come together with community partners, experts in the field, and justice-involved youths and families to learn from each other, better understand problems, and develop multidimensional solutions.

CHAMPION: Help reframe and shape the public discourse about youth justice and related issues, and support effective advocacy and communications aimed at building public awareness.

CONNECTOR: Engage in networks and coalitions and urge fellow philanthropic colleagues, grantees, and systems and community partners to work together to prioritize youth justice within their portfolios and their daily work.

SUSTAINER: Focus strategic, intentional, and thoughtful financial investments on advocacy and policy reform efforts over the long term to achieve systems change, strengthen nonprofit infrastructure, and develop leadership in the field.

A decade from now, this vision can be our reality, and we will be proud to say we live in communities where the following are true:

- Youth prisons have been closed and the hundreds of millions of dollars spent on incarcerating kids have been invested in a comprehensive youth development system—a network of community-based service providers that intervene in the lives of young people through restorative and rehabilitative approaches.
- Rather than getting arrested and incarcerated for minor offenses, such as shoplifting and schoolyard fights, kids are treated like kids. They have access to community-based services through pre-arrest diversion programs that ensure accountability, while providing the care and support required to address their real needs.
- Schools are treated like schools and not environments where youths are criminalized for exhibiting age-appropriate behavior. Kids will not be arrested on campus, but instead will have access to restorative justice and support.
- Homeless people are no longer released from jails, courthouses, and police stations to life on the street. Instead, they receive a "warm handoff" to social services and housing providers for the support they need.
- L.A. County and other communities no longer incarcerate Black and Latino youths and adults at four and five times the rate of White youths and adults.

Through smart, cost-effective reforms, the current county jail population can be reduced to a small fraction of its former size. That's because we have invested in a care-first, decentralized model that dramatically reduces adult arrest and incarceration by prioritizing diversion strategies and community-centered, health-focused treatment facilities.

After all, when youths who commit minor crimes are given the support they need, they are less likely to enter the criminal justice systems as adults.

10 ENVIRONMENT
A DIVERSITY LENS ON TRANSIT POLICY

MARY SKELTON ROBERTS

Although climate change is a global, massively complex problem, as Senior Vice President of Programs at the Energy Foundation, I also believe it's primarily a problem of community, human connection, and the ways we live and interact with each other. The COVID-19 pandemic and accelerated climate impacts in recent years only underscore the importance of caring for each other and finding collective solutions in the face of adversity—values that run deep in Latinx communities.

I experienced this firsthand growing up as a first-generation *afro cubana* immigrant in the working-class neighborhood of Jamaica Plain in Boston. My neighbors were mostly Irish, African American, and, increasingly, Latin American families, who were arriving from Cuba and Puerto Rico and would define that area of Boston (in spite of significant gentrification) for years to come. I now marvel at the connectedness and sense of community in the neighborhood where I grew up. When I was young, and even after I got my driver's license, I never drove, instead accessing the city and all of its culture and resources by foot, bus, or train. On the weekends, we took the bus to Dudley Square (now renamed Nubian Square), another longstanding community of color in Boston, to buy ethnic foods at the markets there. My mother also didn't drive, and whenever we'd go grocery shopping, there was always a group of maybe five or ten men with cars or minivans, waiting outside the store. For a few bucks, they'd load up your bags and drive your family home, an early version of Uber, but built on community trust and support.

This is just one example of how, long before we even knew what climate change was, Latine communities have been living low-carbon, resilient lifestyles. In fact, many of the climate solutions I have worked for—public transit, creative alternatives to driving, shared green spaces, and community resilience—are things Latinx people have been relying on and supporting for many years. Even as the pandemic has rattled our cities and created a host of new challenges, I believe the close-knit, resourceful nature of Latinx communities can serve as a model for a world that is learning to collectively fight and adapt to climate change.

We bring to this challenge certain shared cultural values: family loyalty, extended community, communal pride, and conservation of resources. In addition, in so many Latin American communities, from the Caribbean islands to Southern California, we have already been living with climate change for years. Despite our relatively low contribution to its causes, Latine communities have been disproportionately enduring the consequences of climate change and fossil fuel reliance for a very long time. We need only look to the tropical region my family emigrated from, and the storm damage that is becoming an increasingly perilous and routine fact of life. Drought, record heatwaves, and raging wildfires in the Southwest, not to mention flooding and storms in other regions, are taking huge tolls on our livelihoods.

While Latinx people have deep connections to climate change, you wouldn't know it based on a cursory glance at the historic climate movement. While the field is always evolving, there's been a disconnect between our real-world experiences with climate change and our leadership in mainstream climate action. I've experienced this in my own life. Even well into my career, I didn't identify as part of any climate change movement. To me, climate change represented melting ice caps and hungry polar bears, right? I was working on land use, housing, and economic development! Of course, eventually, it all clicked into place for me. Now I see climate change and its intersectionality in everything, whether it's my work at the foundation, the future of my city, or raising a daughter of my own in these uncertain times. I now recognize that it is impossible to solve the problem of climate change without uplifting the role of Latine communities, for both moral and strategic reasons.

Therefore, I propose that we make these connections even stronger for more Latines (using a gender-neutral term)—connections between the big-picture problem of climate change, the devastating impacts that face the Latine Diaspora, and our capacity to drive solutions.

The Climate Threat and Latine Communities

Climate change is the defining problem of our time. Human activity leading to the emission of greenhouse gases is the dominant cause of rising temperature and disruption of the global climate, impacting every system that we interact with on a daily basis—water, food, labor, health, housing, and more. The wealthiest nations since the Industrial Revolution have been pumping greenhouse gases into the atmosphere at the highest rates for decades, and rapidly electrifying nations, such as China and developing countries in the global south, are catching up.[1] The leading sectors contributing to those emissions are electricity and heat, agriculture, transportation, manufacturing, and land-use change.[2]

Global response to climate change is bending the curve, but we are currently on track for a bit over 3°C (5.4°F) of warming this century, which would yield catastrophic outcomes.[3] A 2018 report from the UN Intergovernmental Panel on Climate Change (IPCC) warned that even the range of consequences within the international goal of between 1.5° and 2°C (about 2.7° F) of warming are severe.[4] For example, in the 2°C scenario, 37 percent of the world's population would be exposed to severe heatwaves at least once every five years. An additional 411 million people in urban areas would be exposed to severe drought. And as many as 80 million people worldwide would be exposed to flooding from sea-level rise.

The 2018 IPCC report urged global collaboration to reach net zero carbon emissions by 2050, a goal that must be met in order to have even a 50 percent chance of limiting global warming to 1.5° C. Encouragingly, many countries are taking real steps toward this goal, but there is a critical role for the United States. We are second only to China in carbon emissions, but under President Donald Trump, the United States exited the Paris Climate Agreement and rolled back over 125 regulations and policies designed to curb emissions—pushing for deregulation on everything from drilling on wildlife refuges and corporate carbon emissions, to lightbulb and dishwasher efficiency standards.[5]

The White House must do more than restore the status quo—to achieve net zero by 2050, the United States must roll out bold, ambitious plans in the next decade. It must take into account the needs of communities of color, including Latinos, who will be the most impacted by the consequences of global warming.

First and Worst

Climate change magnifies longstanding environmental justice concerns over how low-income people and communities of color, while contributing relatively little to environmental degradation, experience disproportionately severe consequences from it.

A 2008 report by researchers at the University of Southern California and the University of California, Berkeley, coined the term *climate gap*, identifying the unequal impact climate change is having on people of color and the poor. Focusing on California, the report found low-income families to be more vulnerable to extreme heat. Agriculture and construction workers, many of whom are Latine, are at increased risk of death from heat-related health effects, and the climate crisis will dramatically impact jobs in these sectors.[6] In my home city, the immigrant communities of East Boston are surrounded on three sides by water and are vulnerable to increased flooding.[7] The working-class community of Dorchester is especially susceptible to heat exposure and stormwater flooding. And the mostly immigrant community of Chelsea is home to environmental hazards like incinerators and fuel storage, many of which lie below the flood plain.[8]

Some of the most destructive climate impacts we've seen threatening Latinx communities are the severe tropical storm seasons that pummel Cuba, Hispaniola, and Puerto Rico. Hurricane Maria was one of the worst disasters in U.S. history, destroying tens of thousands of homes, crippling island infrastructure, and causing thousands of deaths. In addition to human loss and property damages, the impact of these events reverberates to extended families who have relocated overseas, as well as to the disruption of local and regional economies.

We saw communities of color ravaged in 2020 by a global health crisis linked to environmental degradation,[9] a disease that interacts with air pollution in ways that disproportionately harm Black and Latinx people,[10] many of whom are considered "essential workers" and unable to maintain social distance.[11] On top of the COVID-19 pandemic, yet another historic wildfire season raged across the Southwest over the summer. Research has found that majority Black, Hispanic, and Native American census tracts experience 50 percent greater vulnerability to wildfire than others.[12] Failure to direct resources to vulnerable communities, such as undocumented immigrants, during wildfires exacerbates inequality. For many of us, the compounded crises of fire and disease hammered home what life during climate change really means, and the great urgency needed to address the inequities it preys upon.

The Demand for a Response

Clearly, there is a moral imperative to engage Latines in climate solutions, but there is also a strategic one. I have found that the strongest and most durable climate solutions begin in communities, and ours demonstrate a deep understanding of this crisis. One climate strategy that both the Energy Foundation and my former employer, the Barr Foundation, have relied upon is backing research to elevate this understanding.

In September 2020, Barr funded University of Massachusetts Boston polling that found people in Greater Boston widely believe that climate change is happening, and Latines are less likely than others to claim it is not. Asian Americans, Latinxs, and Blacks are more likely than Whites to identify climate change as a "serious problem," and more inclined to view its impacts as being shared equally.[13]

National data reflects similar patterns. A 2017 study from the Yale Program on Climate Change Communications found that "Latinos are much more engaged with the issue of global warming than are non-Latinos. Latinos are more convinced global warming is happening and human-caused, more worried about it, perceive greater risks, are more supportive of climate change policies, and are more willing to get involved politically."[14]

But there are still some key disconnects that have kept us from having a proportionate decision-making role. For one, we can't ignore the fact that the environmental movement, which has historically made up the leadership on climate change, has been overwhelmingly White. In 2018, of the top forty environmental NGOs, 73 percent of full-time staff and 86 percent of senior staff were White. The problem exists in foundations as well, with 67 percent of full-time staff and 96 percent of senior staff being White, according to a major diversity initiative in the field.[15]

It is also not always easy to recognize ourselves as climate change leaders. This disconnect is something I've experienced myself, even though my current life's work is climate change! After I finished my undergraduate degree, I worked on land use and economic opportunity. Green issues certainly caught my interest but hardly made me a dyed-in-the-wool environmentalist. In grad school, I worked on cities and transportation, parks, and environmental health. Although I clearly understood the importance of climate change, I didn't see it as *my issue*. I didn't see myself in the work.

As awareness and urgency around climate change began to

surge, and narratives emerged around the subject, it became undeniably clear that all of this was inextricably connected. Climate change became the umbrella for environment, health, housing, economic development, and other issues that impact people on this planet.

The same coal plants spewing pollution into Latine neighborhoods are also leading to flooding and punishing heatwaves. Quality, affordable housing does little good with hurricanes and wildfires threatening it every year. And the jobs that sustain our communities—in construction, energy, agriculture, and more—will go up in smoke if we don't rally together around solutions.

National Opportunity: A New Economy Centered on Environmental Justice

The election of Joe Biden Jr. in 2020 sparked a collective sigh of relief from climate activists. As the country rebuilds from the pandemic and economic hardships, there is a path forward to enact a climate agenda that centers justice.

Rejoining the Paris Climate Agreement was an important first step, as was restoring the policies that were torpedoed by the Trump administration. But this is a unique moment to reimagine our nation's systems—from health, education, and work training to transportation and energy, and agriculture and food—that intersect with climate and perpetuate injustices.

The ambitious U.S. Climate Plan, which he proposed in April 2021, would reduce our greenhouse gas emissions to half of the 2005 levels by 2030—and potentially reinvent the U.S. economy in the process. The shift to all-electric transportation and energy efficient housing will boost both the environment and the economy.

In addition to the Environmental Protection Agency, his team embedded ecological agendas in Transportation, Housing and Urban Development, and even the Treasury Department.[16] Biden's early selection of diverse leaders for his Cabinet continued an encouraging trend that began with the historic nomination of Vice President Kamala Harris, the first woman and woman of color in that post. Biden's Cabinet appointments included Cuban American Alejandro Mayorkas as Secretary of the Department of Homeland Security, the first Latino and first immigrant to be nominated to the position; California Attorney General Xavier Becerra as Secretary of Health and Human Service, and Connecticut Education Commissioner Miguel Cardona as Secretary of Education. And there's political commentator and campaign organizer Karine Jean-Pierre's hiring as White House Principal Deputy Press Secretary. Born to Haitians in Martinique, the policy expert, who is Black and lesbian, adds broader perspectives to Biden's team. Julie Chávez Rodríguez, an Obama administration appointee and granddaughter of labor leader César Chávez, was named Director of the White House Office of Intergovernmental Relations. Latines in these positions can bring lived experience and advise the new administration on what it feels like to be Latinx, as well as on how proposed policies could impact families like theirs.

The administration would be wise to continue deepening coalitions and partnerships with Latinx leaders and movements, especially those pushing for a bold climate agenda.

AOC and the Green New Deal

If you've been paying attention to the climate leadership that has been happening just outside of the spotlight for years now, then it came as no surprise when a young Latina from the Bronx rose to power as one of the most impactful forces in climate policy today. Alexandria Ocasio-Cortez did, however, surprise the political establishment when she upset ten-term incumbent Joe Crowley in the 2018 Democratic primary.

Her sweeping grassroots campaign mobilized voters in a district that is about 50 percent Latinx, 40 percent Spanish speaking, and 75 percent people of color. The win was hardly a fluke of demographics, as some of her best outcomes were in gentrifying areas.[17] Ocasio-Cortez won because of a powerful campaign fusing economic justice, health, labor, and climate.

Since taking office and through her reelection in 2020, the Representative's signature proposal, the Green New Deal, became a versatile policy blueprint and a rallying cry for climate action. It includes sweeping public investment in infrastructure and energy to meet emissions reduction targets set out by the Intergovernmental Panel on Climate Change. The Green New Deal is important because of what it symbolizes: a reimagining of our COVID-19-impacted economy and the energy system to create a cleaner and more equitable society. It is this kind of big, bold thinking that can address climate change and rebuild the fabric of our country.

There is also a strong economic case for the Green New Deal. Researchers at the Global Commission on the Economy and Climate estimate that reimagining key economic systems in the United States—energy, cities, food and land use, water, and industry—could lead to 65 million low-carbon jobs and add $2.8 trillion in government revenues per year by 2030.[18]

Unlocking Latine Power for Climate Solutions

My work has focused on transportation and land use, so I'll take a moment to outline what meaningful climate action can look like. In Massachusetts, we have a goal of reducing greenhouse gas emissions by 80 percent before the year 2050. That means the way we design our communities and get around have to dramatically change. This includes the following:

Rethinking transportation. In the United States, transportation has surpassed energy as the largest contributor of greenhouse gas emissions, accounting for nearly a third of emissions.[19] Boston and other cities must develop multimodal networks of rail, bus rapid transit, electric vehicles, and bike and pedestrian walkways. Single-passenger vehicle transportation needs to be drastically reduced, and the number of people taking public transit drastically increased. All of this will require difficult decisions, made even more difficult by COVID-19. As I have pointed out in an opinion piece I wrote with Dr. Aaron Bernstein, interim director at the Center for Climate, Health, and the Global Environment at Harvard, rather than retreat to our cars after the pandemic, we must restore confidence in public transit, recognizing that climate solutions are public health solutions.[20]

Greater connectivity. Reducing transportation-related emissions also requires a mix of housing and business development that allows people of all income levels and backgrounds to access the city's opportunities and resources, without getting behind the wheel. Again, the pandemic has complicated this already difficult task, but should not send us fleeing into suburban sprawl. As urban populations almost certainly continue to grow, we must build safe, healthy, and interconnected neighborhoods. We can learn from the pandemic response that there is tremendous hunger for more greenways, biking, and walking paths that are accessible to residents across demographics.

Resilience to shocks and stresses. During the winter of 2014, record snowstorms crippled Boston's transportation system.[21] In 2018, one of our worst winter storms and surging tides flooded Boston and coastal Massachusetts with frigid seawater.[22] In 2020, the pandemic put our social resilience to the test, demanding solidarity and mutual aid when formal institutions were unable to meet all of the city's needs—even before the following winter's blizzards. The future Boston will need to retrofit existing buildings and create new infrastructure to manage flooding and storms. But the city will also need to strengthen its social ties so we are prepared to care for each other should disaster strike.

In all cases, the political will required to create these shifts—not to mention those needed in the energy sector—means we'll need strong community leadership. I'd like to highlight some success stories to provide a sense of what fully realized Latine climate leadership looks like and how it might grow into global change.

Latin America's Transit Leadership

The Barr Foundation and a coalition of stakeholders have been looking to Latin America to find exemplars of bold public transit. Around 2013, the foundation took an interest in bus rapid transit (BRT) as a powerful option for revolutionizing transportation.

One striking example we found was in Medellin, Colombia, where infrastructure improvements became a centerpiece of a radical urban transformation. The city began to reshape itself in the 1990s, after a violent period of drug cartel activity. Its transit agency played a major role in the renaissance, carrying out an education and engagement campaign to build a "Cultura Metro,"[23] a shared sense of cultural identity around world-class public works projects. Transit investments in light rail, gondolas, and BRT were used to revitalize marginalized areas, fostering local ownership and city pride.[24]

Similarly, in Mexico City, the Metrobus is one of the world's most advanced transit systems, moving more than 1.8 million passengers daily. It's the centerpiece of sweeping improvements that arose in the early 2000s, when the city had some of the worst smog and congestion problems in the world. The changes slashed pollution and traffic—and greenhouse gas emissions.[25] The Barr Foundation led four educational trips to Mexico City, inviting local leaders to learn from city planners there. Several bus transit-way projects are now under way in Greater Boston.

Climate Resilience Through Community Connection

Impacted communities lead with the wisdom of lived experience, and island communities in the Caribbean have been coping with the impacts of climate change for many years. I'm inspired, for example, by the innovation and resilience in my family's home country of Cuba, which has been living with intense tropical storms, while working with scarce resources during political isolation. Cubans have very much lived the low-carbon, resilient lifestyle I described in my own upbringing, relying on community connections and neighbor-to-neighbor support for storm preparation. The Cuban government adopted a program called Tarea Vida, which involves restrictions on new building in flood zones, relocation of existing communities, landscape restoration, and an overhaul of the island's agriculture.[26] There is much we can learn from these efforts.

One lesson we've learned is the profound way that this resilience stretches across the Latin Diaspora. Following Hurricane Maria, we received many requests to support efforts in Puerto Rico and chose to help. The strong familial and cultural bonds between Caribbean and Latin American countries and immigrant populations throughout Greater Boston run deep. That strikes me as a significant advantage in climate resilience—not only our longstanding tradition of place-based reliance on community, but also our ability to look at the problem beyond a strictly local lens and realize that our community is global.

Voting and Organizing Power in California

In 2007, California passed one of the strongest pieces of climate change legislation at the time, Assembly Bill 32, California's Global Warming Solutions Act, known as AB 32. In 2010, the oil industry–backed Proposition 23 threatened to essentially repeal the act. In the face of a $100 million campaign, environmental, economic, and racial justice groups formed a partnership, marking the "emergence of a people of color environmental majority with political clout," according to a 2011 case study by the Funders Network on Transforming the Global Economy.

Environmental justice and community groups not only worked alongside a mainstream environmental campaign, but also created a separate coalition to defeat Prop. 23 and build a long-term vision for environmental justice in the state. Prop. 23 was round-ly defeated at the ballot, with 61.6 percent voting no, including 73 percent of voters of color. Predominantly Latinx parts of the state voted as much as 77 percent against. "People of color are environmentalists and are, in fact, the future of the environmental movement,"[27] was a key takeaway from that vote, which the Funders Network report identified.

Since then, Latines have flexed their political clout in Sacramento to pass legislation directing a large portion of AB 32 Solutions Act revenues toward disadvantaged communities.[28] Los Angeles had another major reminder of this influence in 2016, when voters passed Measure M, a "mega transportation measure" that levied a half-cent sales tax to raise tens of billions over forty years for rail, bus rapid transit, and bike projects. A Cal State L.A. poll leading up to the election found that 71 percent of Latinx voters favored the measure, and otherwise found the group to be a defining political force in the state, with around half saying they'd attended a community meeting or signed a petition.[29] Indeed, the measure handily won its required two-thirds vote on Election Day, propelled by millennials and Latinx voters, who came out in huge numbers in support of the transportation package.[30]

A Blueprint to Elevate Latine Power in Climate Action

Going forward, we need to shift the narrative so it reflects the Latine experience and build stronger, more explicit connections between our communities and the climate movement. There are some key strategies that can be put to work in the nonprofit community, as well as in the public and private sectors. The following have particular relevance for donors and funders.

Expand the Climate Narrative

Texas Tech atmospheric scientist and climate communicator Katharine Hayhoe points out that, because climate change is a "threat multiplier," we all care about something that is impacted by it. There are many entry points to climate change, including issues that loom large in Latinx communities, such as public health, economic opportunity, and social justice. We've got to make those connections stronger and more explicit.

We also need to elevate local expertise and success stories, from green infrastructure to urban farming, to community renewable-energy projects.

Talking up climate change in our daily routines will help. But philanthropy is in a strong position to facilitate this shift in the narrative. We can fund nonprofits, or even cities and transit agencies (as in the Cultura Metro campaign). We can also use our platforms as institutions of wealth and power to send that message ourselves, using our own voices to expand this narrative so more of us see ourselves as climate champions and experts.

Meet Communities Where They Are

A few years back, Barr was supporting research to learn more about how Boston's Latino communities were using transportation. Especially in areas that aren't served well by our transit system, it's crucial to understand how these residents were getting where they need to go. I remembered the low-tech community car sharing from my youth, and knew we were likely missing part of the picture.

We partnered with Stephanie Pollack—the Deputy Administrator of the Federal Highway Administration who was then a researcher at Northeastern University—to compile data. The problem was, Stephanie and I knew that largely immigrant communities were not going to freely volunteer information about their daily lives to teams of university researchers, nor could we rely on online surveys or canvassing transit stations. So Northeastern partnered with Neighbor to Neighbor,[31] a Latinx-led nonprofit in Massachusetts, to go into these communities, knock on doors, and have conversations with families. As a result, we discovered that my hunch was true—there was extensive, organized carpooling happening that transit experts had been missing.

The lesson here is, just because not all Latinx communities are participating in systems the way we might expect, it doesn't mean they are not participating. Just because Latines in California may not all be active in green NGOs doesn't mean they aren't environmentalists who are shaping the climate agenda of the state. It is crucial that we proactively and respectfully go into these neighborhoods and engage with them where they are.

Develop the Next Generation of Planners, Scientists, and Engineers

The only way old patterns and ways of thinking change is to change the leadership and workforce in influential fields. That's because even the most "woke" public agency administrator, CEO, or researcher is still limited to their own life experiences and values. That doesn't mean their leadership isn't important, but we've got to elevate Latinxs alongside them to bring our unique cultural perspectives to these problems. This new generation of leaders will have a distinct understanding of our needs and be less likely to trade away our demands and concerns.

Doing this requires changes to hiring and recruitment practices, but we also need to play the longer game of bringing brilliant young minds up the chain of command. We can create pathways for young people to enter the fields of planning, transportation, engineering, and environmental sciences, which might seem inaccessible or unwelcoming at first glance. We can empower and connect mentors in these fields to inspire and guide more Latines to explore these careers.

Support Multi-Issue Coalitions

By using different entry points to onboard a wide variety of communities, interest groups, sector leaders, levels of government, and more, we can build connections that draw in Latine communities and strengthen political power. Philanthropy in particular has a rare ability to link up different players, fund overlapping work, and help to find a shared mission. A large part of that work involves creating a space where leaders from different worlds can come together and build trust so that future collaboration can happen more naturally.

No single government agency, NGO, or private company can handle climate solutions at the scale we need. A series of modest but highly effective bus rapid transit pilots have begun to change the way we prioritize public transit on our roads, but they have carved out new city and state channels of communication and collaboration. Transforming streetscapes (controlled by cities) and transit (controlled by the state) will be a smoother process with those connections in place.

Philanthropy should expand its efforts to fund alliances and collaborations that tackle intersectional issues. For example:

- Groups that work in housing justice, affordability, and/or curbing gentrification can work with transit groups to build support for increasing economic opportunity to their communities without accelerating displacement. Such a coalition can move transit investment while making sure planning and policy take housing needs into account.

- Coalitions should connect public health to the climate movement—for example, programs that focus on pollution and asthma rates in low-income neighborhoods can also prioritize reducing emissions from vehicles and public transit (see California's Prop. 23 example). These communities can offer support for climate policy while securing a seat at the table to ensure such plans don't shift pollution into vulnerable neighborhoods.

- Organizers working on establishing new green spaces and urban parks can also work with planners on flood protection measures, improving public health, and neighborhood livability with outdoor green spaces, all while holding stormwater in place.

- Labor and economic justice groups can ally themselves with mainstream environmental groups to establish a renewable energy industry that trains and benefits local workers.

A Vision for a New Future

The climate crisis does, at times, feel insurmountable and overwhelming. It is true that if we continue on the current track, we are headed for catastrophe. But I wouldn't do this work if I didn't have hope. I am motivated to continue this fight because I have hope for a clean-energy economy that works for everyone. For public transit that is clean, affordable, and efficient. For expanded access to green spaces, clean water, and breathable air. For good jobs that lift people out of poverty and allow them to provide for their families, without wreaking further havoc on the environment. For cities where biking and walking are as safe and easy as driving. For a better future for my daughter.

At the Energy Foundation, we know that there is a path forward for Boston, for our nation, and for the world to emerge from the challenges of the past and build better systems that work for everyone.

We have an opportunity, now, to get people back to work: by building a new public transit system, creating green manufacturing jobs, installing solar panels, and overhauling infrastructure, leading to new trade jobs for electricians and mechanics.

The next decade is critical for getting the United States on track to reach net zero emissions by 2050. We can do it, with this White House and climate activists in Congress. There are countless examples of promising work happening at the local level, such as Boston's work to reimagine transit and California's passage of the Global Warming Solutions Act. Philanthropists who want to support this work can fund research and innovation, bring together problem solvers from across sectors, and partner with government to scale up promising local solutions.

We have the blueprints, but to succeed, Latinxs need to see themselves in this movement. We have so much to offer in the fight against climate change—starting with our shared values around community and resourcefulness—those same values that made it possible for me and my mom to get a safe ride home from the grocery store all those years ago. We are among those most impacted by climate change, and we need to speak up, to push our local, state, and federal governments to accelerate their progress. We need to run for office, and we need to continue to demand policies that work for our families.

Together, we can realize a vision in which Latine communities are leading the way on climate, elevating our insights and power, and building a future in which we avoid certain catastrophe and become more resilient in the face of climate impacts.

11 ARTS AND CULTURE
OUR VOICES AND IMAGES MATTER

OLGA GARAY-ENGLISH

"Art and culture are not just accessories to organizing, they are indispensable. Critical. The blood and fire of our movements. They sustain us and allow us to not only imagine but to feel the world we are building together."

—*Augusto Boal*

The arts are part of the human DNA. They have been integral to every society since time immemorial, and claiming our right to the arts remains vital for all societies, especially marginalized communities. Not only do the arts provide a pathway for creative thinking and action, but they are also a way for us to demand and claim a more equal future for ourselves and our fellow human beings on this increasingly fragile planet. The arts allow us to explore our own individuality as well as bring people in communion to build cohesion, empower communities, increase tolerance, and create the policies that will impact the way we steward our planet and raise our children. In underserved areas, including communities of color, the arts have long been credited with reducing poverty, as well as strengthening cultural identity, ameliorating the effects of trauma, and nurturing a shared vision, according to a 2017 Policy Link report.[1]

Creativity is a muscle that must be constantly conditioned to garner power, and the arts provide a pathway for creative thinking and action—both highly prized tools in business and society. In the same manner, culture helps to build social capital; it is the glue that holds communities together. Although it is important to understand the history and evolution of art and to see the works of the masters and innovators who have contributed to Western culture, here in the United States, the space given to people of color in the art world has been far too limited. If it is true that people are inspired and find cohesion and a sense of self-worth in seeing themselves reflected in a culture, and in the works that are displayed in museums, galleries, and the community theater around the corner from where they live, then much more needs to be done to open opportunities for Black, Indigenous, People of Color (BIPOC) arts in general, and Latino arts in particular, to be developed, created, curated, and appreciated much more broadly.

The White-dominated U.S. arts and culture establishment has discounted people of color: our artists and audiences, the staff members who are hired to lead cultural institutions, and the Boards of Directors that set their policies and strategies. In a breakthrough 2010 study, the American Association of Museums, as part of its Center for the Future of Museums, acknowledged that only 9 percent of core museum visitors and about 20 percent of museum staff were people of color that year. "If museums want to remain relevant to their communities," the study found, "the museum audience will have to look dramatically different as well, particularly in the western and southern U.S. and in most of the larger cities across the country."[2]

The importance of acknowledging and promoting the art, artists, art administration, and audience for and by U.S. Latinos and Hispanic Americans is part of a much bigger future demographic and cultural portrait of the United States. Already, California and other states are majority minority. The demographic shift has already started, and we must think ahead. The U.S. Census Bureau projects that by 2044 the whole country will have no clear racial or ethnic majority. Put another way, the majority will be made up of people of color. By 2050, the Hispanic/Latino populations will have almost doubled again to form 30 percent of the U.S. population. The implications are vast in practical terms, such as workforce, education, and healthcare, among other issues for the United States. But the cultural roots must start to branch and be amended.

"The United States must reckon with the fact that Latinos are essential to its survival and to its splendor, and have been for generations," cultural critics Elizabeth Méndez Berry and Mónica Ramírez wrote in a *New York Times* op-ed in late 2020. "We Latinos need to know it, too."[3]

Of course, I didn't always know it. My conservative parents, who arrived separately in 1961 and 1962, when each got the opportunity to flee from Cuba, sought to "protect" their only child from outside "American" ideas and influences that were too liberal and alien in their view.

At the University of Florida in the early 1970s, however, I developed a more expansive view of the world. New ideas and experiences permeated my life in Gainesville, Florida. This included an increased appreciation of how the arts play a critical role in helping us claim and own our heritage and culture, something that had been squashed in me in the three small U.S. towns where I grew up. In rural Pennsylvania, southeast New Jersey, and northern Florida, blending in with my almost 100 percent White peers was expected, even demanded. Anything that marked you as different was not tolerated. Often, my parents and I were the only Latine family in these small communities, and outside our home the pressure to assimilate was strong.

Later, while getting my master's degree in community psychology at Florida International University (FIU) in the Miami area, I had to conduct a practicum to complete my degree. I was assigned to FIU's Center for Rural Education, which was directed by a former Dominican nun, Sister Magaly Rodriguez O'Hearn. The center used the pedagogy of Paolo Freire, in which advocates challenge learners to consider patterns and structures of inequality as an instrument for liberation.[4] Freire also proposed that "without a sense of identity, there can be no real struggle."[5]

The center used Freirean pedagogy to introduce literacy and

English as a second language to the farmworkers of South Florida. Tens of thousands of seasonal and migrant farmworkers gather there each year to pick citrus and other fruits and vegetables. Of these, 70 percent are originally from Latin American countries. Back in the 1970s, agribusiness tried to keep them in their camps far away from any perceived "negative" outside influence.

Taking a page from Augusto Boal's Theater of the Oppressed, a tool for social change that uses theater for grassroots education, we entered the farmworker camps with Los Callejeros, the center's Latin music group, which was made up of former farmworkers, to build trust through music while gathering the community. Later, we would introduce theater skits related to the farmworkers' experience. The goal was not theater for theater's sake, but a means to reflect the farmworkers' living conditions and their ongoing struggles. People showed up, and it wasn't long before we were a familiar sight at the camps. After showing up consistently and becoming known quantities, we would start the literacy process.

The arts were instrumental in building the trust that was critical for Freire's "*conscientização*," the process of achieving critical consciousness. According to Boal, critical consciousness "focuses on achieving an in-depth understanding of the world, allowing for the perception and exposure of social and political contradictions. Critical consciousness also includes taking action against the oppressive elements in one's life that are illuminated by that understanding."[6] Similarly, in an interview for the University of Southern California Dornsife College of Letters, Arts and Science website, anthropology Professor Dorinne Kondo said, "Making art is a form of cultural work; it is not simply the spontaneous outpouring of creative genius."[7]

Both in this country and throughout Latin America and the Caribbean, grassroots arts organizations understand the perspective of art as cultural work and have used it to achieve important gains alongside their communities. They understand the crucial role that the arts play in empowering vulnerable populations, and the way they can build community strength and individual accomplishment.

"Mexico's performing arts/music scene has deep and diverse roots, which stem from its Indigenous, African and European/Criollo legacy," said Cristina King Miranda, a curator and consultant who splits her time between her Mexico City base and Puerto Rico. "Violence, political-social strife, and uncertainty have always saturated the country, yet Mexico is living a great cultural apogee. The work and creativity are progressive and powerful, and was, in part, shaped by forces of government repression in the late sixties (the massacre of university students in 1968) and the country's renaissance in the 1980s, after the 1985 earthquake.

"In Mexico, artists, festivals, and cultural spaces work with few resources and in fragile conditions," she added. "This has resulted in a plethora of community-initiated projects dealing with issues of social justice, human rights, and equity, combined with sophisticated digital presence to project work around the world."

One can tell a similar, complex story about any one of the countries in this diverse continent, each with its own distinctive social structures and cultural legacies, some with multiple Indigenous languages, such as Quechua, Guaraní, and Aymara, in addition to those of their European colonizers.

The U.S. Latine experience is also extremely multifaceted. Some of us have been here for generations with a sometimes precarious relationship to the Spanish language; others are recent immigrants with little familiarity with English (and some from Indigenous communities arrive in the United States with little knowledge of either English or Spanish). As the art critic Carlos Aguilar wrote in the *New York Times*:[8]

> Latinos are not a monolith. The context, details, and
> nuances that go into telling the story of a family in
> Mexico City won't be the same for the story of a family

in Los Angeles, which would in turn differ for one in
Miami. American-born or -raised Latinos have unique
life experiences, straddling the line between assimilation and pride in their heritage . . .

The active participation of Latinos in this country is generally
ignored in both the media and in history books. "Our presence
is intrinsic to this country," Aguilar wrote. "Yet, American Latinos remain mostly invisible in our collective narrative, a narrative
that very much includes the images we consume."

Yet there are cultural commonalities even in our diverse Latinx
origins, and these are reason to celebrate. By recognizing the
intrinsic worth of all human beings and the communities they
form, the arts are the perfect vehicle for bringing us to a deeper
level of understanding and communion.

Latine immigrants and refugees have always found ways to
stay connected to their countries of origin. Cheaper international
flights, communication platforms such as WhatsApp, and the
internet have provided a level of interconnectedness between U.S.
Latine communities and their countries of origin. They created
an awareness and solidarity across the hemisphere. Even in countries with strict travel limitations, such as Cuba, refugees who
came to this country in the early days of the revolution were able
to maintain a lifeline through the power (and nostalgia) of our
music. More recent immigrants have a more fluid relationship to
the island, and hybrid artistic manifestations, such as Latin Hip
Hop and Latin Rap, have been the result.

Now more than ever, artists have urgently embraced the digital
universe as a means to circumvent the travel restrictions imposed
by governments and world events. And, though many of our communities are still mired in digital deserts, increasingly they too
are being exposed to the digitalization of the arts. International
arts collaborations that previously were not possible due to visa
restrictions and the cost of travel are now flourishing. And this
new way of creating art will be around for a long time to come.

The arts are a means to find new paths for expression, but they are also a means to promote democracy and cultural and social agency. In the United States, Mexico, Central and South America, and the Caribbean, there are countless examples of arts organizations that promote healing, denounce domestic violence, build relationships and the organizational capacity to work within and beyond borders, share technical skills, and nurture cultural leadership.

Here are some examples of the organizations undertaking this transformative work, which prizes equality and denounces discrimination.

FOMMA (Fortaleza de la Mujer Maya), Mexico

FOMMA is a collective of Mayan women that uses theater for education and community building. It was established in 1994 by Petrona de la Cruz (from Zinacantan, Chiapas, Mexico) and Isabel Juárez Espinosa (from Aguacatenango, Chiapas). Creating FOMMA was considered in that area as a reckless act of defiance, but as it has helped collective members move toward artistic fulfillment and respect, the group has become an internationally admired arts and social service organization.

FOMMA, also called Reflejo de la Diosa Luna (Reflection of the Moon Goddess, or Xojobal Jch 'ul Me'tik), uses drama to preserve the languages, cultures, and arts of all its members. Women's rights are the primary focus of the plays that the troupe takes throughout communities small and large around Chiapas, throughout Mexico, and abroad. Based in Chiapas, the group is made up of actresses and playwrights, who often write about tackling challenges and gender oppression in their own lives.

Other FOMMA programs and services for marginalized people and low-income older adults include professional training, language lessons, and psychological, legal, and personal support. They also offer the underserved population a public space for book events, documentary screenings, art exhibits, and concerts.

TransformArte, Puerto Rico

TransformArte supports eight very poorly resourced, once infor-mal settlements in the San Juan metropolitan area of Puerto Rico. Its aim is to provide these neighborhoods with the means, through performing arts and community-based initiatives, to formulate priorities and address their specific needs for local development and improvements. The neighbors in each of the eight areas have worked for thirty-six-week stretches with a ten-hours-a-week facilitator. This project that pairs artistic expression with com-munity building has been funded through the collaboration of three homegrown foundations: the Miranda Foundation and the Flamboyán Fund for the Arts, with additional support from the Segarra Boerman e Hijos Foundation.

As with Florida International University's Center for Rural Education, the project is based on the work of Brazilian theater artist and educator Augusto Boal, whose "forum theater" enables actors to represent the oppressions of everyday life and provides an active role for audience members. Using theatrical language to start, the participants sort out their collective social issues, goals, and priorities and then develop necessary processes to achieve social change. Community recognition and empowerment are the method's ultimate goals. Of course, the marriage of art and community development comes with the unique spin of Puerto Ricans, who are also known as Boricuas.

"Creativity is Boricuas' strength, and it is present in Puerto Rico's everyday life and through diverse expressions of music, dance, literature and theater, food and visual arts," said King Miranda, the art curator whose mother, Lourdes Miranda, estab-lished the Miranda Foundation.

"Boricua artists from the island and from the U.S. mainland are bringing their own unique contributions and experiences to the conversation about Puerto Rico and the evolving concept of Puerto Rican identity."

Caribbean Cultural Center and the Creative Justice Initiative, New York City

East Harlem, New York-born Dr. Marta Moreno Vega is a Yoruba Priestess, an Afro Latino and Caribbean history scholar, and the inspiration for introducing Groot's Abuela Estela character in the *Guardians of Infinity* #3 comic. Moreno Vega was an early Director of New York's acclaimed El Museo del Barrio, and founder of both the Caribbean Cultural Center African Diaspora Institute (CCCADI), an international organization to link communities of Afro-descendants, and the Creative Justice Initiative, which promotes more appropriate funding of cultural organizations from historically disenfranchised communities.

Part of her life's work has also been countering misinterpretations and superstitions that have swirled around non-Christian beliefs of Afro-descendants since their ancestors were brought to the New World—and that persist today. Indeed, one of CCCADI's core lines of work is to build a sense of a community's ancestral roots and its spirituality. As a pre-pandemic example, it sponsored "The Orisha Tradition: An African Worldview," an introductory belief-system workshop.

Dr. Moreno Vega's Creative Justice Initiative was based on the principle of cultural and artistic human rights, including the right to legally protect one's creations, as spelled out in Article 27, Section 1 of the United Nations Universal Declaration of Human Rights. The Initiative's focus is on funding for artistic and cultural organizations serving Black and Afro-descendant, Latine, Indigenous, Arab, Asian, South Asian, Pacific Islander, Appalachian, and LGBTQIA+/Two Spirit[9] people, as well as people with disabilities.

"As our nation reckons with a legacy of structural racism, oppression, and discriminatory policies and practices," its website says, "cultural equity is essential for achieving social justice."

E Quem É Gostabroach, Brazil

The E Quem É Gostabroach company in Brazil started as a research project of Black university students in Sao Paulo, who were looking to explore what it means to be Black, specifically a Black artist, in Brazil today. Its best-known work, *Isto é eu um Negro?* ("Is this a Black?"), which has toured internationally, opposes silence, and demonstrates that racism can be found in all aspects of Brazilian society.

"The evaluation of racist society is striking, in a mixture of dance, theater, music, projected images, that is, art," cultural critic Alvaro Tallarico wrote of *Isto é eu um Negro?* "A different aesthetic and a constant metalanguage, playing with the theater itself all the time. That is, mixing reality and staging—of reality."[10]

Mau Mapuche, Chile

The Mapuche are the largest Indigenous group of Chile and northern Argentina. The Mau was a political and cultural movement in the early twentieth century to preserve Samoa for Samoans when that Pacific Island was under New Zealand's administration. Mau Mapuche is a collective of Mapuche artists under the direction of renowned choreographer Lemi Ponifasio, who is of Indigenous Maori origin and Director of the Mau artistic laboratory. The original idea for the collective was to explore the similarities and differences between the Indigenous people of Chile and those of Ponifasio's native Samoa. Ponifasio and his partner, Helen Todd, developed a residency with twelve Mapuche artists, which led to *I Am Mapuche*, which has won awards and acclaim. They have produced five other works with Indigenous artists, some having toured internationally. Five Mapuche artists visited New Zealand for a month-long residency and a deeper dive into New Zealand's First Nations, which include the Maori, and their struggles to achieve equality. The residency was part of a Chile–New Zealand cultural exchange.

The collective was also active, starting in October 2019, in supporting the plebiscite that led Chile to draft a new Constitution.

El Colegio del Cuerpo (The School of the Body), Colombia

About 8,500 low-income youngsters have been trained at El Colegio del Cuerpo, a nonprofit dance academy established more than twenty years ago in Cartagena de Indias, Colombia, by Álvaro Restrepo and Marie France Delieuvin. Some of their students have been street children. In addition to dance, the academy teaches its youth to seek peace through art and to practice self-respect and self-knowledge.

Restrepo, who performed in 2010 with the Martha Graham Dance Company, developed and directed a ceremony honoring the victims of Colombia's fifty-two-year armed conflict. *INXILE: The Trail of Tears* included three hundred performers, among them hundreds of victims of violence, and was produced in major Colombian cities.

The company has received support from various philanthropic and international entities for specific projects, as well as the Colombian Ministry of Culture. One such project, involving 1,200 schoolchildren from low-income areas of Cartagena, lasted from 2007 to 2010 and was funded by the Japanese government through the World Bank.

INTAR

International Arts Relations, Inc. (INTAR) is an organization committed to the development of "theater arts without borders," and it focuses on the concerns and cultural heritage of the U.S. Hispanic community. Over the past five decades, INTAR has produced classic plays as well as Latinx adaptations of classics from other cultures and cabaret performances. It has commissioned and/or produced works by more than 175 composers, choreographers, and writers, including Pulitzer Prize-winner Nilo

Cruz. It has also helped many playwrights, directors, and actors to get professional theater credits necessary for union memberships, as well as English-language media reviews. The NewWorks Lab was founded in 1994, under the direction of Michael John Garcés, and is designed to support the creative development of artists from the Latino theater community. Garcés is now the Artistic Director of L.A.-based Cornerstone Theater. It launched Teatro Jornalero Sin Fronteras, which is also described here.

INTAR's last main-stage production before the pandemic forced the theater's closure in 2020 was *Bundle of Sticks*, by queer Puerto Rican and Dominican playwright J. Julian Christopher, who holds a master of fine arts in acting from The New School for Drama.

Self Help Graphics & Art, Los Angeles

When a group of printmakers gathered to work together in an East Los Angeles garage back in 1970, they couldn't have known that they were creating a veritable Los Angeles Chicano institution. The group, including the late Sister Karen Boccalero, Carlos Bueno, Antonio Ibáñez, Frank Hernández, and others, helped to launch the Chicano arts movement in Southern California in 1971, when it held its first exhibition at El Mercado Shopping Center in Boyle Heights, a longtime arrival point for Mexican families to join those who had settled there before. With support from Boccalero's order, the Sisters of St. Francis, it wasn't long before Self Help Graphics moved to Boyle Heights. By encouraging and giving space for local artists' creativity and development, it has been long admired by the Los Angeles Latinx community for succeeding at the intersection of arts and social justice.

Self Help Graphics may be best known for the innovative print-making works of its artists and for the yearly Día de los Muertos celebrations that draw audiences from all over the region and have been used to make artistic and political statements. However, its educational programs, such as the Barrio Mobile Art Studio, has sent teams of intergenerational artists to teach and inspire young artists in public schools, community centers, parks, libraries, and other public spaces all over Southern California since 1974.

Teatro Jornalero Sin Fronteras (Day Labor Theater Without Borders), Los Angeles

Day laborers work for whomever will hire them by the day for construction, gardening, painting, and other unskilled duties. They also make up this ensemble theater group. Cornerstone Theater and its Artistic Director, Michael John Garcés, formerly of INTAR, launched the ten-member troupe as an initiative in 2008. Its mission calls for creating plays by and for the day-labor community of more than 25,000 people in the L.A. area. The fifteen plays they developed since then use theater, specific dialogue, and music to teach about worker and immigrant rights, building healthy families and work sites, and explorations of transnational cultures, while empowering them by sharing their experiences and voices. Since 2011, Teatro Jornalero Sin Fronteras has developed programs in Northern California and El Salvador, where a residency has aimed to offer training to youngsters in improvisational theater techniques, using themes based on the challenges that they live, particularly around immigration and its effects on loved ones who are left behind.

The Hemispheric Institute of Performance and Politics, New York University, New York

The Hemispheric Institute of Performance and Politics, housed at the New York University Tisch School of the Arts, has developed a network of sixty universities, libraries, and cultural centers, as well as human rights and social justice organizations, to study cultural and political performances around the Americas and to create archives to facilitate future research. Affectionately known as the HEMI, it also convenes international gatherings every two years of artists, scholars, students, and writers, and publishes scholarship via online platforms, among other activities. The institute has a social justice focus and seeks to shed light on how theater, music, and dance have been tied to the history of colonialism in the Western Hemisphere.

The HEMI was born of the work of four professors, from the U.S., Brazil, Mexico, and Peru, who wanted to create an academic consortium to house scholars at the intersection of performance and politics. Their work succeeded in attracting seed money from The Ford Foundation, which subsequently endowed the HEMI. It has received major funding as well from other U.S. philanthropies. It has since spawned multiple programs and initiatives, including the Critical Tactics Lab (CTL), which serves as a political action forum for critical reflection about political activism and social movements.

In addition to the video archive and a wealth of other instructional material available through its website, HEMI programs and initiatives include Transnational Arts Initiatives that bring U.S. Latine artists and arts nonprofits together with their Western Hemisphere counterparts to work transnationally; its Helix Queer Performance Network—a collaboration with New York City-based La MaMa Experimental Theater Club and BAX/Brooklyn Arts Exchange. The network fosters the development of queer performers and unity among diverse queer communities in that city through educational initiatives, state productions, and public ones. It prioritizes age, race, class, and gender diversity.

Each of the organizations we are highlighting has chosen dance, music, theater, and the visual arts to tell the stories of their communities with the local artists who shared their lived experiences and who have joined forces with them to use the arts as a tool for empowerment, self-expression, knowledge building, and solidarity.

Colombia's El Colegio del Cuerpo was started by a world-renowned choreographer, Álvaro Restrepo, who combined his passions for contemporary dance and social justice, offering a pathway out of poverty for inner-city, low-income youth. He often chronicles his circuitous route from schoolboy at a Benedictine school to working with street kids, starting in Bogota and later in Cartagena de Indias. For the participating youth, he sets an example of what it takes to be a consummate artist in today's global community and has taken the company, made up of the best dancers of El Colegio del Cuerpo, throughout the world.

El Colegio del Cuerpo's path could not be more different than the journey taken by the largely self-taught members of Teatro Jornalero Sin Fronteras as they give voice to the thousands of day workers, or the groundbreaking work of the Caribbean Cultural Center, which draws on the deep spiritual beliefs of people of African descent throughout the Americas and the Caribbean as a unifying force and vessel for artistry and community grounding.

The through-line in all these cases is a commitment to giving voice to marginalized Latine communities in the United States and throughout Latin America and the Caribbean, celebrating diversity and addressing the real-life issues that we constantly confront. And these lofty goals are accomplished by embracing the arts and culture to express and reflect on the challenges we have faced in the past and present and that we aim to conquer in the future.

They also show how life for all of us can be better in a world with diversity and equity. In some ways, they all point toward the future, even though there is now a wealth of data showing that, in the United States, the nonprofit arts sector suffers from a lack of racial and other forms of diversity, particularly at larger-budget institutions working in European art forms. Just 2 percent of U.S. arts organizations receive more than half of the total contributed income, according to the Helicon Collaborative,[11] which has researched funding patterns at the national and local levels and the demographics of decision makers in the nonprofit cultural sector. The research it conducted in 2011 and 2017 found that overall funding in the nonprofit cultural sector has become *less* equitable. Pre-pandemic arts funding for organizations of color stood at 4 percent of all philanthropic support, yet people of color already made up more than 37 percent of the population.

"There are clear signs that current funding patterns disfavor people of color, rural communities, and low-income neighborhoods," Createquity, an arts research think tank that operated until 2017, said on its website.

The U.S. philanthropic community started to respond to this disparity in funding equity after being riveted by the social unrest that consumed our country after the murders of George Floyd in Minneapolis; Andrés Guardado in the L.A. area; Sean Monterrosa in Vallejo, California; Breonna Taylor in Louisville, Kentucky; Antonio Valenzuela, in Las Cruces, New Mexico; and many others. In "Mapping COVID 19: Understanding Our Past to Create an Equitable Future," a group of Chicago-based philanthropies highlighted the disproportionate impact of the coronavirus pandemic on Latinx, Black, and Indigenous communities. Angelique Power, President of the Field Foundation, wrote: "Policies and lack of investment created the tinderbox."

In response to the perennial lack of investment in disenfranchised communities, The Ford Foundation[12] announced in the fall of 2020 that, alongside sixteen other national philanthropies and many more that are focused on specific U.S. regions, an unprecedented $156 million would be dedicated to Black, Latine, Asian, and Indigenous arts organizations in response to the COVID-19 pandemic that has devastated America's arts and culture and that will have dire economic repercussions for years to come.

But one has to wonder whether this is a one-time initiative, or is this the beginning of a new path toward establishing arts-funding equity in our country? It is incumbent upon us to not waste this unprecedented period of reflection. The arts have a rightful place in the conversation about cultural justice and economic fairness, and it is imperative that we provide platforms for artists and arts workers from U.S. Latinx communities and throughout Latin America/the Caribbean.

This absence of Latines in media was also addressed in the *New York Times* op-ed by Méndez Berry and Ramírez. "Funders and investors working to build Latino power must understand that information is essential community infrastructure," they wrote. "They should invest in independent Latino journalism like Futuro Media Group, L.A. Taco, Revista Étnica, Conecta Arizona, 80grados, Radio Ambulante, and Latino Rebels, instead of bankrolling perennially 'diversifying' but never 'diverse' organizations."[13]

The same goes for the arts, which are critical to our democratic state. Jaroslav Andel, a Prague- and New York-based independent curator and former consultant to the Council of Europe, wrote about how arts and culture help societies face multifaceted issues in *Policy Journal*. "Art invites participation and thus transcends the division between observation and activism. Art inspires insights that resonate across disciplines," he wrote. "Art helps to situate science and technology in public space by symbolically and reflexively representing their roles in society. Art fosters imagination and creativity, capacities that are crucial in its impact on the individual and the community."[14]

Art can also be empowering, as Boal knew. As we move further into a new decade, we must strengthen the arts to fight racial and social injustice. For instance, in 2022, Chileans will decide whether to adopt a newly written constitution to replace the law of the land instituted during the Pinochet dictatorship. The new document was expected to include the arts and culture as a human right. The United States and other countries in this hemisphere, and indeed the world, should take inspiration from Chile.

It is also imperative that governments and private philanthropy acknowledge and sustainably fund arts organizations and artists that come from our communities of color. Key to this struggle is the voice of our young people. Amalia Mesa-Baines, pioneering Chicana curator, author, visual artist, educator, and MacArthur Fellowship winner, rightfully said to me in an interview for this chapter, "They need our history just as we need their future."

PROFILE: MANUEL ARANGO

Some people know Manuel Arango as a Mexican businessman. Others know him as an Oscar-winning filmmaker, or as a key driver behind ecological and cultural preservation movements in his homeland, or as a doting father and husband. But many know him as the father of modern Mexican philanthropy.

His father, Jerónimo Arango Díaz, was a Spaniard from Asturias who traveled to Mexico in the early 1900s in search of opportunity. Manuel Arango, the youngest of five siblings, was born in Tampico, Tamaulipas, and attended boarding school at the Culver Military Academy in Indiana. He studied economics for three years at Lawrence College, in Appleton, Wisconsin, before dropping out to start a business with his brothers, Jerónimo and Plácido. Their store, called Aurrerá, grew to become a pioneering chain of self-service general stores.

Over the years, the brothers diversified their business, opening restaurants, department stores, and discount stores, and in 1971, they founded the public company Grupo Cifra. Twenty years later, Walmart partnered with Grupo Cifra in order to enter the Mexican market, and in 1997, it acquired a majority stake in Grupo Cifra. The supermarkets became Walmart de México and later Walmart de México y Centroamérica.

Now retired from business, in which he was actively involved for more than forty years, he pursues other interests, such as publishing, documentary films, and mostly nonprofit sector activities. Arango established several civil society organizations, beginning with Compartir Fundación Social in 1983, which awards outstanding nonprofit organizations in areas such as community development and volunteer work. In 1984, he founded the Fundación Mexicana para la Educación Ambiental (Mexican Foundation for Environmental Education), and in 1988, the Mexican Center for Philanthropy (CEMEFI), to promote civic engagement among Mexican citizens, as well as to grow a culture of philanthropy among corporations and wealthy individuals.

In 1975, he married Marie Thérèse Hermand. They have two daughters, Manuela and Paula. Still very active, Arango likes to spend time with his family, especially his five grandchildren.

Arango is a lifelong learner. He continues to advocate for environmental causes, to promote civic engagement, and to push the corporate sector in Mexico to adopt philanthropic models that benefit society.

Leadership Lesson #1: Communication is a powerful tool for change

Early in his business career, Arango grew concerned about pollution, especially the persistently poor air quality in Mexico City, where he and his family lived. The 1951 book *Land Hunger in Mexico* by Thomas Harvey Gill had a particular impact on him. His inquisitive mind, which led him to succeed in his business career, also sparked his explorations of a wide variety of other personal interests.

"Traveling with some tourists to Oaxaca. . . . By that chance occurrence, I discovered the richness of the pre-Hispanic world and its immense legacy that can make all Mexicans proud."

He subsequently supported Dr. Ignacio Bernal, renowned archaeologist and former Director of the National Institute of Anthropology and History, in the excavation of Dainzú, a previously unexplored site in the state of Oaxaca.

"That's when I decided that it was important to show Mexicans and the world the amazing things that I had seen," he said, "so I decided to do a documentary, without any idea of what that entailed. It's funny: just as I got into philanthropy through ecology, I went into movies." He has at least five producing credits in his filmography, and he won two Oscars for his debut documentary in 1971, *Sentinels of Silence,* narrated by Orson Welles in English and Ricardo Montalbán in Spanish. The film takes viewers on a twenty-minute helicopter tour of Mexico's impressive pre-Hispanic monuments, including Monte Albán, Teotihuacán, Mitla, Tulum, Palenque, Chichén Itzá, and Uxmal. It is the only time that a short film has won an Oscar in two categories. He shared the Oscars for Best Short Subject, Live Action Films, and Best Documentary in the Short Subjects category with the film's writer-director, Robert Amram, and was thrilled to join Charlie Chaplin on stage at the Oscars ceremony.

Preserving Nature for the Public

In the early 2000s, Arango worked to stop illegal development from destroying Espiritu Santo Island, which is located in the Gulf of California, off the east coast of Baja California Sur state. It is the twelfth largest of Mexico's islands and, at thirty-one square miles, it is bigger than Manhattan. He lights up when describing the island: "It's one of the most beautiful places in the world." Arango rallied nonprofits, corporations, and local and international donors to acquire Isla Espiritu Santo for $3 million from *ejidatarios,* or common-use landowners, thereby conserving its natural beauty.

"The intention was never to keep the island in private hands," he said. "We donated it to the government for its conservation in perpetuity, much to the surprise of those who doubted our motives. It's a nice story in which many people participated, and it took six years to come to fruition. It's there today for everyone to enjoy, hopefully, forever."

After visiting Espiritu Santo Island, Spanish sculptor Cristina Iglesias was inspired to create an artwork to recognize and thank those who participated in its rescue and conservation. In order to maintain the island's pristine natural appearance, she designed an underwater sculpture that she called *Estancias Sumergidas* ("Underwater Dwellings"). Installed at a depth of 44 feet, it consists of a series of fourteen concrete panels, each nine feet tall, with a sixteenth-century text interwoven in the design.

To complement the work, Arango teamed with writer-filmmaker Thomas Riedelsheimer to document the process. The resulting film, *Jardín del Mar* ("Garden in the Sea"), celebrates the relationship between art and nature.

Arango's passion for conservation has continued unabated. In late 2020, he was working on a book that showcases fifty of Mexico's approximately three thousand islands that he believes are particularly worth knowing more about. He laments that Mexicans generally don't think of their country as having any islands at all. They are all worthy of protection—and enjoyment.

Another one of Arango's major conservation efforts emerged from his hobby of flying glider planes. A piece of land was purchased to create an airstrip for a group of gliding aficionados in Mexico State, which lies just north of Mexico City. He chose an area of Tepotzotlan near an old Jesuit site that has been turned into the present-day National Museum of the Viceroyalty. The airstrip had 173 acres (70 hectares) of land. When the gliding days passed in the late 1980s, the land was donated to the Fundación Xochitla ("place where flowers are plentiful" in a local Indigenous language). The foundation operates Xochitla Park as a much-needed urban green space and, before the pandemic, scheduled family-oriented activities that drew about three hundred thousand people a year.

"We're surrounded by an industrial warehouse zone, we're like a big green patch surrounded by concrete slabs," Arango said. "And to confound things, we pay as much in taxes as they do. But it's really worth it!"

Leadership Lesson #2: Find the path where you can make the biggest difference

Arango's interest in environmental causes led him into the international world of NGOs. He was curious to learn more about these organizations that exist outside of partisan politics and represent diverse causes to which he could offer his talent, time, and experience. "That world grabbed me because I discovered the possibility of contributing to purposeful change without necessarily getting involved in, or belonging to, a political party," he recalled. Speaking about Mexico, he said, "Political representation through the parties worked for many years, but the citizenry today does not believe that's enough; it wants to participate." He agrees with the Dalai Lama's view that NGOs "are a civic space for citizens of conscience."

For Arango, the nonprofit sector plays a key role, alongside the government and the business sector, in promoting civic participation and strengthening democracy in Mexico. If one reduces the sources of power in society to the marketplace and the government, then all that's left for the citizenry to do is to vote for its government representatives and go home, he said when interviewed for this profile. "But many citizens, myself included, aren't willing to stop there. We want to go further, we wish to participate, to be part of the changes, to be active," Arango said.

It was this drive that led Arango to found CEMEFI in the late 1980s. While there were many institutions in the United States that organize the philanthropic sector, educate donors, and advocate for different causes to receive funding, this was rare, almost nonexistent, in Mexico.

"I thought more needed to be done to promote this culture of getting involved and giving some of your time, talent and money for the benefit of the common good—a culture of participation and generosity," explained Arango in a 2004 interview with *Alliance Magazine*, wherein he reflected on CEMEFI's founding. "We didn't have any organizations in Mexico whose role was to help the whole sector."

He remains involved in CEMEFI, holding the title of Honorary Lifetime Chairman. He is currently promoting an important initiative within its corporate social responsibility program, which encourages Mexican companies and conglomerates to direct a minimum of 1 percent of pre-tax income to fund programs that benefit the public.

Leadership Lesson #3: For a better future, never stop learning or working

Arango is a man for all seasons. He realizes the value of the past, supporting the preservation of his country's ancient history as a way to increase awareness of Mexico's rich cultural heritage. Yet he also favors change and, as such, is very interested in technological developments and how they can be harnessed to facilitate communications in ways that strengthen democracy.

He acknowledges the benefits of technology and is committed to learning to use newer platforms for communication, including Twitter (find him on Twitter @manuelarangoa). He jokes that he might be among the social media platform's oldest Twitter users. "It's unbelievable. I started to use text messages, WhatsApp, and social media to be close to my daughters," he said, "because it is a new language and, if one doesn't use it, you become technologically illiterate." The use of Twitter and other social media is empowering, he said, and pointed out that it has potential for good in increasing democratic representation. "I have lived through this revolution, and it fills me with hope, with optimism," he said of social media. "We will have a better world with it, as long as we use it appropriately. This revolution to benefit humanity depends on that. And I have faith that it will be so."

At eighty-four in late 2020, he was hardly ready to hang up his hat and rest. "I always have at least ten projects I'd like to carry out. And I have at least a hundred books at home that I'd like to read."

Looking Forward: Spark Civic Engagement for Strong Democracies

As nations including Mexico and the United States become more and more polarized politically, Arango considers the nonprofit sector—especially philanthropy—as a place for coming together. "Intention is crucial, as we are all doing the same thing along different paths," he said. "We all dedicate time, talent, and resources from the local up to the global levels, with the desire to improve everybody's living conditions. That is what unites us, no matter whether we call ourselves left, right, center, conservative, progressive, liberal, crazy, romantics, good, bad. It is precisely that diversity—that we have all kinds—that makes this sector so valuable; it's what makes it strong."

Arango believes strong democracies need government, businesses, and nonprofits in order to balance competing interests and find appropriate solutions to societal challenges that are not dominated by either the market or the political parties. He also has a message for people who do not participate actively in society, who prefer to sit on the sidelines and be spectators:

> It bothers me when people say, "Let's see what happens." I say, "Please don't say that." Because something you don't want to happen is going to happen. Get involved! I think all this anxiety in the world, all this uncertainty, should be translated into personal involvement. Everyone should do their part to create a better world.
>
> We continue and will keep going in the civic battle to guarantee democracy and freedom of expression in our country. All of this, and more, I have seen, I have lived. It has been exciting. However, there is still a lot to get done, although I fear that I don't have much time left. It will be for those who come after.

PART IV

DEMOCRACY IN OUR HOMELANDS

12 CENTRAL AMERICA
A MODEL OF DIASPORA ACTIVISM

ALEXANDRA AQUINO-FIKE AND REAVEY FIKE

I was four years old when I fled with my mother to the United States. We were escaping the perils of civil war and state-sanctioned violence in our home country of El Salvador. And we were not alone. The 1980s saw an exodus of more than one million refugees from Central America. By 1990, the U.S. Salvadoran population had increased fivefold.

Most of us left because we feared for our lives. In my case, we were fleeing the government's persecution of my family. My father had been forcibly disappeared for his involvement with left-wing political groups. My mother, left widowed with a young child, began to receive death threats for her continued organizing efforts following his disappearance.

It has been more than three decades since I left El Salvador. In many ways, my life in the United States has been one of privilege. We were able to enter the country with visas and settled in San Francisco, where we were protected by a small yet privileged group of American activists, who offered us safety and support during our period of transition. My mother came from a well-educated family and spoke relatively good English. Within a few years, she remarried. Her new husband was an American citizen from a middle-class family, cementing my access to a high-quality education and a promising career trajectory.

In contrast, most Central Americans leaving their home countries in the 1980s came from poor families, from towns with little economic opportunity, and from areas ravaged by violence. As it has been in more recent years, opportunities for legal entry were scarce. Many were forced to enter clandestinely, choosing to risk possible deportation and a life with undocumented status over the higher probability of suffering violence or death back home. Now, as then, safety remains elusive. Although today's immigrants are fleeing largely from gang-related terror, not civil war, violence continues in Central America. Since 2012 alone, the number of asylum seekers originating from the region has increased more than tenfold.[1]

The worldwide Central American Diaspora had reached an estimated 4.4 million by 2017 (nearly 10 percent of the region's 42,688,190 people), according to the Migration Policy Institute's August 2019 report,[2] which cited UN Population Division data. Almost 80 percent settled in the United States.

Although the civil war has ended, the armed conflict is over, and El Salvador now has a democracy, the legacy of the war has left deep, enduring trauma and ever-fresh cycles of violence. In my own case, while I've lived a life of relative security since leaving El Salvador, the trauma of having my father so brutally erased from my life has left deep wounds that I am only now unpacking and addressing. I am lucky to have the support to recognize and try to heal my wounds; most of us have not addressed our trauma.

How do we end these cycles of violence? How do we reckon with our trauma? I believe that the violence in El Salvador and the weakening of its democratic institutions is partly rooted in our society's failure to properly face our past. It has yet to confront the legacy of trauma dating from the *Conquista,* the massacres of our Indigenous ancestors, and the seemingly endless cycles of trauma.

I begin with a story—a story about an unlikely group of people banding together across borders to attempt the impossible. This is a story about children, mothers, fathers, brothers, and sisters forced to leave due to cycles of violence and poverty deeply rooted in U.S. foreign policy. Ours is a story of state-led family separations and extreme violence (first in El Salvador, and more recently in the United States). Ours is a story of trauma inflicted in childhood leading to further violence and pain. Ours is a story of international solidarity—with religious leaders, human rights activists, political leaders, lawyers and judges, and generous families and individuals daring to put children and families' health first. Ours is a story of Salvadorans, Salvadoran Americans, and Americans of all backgrounds uniting across borders to give voice and tell what happened to the victims of state-sanctioned violence, poverty, and corruption.

I believe that only when we tell these stories and lift up models of truth, reconciliation, and healing will we be able to imagine a more peaceful future for Central America.

Building a Movement to Locate Los Desaparecidos

In 2014, with the support of my mother, I launched a campaign to find my father's remains. What began as a personal journey soon became a collective movement to confront El Salvador's past in search of the remains of those who were forcibly disappeared during the war—Los Desaparecidos, or The Disappeared. The voices and protagonists of this campaign are the daughters and sons of those who vanished.

Through this work, I have come to see the power of transnational organizing in reconciliation and peacebuilding. With such a significant proportion of Central Americans living abroad, cross-border work is particularly critical to advancing the future I envision.

Scholars have written extensively about the capacity for Diaspora communities—like ours—to influence countries of origin. Salvadorans living in the United States, they agree, hold massive economic and political potential. In 2017, United States residents sent over $5 billion in remittances to El Salvador, accounting for more than 18 percent of the country's GDP, according to Central Bank data. And, with voting laws in El Salvador recently amended, an even greater number of United States residents (almost three hundred thousand, or the equivalent of 5.6 percent of the turnout for the 2019 presidential election) are eligible to cast ballots in

Salvadoran elections. Capitalizing on this potential could mean significant gains for Salvadorans living across borders.

But, economic potential aside, I have a vision of Salvadorans living across borders coming together under an international human rights framework, not only to tell our stories, but also to begin to tackle the root causes of violence in the region. This vision requires that we confront our past traumas and work to heal our collective wounds.

Looking Ahead

In the next decade, I see a robust, transnational human rights agenda that centers on the voices and experiences of those who were forced to flee. I see the model of organizing I've undertaken to find my father's remains having an impact beyond just the issue of forced disappearances.

My vision is for Salvadorans working across borders to influence a broad range of policy issues that advance a human rights agenda. This includes Salvadoran Americans helping to enact policies in El Salvador that address migration causes. These include investment in social services, judicial reform, gang-violence prevention, and the protection of our sacred democracy and the rule of law (rather than the current weakening of such institutions by the administration of President Nayib Bukele).[3] It also involves the resolution of past human rights violations from the armed conflict, among others. This also includes Salvadorans in El Salvador pushing Salvadoran Americans to organize around key human rights issues, such as pressuring the U.S. government to treat our migrant brothers and sisters with dignity and humanity, to develop a comprehensive immigration reform bill, and to make smart and human-centered economic (rather than militaristic) investments in our region.

The example of transnational organizing undertaken by the Our Parents' Bones network and campaign, which I helped to establish, can serve as a resource to other Latinx/Latin American communities. This Mauricio Aquino Foundation project may help others who seek to center their work within a human rights framework, although it is not a one-size-fits-all model.

Violence That Engenders More Violence

The parallels between the immigration crisis of the 1980s and the past few years are striking. It is important to note that the newest wave of migration is not simply reminiscent of the past; it is rooted in it.

Experts point to the persistent violence in El Salvador as being a direct result of the destruction of the country's social fabric during the civil war.[4] In the decade from 1979 to 1989, the military-backed Salvadoran regime received more than $4.3 billion in training and aid from the United States,[5] enabling Salvadoran military and paramilitary officers to become forces of unimaginable violence. By the time the civil war ended, over 75,000 people were killed, a million Salvadorans were displaced, and at least another 10,000 had been forcibly disappeared.[6]

My father was taken from our home in San Salvador on the Wednesday of Holy Week in 1981. Members of the Policía de Hacienda came at close to midnight. They asked for my father, Mauricio Aquino Chacón, forced him into a white pickup truck, and drove him away with other detained people, despite the protests of my distraught mother and my great-uncle. My mother and I never saw him again. I was only eighteen months old.

My father was "disappeared" from his family, friends, and community without any formal charge or adjudication. To this day, the government has not acknowledged that my father was taken by government forces; my family never received any acknowledgment that he was being detained, and we never received any notification, formal or informal, that he had been executed.

My father's family and my mother sought answers through meetings with various government officials, through newspaper ads begging for information, and, more recently, in a legal inquiry through El Salvador's version of the Freedom of Information Act. Still, we have not received an official answer regarding what happened. My father's official status remains Disappeared.

Scholarship on post-conflict societies finds that violence does not cease when armed conflict is resolved, but rather devolves into high levels of crime, vigilantism, and other forms of community violence.

In cases of prolonged armed conflict, such as El Salvador's, this leads to a "culture of violence"—in other words, "a socially permissive environment within which violence can continue even after peace accords have been signed and the violent political conflict has ended."[7] In El Salvador, experts note that the civil war "left behind a militarized society with most of its population unable to earn enough to survive, creating fertile recruitment ground for drug cartels and various organized-crime groups."[8]

What many fail to see is that at the root of the surge in recent years of out-migration from Central America is not only the destruction of our socioeconomic fabric, but also enduring psychological and physical trauma.

As I enter this new phase of my life, that of a parent and a middle-aged professional, I realize that the trauma of having my father forcibly disappeared continues to impact me in deep and painful ways. Not a day goes by when I do not think of my father and ask what is the purpose of my life—why was he taken and yet I live? Not a day goes by when I do not ask if I am making him proud.

Very little attention has been given to how Salvadorans contend with our legacy of trauma. Although four decades have passed since the start of the civil war, El Salvador has largely failed to confront, let alone reconcile with, its tragic past. Unlike other countries that have experienced brutal wars or government-sanctioned repression (e.g., Serbia-Bosnia, Rwanda, South Africa), the Salvadoran state provided only limited opportunity for the victims of violence to pursue reconciliation.

Peace accords signed by government and rebel forces activated

an immediate and complete amnesty for individuals on both sides
of the armed conflict. For almost three decades, this amnesty
has effectively translated into a "Don't Ask, Don't Tell" culture
in the country. Despite the Salvadoran Supreme Court having
annulled the amnesty law in 2016, most people turn a blind eye
to El Salvador's violent past and to the terrors that have impacted
so many. We realize that we are not unique. The lack of reconciliation haunted generations of people after the Spanish Civil War
in the 1930s, and the Dirty War in Argentina (1976–1983), just to
name two. And people joining together to seek information on
loved ones led to creation of the Dirty War's Asociación Madres
de la Plaza de Mayo, the Agrupación de Familiares de Detenidos
Desaparecidos in Chile, and national registries and governmen-
tal commissions charged with determining the fate of disappeared persons in Mexico and Colombia, among others. Mexico's
National Human Rights Commission also pursues information
on forced disappearances.

Despite the establishment of a Salvadoran Truth Commission
in 1992, most documentation of wartime violence remains classi-
fied or has been destroyed. It's not just families like mine that have
been denied information. Even the acknowledgment of incredibly
well-documented human rights abuses, such as the assassination
of Roman Catholic Archbishop Oscar Romero in 1980 and the
massacre of the entire village of El Mozote in 1981, have been met
with intense resistance by the Salvadoran government. Channels
through which to pursue justice, let alone truth, remain scarce.

Until El Salvador and the United States engage in a process of
confronting and atoning for the past violence and trauma committed against Salvadorans, the continued cycles of violence will
never fully end.

Organizing for Ghosts

It is now about forty years since I lost my father, and the search to
find out what happened to him is, in some ways, just beginning.

In 2013, I met a woman who awoke long-buried questions. That year, I had the honor of joining the Board of Directors of the SHARE Foundation, a Berkeley, California-based nonprofit that has long advocated for human rights in El Salvador.

I was one of two new Board members—each of us women in our mid-thirties. In our first meeting as a Board, we were asked to explain what had drawn us to SHARE. I spoke first, expressing my desire to support human rights in El Salvador and discussing how my father's disappearance had inspired me to pursue a life dedicated to justice. The second new member, who requested that her name not be published here, spoke next: "My mother was also disappeared."

There were others like me, I knew. Children whose parents had been forcibly disappeared. Children who, like me, were now adults.

Yet, it was the first time in my life that I had met another young person like me; another person who had lost a parent in such a brutal way—another person with unanswered questions. My Board colleague's story was horrific. As a three-year-old, she had been taken and detained along with her mother. She was eventually released, but her mother remains Disappeared to this day.

Perhaps SHARE Foundation Executive Director José Artigá had something in mind that year when he invited the two of us to join the Board of SHARE. That colleague and I gravitated toward each other, sharing our experiences growing up and the impact of disappearance on our families and on the nation as a whole. And we began to wonder: "There must be more of us."

With the support of my mother, we began to think about organizing an effort to locate the remains of our parents and to finally give them a sacred burial. We envisioned a campaign that would share the faces and stories of our parents in a bold way—to give them life that could not be erased. Slowly, the group of children with Disappeared parents grew from two, to ten, to hundreds of grieving relatives.

In time, we wondered: if a generation of Salvadoran Ameri-

cans in the United States were suffering in this way, what did this trauma look like for Salvadorans living at home? We realized that the quest to find out what happened to our parents—to properly honor them and to respectfully bury their remains—would not only help to heal our own wounds but could also compel El Salvador (and to a certain extent, the United States) to engage in a collective, and much-needed, reckoning with the past. Our Parents' Bones now spans generations of Salvadorans and Americans who are still haunted by the war and the ghosts of our disappeared loved ones.

Remarkable Progress

In five years, this small but mighty coalition has had a historic impact on the human rights landscape in El Salvador. We have met milestones that, for decades, seemed out of reach. In 2016, the forced disappearance of adults during the war was acknowledged for the first time by a sitting Salvadoran President (former Salvadoran President Salvador Sánchez Cerén). And, in 2018, we witnessed the official opening of the Commission for the Search of the Disappeared Adults During the Armed Conflict (CONABUSQUEDA), the first government-sanctioned commission charged with investigating cases of our disappeared relatives. As a result:

- A team of eight investigators, anthropologists, and forensic specialists was formed to find the remains of the disappeared throughout El Salvador;
- The case of thirty students forcibly disappeared during the July 30, 1975, massacre in San Salvador has been under investigation for future excavation; and
- A coalition of eleven organizations representing the voices of victims and human rights advocates, including the Our Parents' Bones/Mauricio Aquino Foundation, is working in tandem with CONABUSQUEDA commissioners to

ensure independence and effectiveness in the search for the bones of our disappeared. El Salvador has approved the creation of a DNA bank to ultimately match the remains of people found to have been killed during the war with their living relatives.

There have been many obstacles in our path, and plenty more challenges lie ahead of us. But I don't think anyone in the campaign would have imagined that some of us would one day be talking face-to-face about our disappeared parents with members of the U.S. Congress and high-level officials at the U.S. State Department, or ministers of various Salvadoran government agencies, let alone the President of El Salvador. We never expected anyone to listen to our stories.

And yet, as we began to speak out, we realized that our stories—individually and as a collective—held power. We realized that people were moved and inspired. Most agreed that no child deserves to lose a parent, much less in the horrific way we have. Most agreed that we—children and other relatives of the Disappeared—deserve to know what happened to them. Why were they taken? When did they die? How? Where are their remains? As difficult as it is to speak about our parents, we continue to do so, and we hold each other up every time it becomes unbearable.

Early Organizing Steps

Serendipity may have had a role in the birth of this campaign, but the achievements that followed were a result of highly strategic and coordinated efforts. From our meeting in spring 2013, it took us over a year and a half of actual organizing with Salvadorans in the United States and El Salvador to officially launch our mission.

Several critical actions were needed for the campaign to take a structure, gain support, and start to gain legitimacy. We began by recruiting three main membership clusters: 1) a small but dedicated group of children and other relatives of disappeared parents who were willing to publicly share their stories; 2) campaign volunteers with community organizing experience; and 3) an advisory committee with direct access to key political and human rights leaders, both in the United States and El Salvador, who were willing to provide campaign leaders personal support and access.

Voice/Storytelling/Messaging

Our first step as a newly formed coalition was to think about the voice of the campaign. Together, we represented children, wives, mothers, siblings, and other relatives of the Disappeared. When we imagined our campaign going public, we thought: which voice could most effectively tell the story?

In many ways, the question of *voice* and *story* formed the soul of our campaign. In El Salvador, the Mothers of the Disappeared and other groups were already dedicated to addressing human rights abuses during the civil war. For decades, these groups have sought justice and have often faced swift sabotage and silencing.

But the voices of the *children* of the Disappeared had not yet been lifted. In our initial planning meetings, some of the children of the Disappeared—including me—began to quietly share our stories about what growing up with the ghost of a Disappeared parent had been like. Seasoned human rights leaders and older relatives of the Disappeared came to us in tears and hugged us tightly. The stories of pain and of longing were familiar, but they were incredibly moved. For many, the notion of a child's lost innocence was like a lightning bolt.

These were new voices, new stories that served to wake up the listener, inspire immediate empathy, and create a space for dialogue without immediate animosity or criticism. From a strategic political messaging perspective, we realized that having this group of Salvadoran American children, now all professionals in the United States, as protagonists of the campaign created a real potential avenue.

Storytelling has never been easy for us. Discussing the loss of a parent is difficult in any setting, but we have committed to telling our stories in often very public settings. Even though we are adults, our stories take people—whether it was a hardened and cynical congressional aide, a State Department official, or a skeptical and weary Salvadoran human rights leader—back to their childhood, or their time as a young parent. Suddenly, they can see the innocent babies, toddlers, and young children who lost a beloved mother or father. Because our generation was so young during the armed conflict, we are not viewed as having the same political agenda, or baggage, that our parents' and grandparents' generations had.

We saw this communications potential and seized it. We quickly focused the campaign on the children of the Disappeared. Together, we developed a set of concrete goals for the campaign:

1) Access information and determine the truth about our parents' disappearances. (Why were they taken, where were they taken, and how and when did they die?)
2) Secure their remains to give them sacred burial.

But, in addition to these publicly stated goals, I believe that each daughter or son of a Disappeared also joined this campaign to find some form of healing. Just being with each other has been a gift. It is a strange club. Most often, we are quite alone in our grief and trauma. But having a safe space to share our anxieties, our fears, and the triggers of grief has been a real source of growth and healing.

In September 2017, when I had the honor of representing the campaign and my fellow *hijas* and *hijos de los Desaparecidos* before then-President Sánchez Cerén and then-Foreign Minister Hugo Martínez, I related the story of my father.

There came a moment when I felt that I could not breathe, and I could feel my throat choking with rage and tears. I stopped talking and just held onto the podium. An elderly woman—

Guadalupe Mejía, known as "Madre Lupe" for her historic leadership of mothers searching for the Disappeared—stood up, came over to me, put one hand on my back, and the other on my arm.

In that moment, she literally held me up. I felt her strength flow through me, and I knew I had to keep going. It was a moment of deep meaning: a woman who had been fighting for over forty years to find her sons holding up and gently pushing a young woman, a daughter of a disappeared father, to speak up and, perhaps, help take on the mantle of this crusade.

Leveraging Existing Networks/Relationships

I mention that moment because it also speaks to the essential role that existing relationships have played in our campaign. Our Parents' Bones is intentionally centered on new voices. But, as a collective of young leaders, we found immense strength in human rights networks dating back to the 1980s.

Despite this history of U.S. intervention in El Salvador, and in Central America generally, there is a strong foundation for current transnational organizing efforts to build upon, because Salvadorans have a deep history of organizing and resisting inequity and injustice. There is also a rich history of transnational political organizing, namely, the U.S.–El Salvador Solidarity Movement, which sought in the 1980s to end U.S. aid until the Salvadoran government ceased its human rights abuses.

Key leaders of the immigrant rights and sanctuary movements of the 1980s again rose to the occasion as campaign representatives for Our Parents' Bones. We drew heavily on their insights, lessons learned and experiences. They had organized the movement of resources and people to bring public awareness among U.S. citizens to the human rights atrocities of the civil war occurring in El Salvador and to pressure both governments to put an end to the human rights abuses and to allow Salvadorans in the United States to remain with some type of legal status.

Coalition-Building

Campaign representatives made it a priority to set up an advisory committee with U.S.–Salvadoran human rights leaders from the Solidarity movement in the United States, but we also made it a priority to build a strong coalition of diverse supporters in El Salvador. Through the years, some campaign members had maintained strong relationships with leaders of the Farabundo Martí National Liberation Front (FMLN). The FMLN was originally the umbrella group of guerilla forces in the civil war. Its units were demobilized after the peace accords were signed in 1992. The FMLN became a political party, which came into power in 2009 under Mauricio Funes, and then again in 2014 under the Sánchez Cerén administration.

Some of our advisors and directors found themselves with former FMLN *compadres*, friends, and colleagues who had risen through the ranks to be high government officials, even ministers, and had the ear of then-President Sánchez Cerén. Relationships with these officials, and institutions like the Jesuit University, were instrumental in garnering his administration's support for the issue of the Disappeared generally and, in our case, for the establishment of CONABUSQUEDA.

We also knew that the support of longstanding human rights organizations in El Salvador would be key. There was a strong risk, however, that our campaign would be viewed as "competition" for resources, or as "not legitimate," by these actors. Building a coalition with human rights leaders in El Salvador took years of carefully planned meetings, phone calls, and other small actions to build trust. We had to stress at every step of the way that we were there to support their work, but we also needed to make clear that our agenda was slightly different.

We touted the contributions we were bringing to the struggle—specifically, our access to U.S. political leaders and to U.S. audiences—without putting undue pressure on these players. Those of us with U.S. citizenship learned to exercise caution

in how and when we used our privilege. As a Salvadoran American who arrived in the United States with greater class privilege
than most of my fellow Salvadoran migrants, I had to quickly
learn when to step back and let other Salvadorans or Salvadoran
Americans step up. I learned that in certain meetings, which my
privilege had helped to secure, it was important for me to yield the
platform to other Salvadoran leaders who had been fighting this
fight for decades. And I learned when it was strategic to step up
using my voice and privilege (e.g., in certain congressional meetings). Facing privilege is critical to building lasting trust and a
stable coalition.

Lessons Learned

Through storytelling, coalition-building, and strategic political
partnerships, we have leveraged our collective voice to achieve
something profound. Our achievements help paint a broader
vision for peace, reconciliation, and human rights in El Salvador.
Still, there have been significant obstacles along the way. Core
challenges have included the following:

- Securing the trust of Salvadoran human rights leaders and
  building a transnational coalition that sufficiently satisfies
  the main goals of Salvadorans, both in El Salvador and in
  the United States
- Maintaining the participation of a volunteer-based network
- Dealing with government/leadership transitions
- Ongoing scarcity of funding for our work
- Learning to unlock the power of binational citizenship

We have learned several key lessons through this transnational
campaign. First and most important, this kind of work at its core
is emotional, painful, and can bring up or trigger long-suppressed
trauma. We all had to learn how to reach out for support, including

professional care, when needed. We all had to learn when to lean on someone to move past their fear or paralysis, and when to give that person the space to be alone with their pain. We've lost members along the way for whom the work triggered too much pain. We learned to support and respect each person's individual healing process and engagement capacity.

Given that this all-volunteer network has no paid staff, we've learned the hard way that this work (for better or worse) will go slowly and that we have to accept that our work will often go forward in spurts based on key opportunities or people's availability.

We've also learned that building trust with our longtime Salvadoran human rights colleagues was a key resource. We collaborated by spending sufficient time with them and identifying where and when we could support their agendas, being clear about our own agenda and the commonly shared agenda. Most important, by really showing up to meetings and events to support them, we were able to slowly build sufficient trust to begin to call ourselves a true coalition. They have in turn supported us in key meetings and requests to the Salvadoran government. They have served as our champions and spokespeople in El Salvador. The struggle for the Disappeared is our joint struggle now.

Lastly, we've learned that this practice of patience must also apply to our work with the Salvadoran and U.S. governments and that we must be prepared to move quickly and with agility when a political opportunity appears.

For example, when former President Obama was in his last year in office, we realized we had a window of time to draft and communicate a letter to him from several supportive Congress members requesting the declassification of certain CIA and State Department records pertaining to U.S. military knowledge of covert operations (including forced disappearances) in El Salvador during the civil war. We were able to quickly secure key support from twenty-plus members of the U.S. Congress, including Representatives Jim McGovern and Norma Torres (who were the lead signers). Although the letter did not lead to an actual declassification of records, we put ourselves on the radar of many members of Congress.

In 2018 and 2019, we took advantage of these U.S. congressional relationships to pressure the outgoing President Sánchez Cerén to fund at least the majority of the budget for the established CONA-BUSQUEDA commission.

Once again, the environment has changed. Salvadoran President Bukele, who took office in June 2019, has unfortunately not made human rights and the Disappeared a priority. To the contrary, the Bukele administration appeared to be following the authoritarian style of Latin America's brutal dictatorships, all condoned and supported by the Trump administration.[9] Human rights leaders and organizations around the world are sounding the alarm about the state of human rights in El Salvador.[10]

But we eventually realized that we needed to pivot our priorities and strategies away from what hasn't worked: an open letter calling for continued support for CONABUSQUEDA and sending a delegation to El Salvador in the fall of 2019 to meet Bukele administration officials, including the Salvadoran Attorney General. We have come to this conclusion due to the lack of real support for our demands and CONABUSQUEDA's work, and the increasingly frightening state of human rights in the country.

Since President Joe Biden took office, we have geared up to lobby key members of the U.S. Congress and the State Department to assist us with pressuring the Bukele administration on the issue of the Disappeared. We aim to work within the framework of pushing El Salvador to invest in resolving human rights abuses and ensuring the ongoing protection of human rights. Our hope is that the Biden administration will support the protection of human rights in El Salvador. For the children of El Salvador's Disappeared, we will certainly demand it.

A Vision for a Better and More Engaged Future

I believe that El Salvador, like many other countries in Latin America, must confront its painful past in order to truly build a strong and healthy future. This is a process that necessarily requires transnational organizing.

My personal experience in organizing Salvadorans in the United States and in El Salvador for more than eight years has shown me that there is a desire to revisit our stories, to confront our trauma, and to heal our collective wounds. *It has revealed that truth is as valuable as a process as it is as a product.* Telling our stories, and the stories of our parents, is as important as our mission to find the truth about what happened to them. The process of publicly naming the violence and trauma committed against our families and against us, and the process of remembering our parents as human beings and as parents, alone and together, have changed each of us in incredibly deep ways. It has reopened old wounds and forced us to face decades-old nightmares and fears, but it also has created true healing and community across generations, within families, and across borders.

This *process* also has implications extending far beyond the issue of forced disappearances. While our campaign centered on finding truth and reconciliation in the context of the Disappeared, the strategies we undertook to achieve our goals offer a model for organizing that can be applied to a broad set of issues and stakeholders.

Three characteristics, in particular, have proven essential to Our Parents' Bones' success:

1) Strategic messaging/voice: Stories of the grown children proved most effective.
2) Leveraging partnerships by seeking common cause: Existing human rights infrastructure, transnational networks, and personal relationships were invaluable to us. In our case, the Solidarity Movement and longstanding U.S.–El Salvador human rights networks have proven very supportive.
3) Coalition-building: Conscientiously working to develop trust and a shared agenda with groups across

borders—including recognition of varying levels of privilege, assets different groups bring to the table, compromises, and creation of new strategies—has been very helpful.

I see a robust transnational agenda of Salvadoran healing and Salvadoran human rights taking shape over the next decade. We cannot *resolve* issues related to migration without thinking about economic investments, educational access, the prevention and treatment of gang violence, and other elements that contribute to the root causes of the persistent violence and poverty.

Beyond healing for our families and communities, this work leaves no doubt that strengthening human rights protections and inter-American policies will not only help Central Americans everywhere but propel progress for the Western Hemisphere as a whole.

When Luz Vega-Marquis began her career in philanthropy in the late 1970s, she was often the only Latina in the room. Concerned about the lack of diversity on philanthropic Boards, and among staff and funding recipients, she has dedicated her career to making change. She became a champion of under-resourced communities, of women's rights, of an immigration system that respects human rights, and of diversity and minority inclusiveness in American philanthropy and society in general.

Born in Nicaragua, Vega-Marquis and her family fled that country's political turmoil in the late 1960s, when she was just thirteen. She had a half-brother already living in San Francisco, so her parents chose it as the gathering point as the family managed to leave in small groups. Vega-Marquis also had six sisters and two brothers.

After high school, Vega-Marquis intended to become an accountant. But she switched majors to study part-time so that she could work and help her family make ends meet. She eventually earned a bachelor's degree in modern languages from the University of San Francisco and a master's degree in Latin American studies from Stanford University.

Through her college's work-study program, she secured a part-time job at the James Irvine Foundation offices in San Francisco. This was her first glimpse into the world of philanthropy. As a student, she had no idea of what took place in those old San Francisco offices, with their leather couches and a huge boardroom, but she was eager to learn. After graduation, she returned to the Irvine

Foundation, where she worked her way up to Director of Grants and stayed for two decades.

Along the way, she married William "Bill" Marquis, an executive in a nonprofit that prepared and encouraged youths to love education. Marquis was an up-and-coming politician in San Francisco with whom she had two children and six grandchildren.

In 1993, however, their world collapsed when Marquis almost died in a freak traffic accident. His left side was shattered, and he suffered head trauma, necessitating many surgeries. "He fought this," she recalled in an interview for this profile. "You know, they told him, 'You're not going to walk for a whole year.' Within five months, he was walking. They said, 'He's going to be a vegetable.' He was talking."

A long convalescence followed, during which they reshaped their lives around their deep love for each other, their family, and their commitment to racial justice and social change.

She put her career aside and spent two years caring for her husband.

Eventually, she transitioned to leading nonprofits and returned to philanthropy as a grantmaker. In 2020, after almost two decades at the helm, she retired as founding President and CEO of the Marguerite Casey Foundation. During her years there, Vega-Marquis had led a bold effort to support grassroots movements, with a focus on empowering communities to find their voice, and advocate for and create their own solutions. Under her leadership, the foundation gave its grantees the power to decide how to spend their grant funds, and empowered families to create their own solutions. In her book *Ask, Listen, Act*, she detailed the foundation's process for moving its grantmaking strategies from a donor-centric to a community-empowerment perspective.

Meanwhile, Vega-Marquis also encouraged other Latinos in foundations to form their own network, leading to the creation of Hispanics in Philanthropy (HIP), now the premier transnational network for funding Latinx communities.

Like other resilient pioneers who push for change, Vega-Marquis and her allies had to devise their own strategies, develop their own resources, and at times take personal and professional risks to pave the way.

Leadership Lesson #1: Create the spaces you wish existed

Early in her career, while Vega-Marquis was working at the James Irvine Foundation in California, she attended the 1979 annual meeting in Seattle of the Council on Foundations, a leading network of foundation staff and leaders. She quickly noticed that, despite the hundreds of people in attendance, there were no other Latinos there.

"And I was like, eyes wide open, trying to look for Latinos in the field," she recalled. A couple of Latino-sounding names in the crowd didn't pan out. "I'm by myself, so I'm going through the registration book, looking for names of people that look like me—nobody, nobody!"

After that experience, she was greatly determined to find more Latinos working in the philanthropic sector. The Irvine Foundation encouraged her search.

"I started my research and tried to identify folks. And, actually, we came up with about five people," she recalled. "And we started meeting and were trying to figure out what we wanted to do . . . trying to put something together for Latinos."

"I started with the notion of how do we help each other, not only to figure out where we are, but help each other to grow in this field. I didn't know anything about philanthropy, and I was still trying to learn, I was still trying to figure out where people are."

The group first had to decide on a name. As is the case now, not everyone identified with the term *Hispanic*, or *Latino*, or *Chicano*. As a Nicaraguan, she was not thrilled with *Chicano* and the acronym of CHIP, as much as she appreciated and respected California's Mexican American community. After six months or so of debate, *Hispanics* prevailed, and the group was named Hispanics in Philanthropy.

That done, Vega-Marquis continued her quest to find new

members, fundraise, and to ensure that it was given due recognition in the philanthropic world. Inevitably, they faced pushback. "People were not supportive of the ideas that we had. Why do you want to organize? Why do you want to have this?" she said. "But little by little, the Council on Foundations had to accept us."

By 1981, she was even named to the Council on Foundations Conference Program Committee and was able to have an impact on the conference that just years before had had no Latino representation.

"I was able to get one presentation that had a Latino in it. You know, it was a big deal!" she recalled.

By 1983, Hispanics in Philanthropy had made the decision to incorporate. In this, Vega-Marquis was joined by Wells Fargo executive Elisa Arévalo and Herman Gallegos, a former Rockefeller Foundation Trustee who encouraged funding for and helped to organize in San Francisco the precursor of the National Council of La Raza (now UnidosUS). All three are Emeritus Members of the HIP Board.

Leadership Lesson #2: Change may come slowly, but stick to your guns

While at the Irvine Foundation, Vega-Marquis made a point of advancing new ideas and advocating for funding for organizations that were ahead of their time—those with leaders that were pushing for equity and social change. Change was at times slow, but she continued to push the foundation's leadership.

She recalled when Irvine planned to make a series of grants to women's organizations as part of its 1997 Women's Economic Development Initiative. The foundation intended to focus sizeable grants on a handful of organizations, but a number of women's nonprofits expressed frustration that such an approach still left many groups without funding. They pushed the foundation to consider making smaller grants to a broader variety of women's organizations. Vega-Marquis urged the foundation to stand its ground, avoid a scattergun approach that might fail to achieve the goals and give larger grants to just a few groups.

"We defended our position in the open forum meeting that we had," she said.

Later, an organization called Equal Rights Advocates brought her a proposal for work to combat sexual harassment in the workplace. This was long before the #MeToo movement and its far-reaching cultural impact. Back then, activism made many foundation directors nervous. It still does.

"I've been advocating for more than thirty years about inclusion and diversity in this field of philanthropy . . . I've been called a 'one-track mind—that's all you talk about . . .' And I always have to defend myself by saying, 'Well, if you did care about it, I wouldn't have to.'"

Vega-Marquis was honest with the organization's leader: the proposal was a longshot for funding at that moment, but she was committed to presenting the idea to the Irvine Foundation, encouraging the Board to learn about what was happening to women in the workforce and to at least discuss the proposal.

"It took me two years to get a grant to them, but I did," she said. "My strategy became that every time the Board met, I would bring one organization not in the traditional mold of the foundation." As a result, grantees have become much more diversified in size, mission, and racial and ethnic leadership. Vega-Marquis continued to bring up tough conversations and push for change throughout her career. She is proud of the diversity of her staff over the years and has no patience for people who dance around the topic of diversity.

"You know, I've been advocating for more than thirty years about inclusion and diversity in philanthropy," she said. "I've been accused of everything, and I've been called many names. I've been called a 'one-track mind—that's all you talk about.' And I always have to defend myself by saying, 'Well, if you *did* care about it, I wouldn't have to.'"

Leadership Lesson #3: Commit to your values and stand firm

Prioritizing Family Over Work

In 1992, after her husband's near-fatal car accident, Vega-Marquis' career took a backseat. It was an extremely difficult time in her life.

"Come on, wake up," she recalled telling him one day as he lay in a coma. "'You told me that you were going to spend the rest of your life with me; you can't quit now!' You know, he squeezed my hand!"

Her family and friends were invaluable in keeping her going. She credits their support for her resilience and for her ability to embrace the new reality of her life.

Nowadays, Vega-Marquis and her husband travel everywhere together, and the marriage has stayed strong.

Rebuilding by Marshalling Resilience

Two years later, she was ready to restart her work life. A job as Vice President of the National Economic Development and Law Center helped her rebuild her confidence in her skills. She knew she could help move organizations in the right direction.

She next agreed to start up a high-tech nonprofit. Community Technology Foundation of California, later known as Zero Divide, sought to help underserved communities harness the transformative power of technology to improve economic opportunities, civic engagement, and healthy outcomes. She helped to build the foundation's operations from scratch and made sure that the communities they served were heard in the decision-making process.

Through her work, Vega-Marquis gained a more nuanced understanding of racial tensions in local communities and the importance of building multiracial coalitions. "Having an African American man as a husband for forty years really helped me in this job," she said. "You just have to tell people, 'You know, I think broader than this because I think we're all in the same boat. Just gotta get our boats together!'"

In 2001, Vega-Marquis was recruited to be the President of the Casey Family's new foundation, which became the Marguerite Casey Foundation and was funded by their United Parcel Service fortune. Its mission is to help low-income families strengthen their voice and mobilize their communities in order to achieve a more just and equitable society.

The foundation stands out for its willingness to let grantees best decide how to use their unrestricted grant funds. "We had a magnificent group of leaders that believed in activism and advocacy," she recalled.

As President, Vega-Marquis had her fair share of detractors, including among her own staff. "I have let go some people from this organization," she said in early 2019. "The challenge for me is this: we have this set of values that undergird a new way of doing business, with grantees at the center. We engage them where they are. As a woman of color, as an immigrant woman, [program officers] would come and challenge what I wanted to do. Because they think that I don't have the authority, or whatever they might believe. That's racism and sexism. So, they don't stay."

Yet Vega-Marquis appreciates those who challenged her respectfully, who helped her learn and grow. She especially admires the nonprofit leaders with whom she and the foundation developed deep partnerships over the years.

"What I love about our grantees is that they have no problem calling me on the carpet all the time!" she said with a smile about grantee pushback. "But they're very good because I trust them to tell me the truth."

"Oftentimes, I give them my definition of loyalty. And I say, 'Loyalty is when you challenge me respectfully, and you tell me the truth. Then I'll know you're loyal to me. When you come here and tell me I'm great, that doesn't help me.'"

Looking Forward: A Call to Transform Philanthropy

Thinking about the state of philanthropy today, Vega-Marquis is glad to see more diversity and is proud of her decades of work building networks and opportunities for people of color in philanthropy. Certainly, much has changed since she flipped through the Council on Foundations registration list and foundations' annual reports, searching for other Latino-sounding names.

Philanthropy is still far from reaching parity for minorities or women in its executive suites, but she noted that the leadership in the field has marked a milestone by being more than 50 percent female. And she still hopes that philanthropy will devote more resources to Latino communities.

"Most of the people in philanthropy are not there," she said. "We don't see five thousand foundations trying to help at the border. We don't see five thousand foundations trying to change the conditions for Latino children in schools and helping them learn, or helping our artists and creators or art."

"There are a few here and there. But it's not the deep commitment that you and I have to our community."

Whether dealing with draconian immigration policies or racial unrest, she said, "I really appreciate the people who are standing up and saying, 'No, that's not who we are.'"

It is important for philanthropy to support those leaders and organizations who are fighting to protect immigrants and counter racism, and who understand that Latino issues are broader than immigration policies.

"We have to hire people of color," she said. "We have to let them do what they do. It's not inviting people to dinner and not letting them eat. At the dinner table, you also have the tamales, and empanadas and *chicharrón con yuca*, and all of the other things that are part of the cultural milieu . . ."

"It is a transformation, and I see the beginning of that transformation, and I hope it takes hold. I really do hope it takes hold."

13 PUERTO RICO
RACIAL EQUITY AND THE ISLAND'S FUTURE

NELSON I. COLÓN

Some of us look at the many challenges that Puerto Rico has had to face and we clearly see a brighter path forward. We aren't being Pollyannas. As the head of the island's only community foundation, I've lived among the people here, through good times and bad, through calamities and progress, through hope and disillusionment in the political system, always with a bottomless faith in the strengths and abilities of communities and nonprofit organizations.

The physical and emotional traumas experienced throughout the island since the early 2000s are undeniable. Its 2.87 million people struggle with high unemployment in the aftermath of Puerto Rico's bankruptcy and hurricanes Irma and Maria in 2017, which destroyed the already fragile and outdated electric power grid. The island spiraled into social upheaval, with unprecedented protests that forced one governor from office, while a former member of his Cabinet and five top aides faced federal corruption charges. His replacement at the helm came under investigation in 2020 for using earthquake humanitarian assistance for political gain and for overlooking the sale of COVID-19 test kits to the government for $39 million when the real market price was $3 million. Meanwhile, more than one thousand earthquakes struck just as the long pandemic lockdown was getting under way, with additional tremors occurring many months afterward. The survival skills and resourcefulness of everyone here have been tested.

And Puerto Ricans have risen to these challenges, with the energy and goodwill to help each other. From my perch as President and CEO of the Puerto Rico Community Foundation, I join those who believe that community-level efforts will be the key to opening our society to a more equitable future.

In the interim, our work is cut out for us. On top of those more recent traumas, Puerto Ricans continue to grapple with ongoing, deep-rooted discrimination. It seems ironic that Puerto Ricans stand up to discrimination on the U.S. mainland, yet fail to see the effects of racism and colorism when they are on the island.

The Commonwealth of Puerto Rico's Constitution unequivocally prohibits discrimination "based on race, color, sex, birth, origin or social condition, nor political or religious ideas." Yet, it is clear that Puerto Rican culture, despite its many virtues, is one that tolerates not only racism and colorism but also the silence that accompanies them. As long as this is not addressed, there is little incentive to fix it. Most telling is the fact that so many Puerto Ricans have African and Indigenous roots yet insist on marking White when asked to give their race. It is not by chance that those who identify as Black or African-descendant are mostly from low- and very-low-income communities. On the rare occasions that it has come up, it was largely ignored on the island, as was the case with the killings that spurred the Black Lives Matter protests.

I've experienced the corrosive effects of being Black in this society up close. It must be addressed openly at all levels throughout the island, in the United States, and in the Americas.

So why do I see a bright future for addressing racial bias? Because the antiracist movements sparked around the world by the racist killings in the United States open the space for a knowledge development center—as visualized by the late Jamaican economist Norman Girvan—for shared learning, dialogue, and interconnection. This Racial Equity Building Institute of the Americas will benefit from Puerto Rico's unique position culturally and geographically as a bridge between the Americas, providing a unique space to address racism, not only for Puerto Ricans on and off the island but for everyone living in the United States, the Caribbean, and the Americas. It can offer a broader vision and greater inclusivity than the North–South division that persists even today in the U.S. Black experience.

In addition to treating and curing the pernicious societal disease of racism, the best approach to setting Puerto Rico on the right path—beyond the island's intractable political divisions, the asset disparities, and the brain drain of more than six hundred thousand people who have fled to the U.S. mainland over the past decade—lies in grassroots community organizing. We can empower people by allowing them to choose how best to build their communities.

To do this within a relatively short time frame, financial investment will be needed in the areas of racial equity, civic empowerment, K-12 education, and microfinancing for housing, the environment, and other projects. For example, at the Puerto Rico Community Foundation, we have been shaping a transformative model of grantmaking tailored to meet these challenges.

"Our overall goal is to build equity by promoting the growth of human, financial, social, [cultural], environmental and hard assets," is how I put it in testimony before the U.S. House Committee on Natural Resources in April 2019. These six key components make up the collective capital of communities, through which they can transform and empower themselves.

The growth of capital is a way for the islanders to seek social justice, starting with rural areas, which were hit hard by the hurricanes and traditionally have higher poverty rates. The Census Bureau's American Community Survey showed rural poverty in 2018 to be 52.8 percent, compared with 42.5 percent for urban areas. (The U.S. national rate for 2018 was 13.1 percent.) The high poverty rates reflect the low standard of living and unemployment, as well as the pervasive racial and colorist biases that date back to the island's Spanish colonial-era slavery. Racism is a dangerous and damaging legacy, not to mention the excellent work and thought leadership that *doesn't* take place. It is a reality that many on the island share with Blacks on the U.S. mainland.

The Bridge to Solidarity

According to estimates by the Federal Emergency Management Agency, Puerto Rico suffered about $90 billion in damages from the hurricanes in 2017. The total federal disaster relief aid allocated to Puerto Rico was $45.3 billion, although only just over a third, $16.4 billion, had been outlaid by the summer of 2020—almost three years after the storms struck. About six weeks prior to the national election, the Trump administration announced the release of a further $13 billion of the disaster funding to improve the electrical grid and education infrastructure. On its last day in office, $4.9 billion more was released. As soon as President Joe Biden took office, he announced that $1.3 billion, which had been tied up by the U.S. Department of Housing and Urban Development, would also be made available, leaving about $10 billion still to be released almost four years after the disasters.

Prior to the hurricanes, the Foundation Center estimated mainland civil-sector support for Puerto Rico at about $6 million yearly. That historically low level was upended almost overnight.

The disastrous storms blew the civil sector and the mainland Puerto Rican Diaspora into action. Within a year, according to a 2018 Red de Fundaciones de Puerto Rico study, more than $375 million—not counting in-kind donations—was raised and channeled as grants, largely through local nonprofits. Puerto Rico's civil sector quickly provided direct support while serving as intermediaries and advisors to funders from the mainland and elsewhere.

Many new funds were established by the Diaspora, large mainland foundations, and Puerto Rican funders between September 2017 and September 2018, according to a year-after survey also by the Red de Fundaciones de Puerto Rico. (It subsequently changed its name to Puerto Rico Funders Network and Filantropía Puerto Rico.) Our foundation's Puerto Rico Community Recovery Fund, at $13 million, was the seventh largest established, behind funds by Red Ventures ($100 million); Hispanic Federation ($43 million); Unidos por Puerto Rico ($38.2 million); the Bravo Family Foundation ($25 million); Save the Children ($18.5 million); and Flamboyán Foundation ($15 million).

A few months after Hurricane Maria, the Puerto Rico Community Foundation decided to switch to encouraging community networks of neighbors helping neighbors. The system is already paying off. For starters, it has helped provide basic infrastructure, such as neighborhood electricity and lighting for emergency clinics at solar-powered public health centers, as well as clean drinking water through community aqueducts that have been upgraded to receive Environmental Protection Agency (EPA) certification. A decade from now, we should see how these interconnected community microgrids and upgraded aqueducts will cover the island, assuring access to low-cost power and clean water for all Puerto Ricans. After all, access to clean water, healthcare, electricity, and education are basic human rights.

Equal Opportunities

My sense of community empowerment started to develop early on, during my upbringing in Ponce, the largest Caribbean coastal city near the initial swarm of earthquakes in 2020. I was the youngest of seven children who grew up in a poor Black neighborhood of Ponce in the 1940s and moved during the fifties to a mixed low- to mid-income area near the center of town. My father had started out as a sugar-cane cutter, and my mom earned a penny a piece embroidering ladies' handkerchiefs. Isaac Colón, whose first name is my middle name, had finished eighth grade; Luz María Tarrats had only completed sixth.

They met in Ponce, where my father got a job as a messenger at a diamond factory near El Vigía, the hill overlooking that city and its ports and that once served as a lookout post for arriving ships. He was promoted and became such an excellent diamond polisher that he was sent in a team to New York to work on The

Jonker, a huge stone that, when found in 1934, was one of the largest uncut diamonds in the world. Once it had been cleaved into twelve raw stones, Lazare Kaplan, the diamond company that owned the stone, recruited twelve highly skilled diamond cutters and polishers—including my father—to work on them.

While they were in New York, my mom became a beautician. When they returned to the island, which was before I was born, she opened the first beauty parlor for Black women in Ponce, where housing was segregated and discrimination was pervasive. Both my parents returned to school, and eventually my mother graduated from Ponce's only university at the time, Catholic University.

By the 1950s, Dad became the manager at the diamond factory, and the family entered the middle class. Mom became an elementary school teacher and was a well-known Baptist leader. Sadly, both passed away in the early 1970s.

They were obsessed with schooling. All of their children had to go to the university. We were raised—as former President Barack Obama would say—with a sense that we were exceptional. We grew up with a very strong sense of self-worth. We grew up convinced that we were destined for greater things, beyond the limitations that racism would try to place on us.

But just as housing in Ponce was segregated, racism pervaded public and private K-12 education. My siblings and I learned that Black students were not valued as highly as our lighter-skinned classmates. My sister Leyda remembers too well how Blacks were treated differently from other students at Ponce High School. Students had to get their college application from a school counselor. She requested the application three times and was turned down each time.

"If you're not going to the university, why do you want an application?" the counselor kept asking her. Finally, my mother confronted the counselor and came away with the application that allowed Leyda to attend the religious Instituto Politécnico, precursor to Puerto Rico's Universidad Interamericana, where I would later be hired as a professor.

Leyda, now my oldest living sister, recalled having passed the entrance exam, only to encounter trouble in the classroom. Always an excellent student in English, she discovered that one professor had extracted two of the 4.5 pages from an English exam book. Without the missing material, she could only get a C on the exam. But she went on to earn her degree.

"Back in those days, you didn't know," she said. "I didn't know what racism was. And later, when one grows a little more and studies and gets a greater understanding, you realize. A little Black girl like me couldn't get an A in English. That was just for the Whites."

Despite the rough times, we have all gone on to have successful careers. Our hearts still beat affectionately for Puerto Rico, where we have countless nephews and nieces. Leyda, a retired teacher, had three wonderful careers and landed, in her senior years, as a well-regarded fashion designer for Latinxs, Blacks, and physically challenged youth in Southern Arizona. My next surviving brother, Rubén, is one of the most accomplished arrangers and conductors of choir music in Puerto Rico. And Myrna, my youngest surviving sister, is an elementary school teacher with a profound spiritual strength that helped her navigate through the horrifying passing of her son.

Most people would say there is no racism in Puerto Rico now. But it does exist. It may no longer be as it was as late as the 1970s, when Black people were explicitly excluded from certain neighborhoods, fraternities, and social clubs. Most of those types of structures and organizations may have disappeared. But the racism now is not openly discussed. It is not part of the public discourse, even as most of the people in the criminal justice system and in the jails are dark-skinned.

The rare times that the matter has come up in public discourse, it gets swept under the rug. The late author and academic Isabelo Zenón Cruz opened the islandwide conversation in 1974 with the seminal book *Narciso descubre su trasero: El negro en la cultura puertorriqueña* (A rough translation: "Narciso Discovers His Rear End: Blacks in Puerto Rican Culture"). The issue was broadened by the Puerto Rico Commission on Civil Rights with its "¿Somos racistas?" ("Are We Racists?") report, which posited in its second edition in 1998 that the only race worthy of development and empowerment is the human race. The Commission followed rapidly with its deeper dive, "El discrimen por razón de raza y el sistema de justicia" (roughly: "Race-Based Bias and the Justice System"). This latter study about the island, among other issues, found: "Racism is activated to the highest power when a 'Black' person tries to obtain financial or social resources. In other words, racism is a regulating mechanism in the distribution of resources."

Ten years later, when Doudou Diène, former UN Special Rapporteur on contemporary forms of racism, racial discrimination, xenophobia, and related intolerance, held hearings on the persistence of individual and structural racism, he visited not only Chicago, New York, Omaha, Los Angeles, New Orleans, Miami, and Washington, DC, but also San Juan. His report, after hearing testimony about police beatings and institutional racism, was presented to the UN Human Rights Council in June 2009.

After the death in Minneapolis of George Floyd on May 25, 2020, a building trades feminist collective organized a small march and vigil to the Governor's Mansion in Old San Juan, and then-San Juan Mayor Carmen Yulín Cruz made a statement denouncing racism and ordered flags to fly at half-staff for forty-six days, honoring each year of Floyd's life. Public reactions were otherwise muted, although the massive protests in the United States and around the world were reported by the island press.

One of the consequences of racism is the monumental loss of human capital, evidenced by the noticeable absence of Black people among Puerto Rico's public figures. For example, there were no Black-identified members in the Cabinet of Governor Wanda Vázquez, who left office in January 2021. For me, not having Blacks in senior government positions and in social leadership is an enormous loss.

I remember looking at an old family photo with my wife, Nely Torres. "I was a handsome young boy, but I grew up thinking that

I was ugly," I told her. Blacks were portrayed as ugly, dumb, and dirty ("*negro sucio*"), and as objects of derision; for instance, making fun of the large lips ("*negro bembón*"). The effect this has on self-esteem is brutal. For many, it can be isolating. The wounds of racism often remain hidden. Discrimination spreads and evolves when you can't discuss it publicly.

Learning to Survive

I went to study sociology at the University of Puerto Rico, in the Rio Piedras area of San Juan. After graduating, I spent ten months at the Evangelical Seminary while employed as a cleaner at the Methodist Students Foundation in San Juan. That's where I learned to clean bathrooms *really* well.

It was the time of the Vietnam War, and I became a conscientious objector. While still at the university, I was eighteen and Nely was sixteen when we met at a gathering of the progressive Christian Students' Movement. She would go on to become a mental health therapist and a university lecturer, and she would also work for the Puerto Rico Women's Rights Commission. She capped her career as a researcher and administrator prior to her retirement.

We were married in 1969, and, shortly after my mother died in 1970, we moved to Binghamton, New York, where I earned a master's degree in social and cultural anthropology at the State University of New York.

We returned to Puerto Rico, and in 1972 I started teaching part-time at the University of Puerto Rico while working as the Director for a youth development program at the Puerto Rico Planning Board. I moved to a full-time position at Universidad Interamericana and was considered a rising star as a young, pro-Puerto Rican independence professor at a time of great student activism. I looked a lot like Stokely Carmichael, the late "honorary prime minister" of the Black Panther Party, leader of the Student Nonviolent Coordinating Committee, and a Black Power advocate. I had an afro and went around with my bracelets and necklaces.

I sure didn't pass unnoticed. The Puerto Rico Police had an intelligence division to pursue "subversive elements." They fabricated a case against me, falsely accusing me of selling weapons to a policeman. It was a three-year court ordeal, from the time of my arrest in 1975 until my exoneration. It scarred me. Once it was officially over, I didn't want to stick around to find out what might happen if I just went about my business as usual, so I went back to studying. I left the island to study at Harvard University, completing my doctorate in education anthropology in 1987.

Nely and I returned to Puerto Rico with our two daughters the next year. I was offered two jobs: the Education Department Chair at a private university, or the Program Director at the Puerto Rico Community Foundation. Although about thirteen years had passed since my arrest, the trauma still seemed fresh. I understood that being a university professor in Puerto Rico meant being very vulnerable, and I wanted something more stable. And it didn't hurt that the Puerto Rico Community Foundation was offering innovative work. So I became its Program Director.

From Traditional Philanthropy to Innovation

Puerto Rico's string of cataclysms has wreaked havoc on its population and hampered the island government's uneven attempts to forestall economic collapse and address the yawning gap between the rich and the poor.

According to a 2019 Census estimate, the median household income on this island of 2.87 million people was $20,166 in 2018 dollars. That is roughly a third of the U.S. median of $60,293. The poverty rate in Puerto Rico was 43.1 percent in 2018, according to the American Community Survey, more than double the 19.7 percent in 2018 in Mississippi, one of the poorest states. Small wonder that so many people fled to the U.S. mainland in the 2010s.

The long slog through the 2010s undoubtedly weighed heavily on Puerto Rico's philanthropic sector, which traditionally had consisted of well-heeled individual donors channeling funds to arts and cultural institutions on the island.

When I was hired in 1988 as Program Director, I gladly supported the foundation's priority to fund pilot projects but eventually realized that they too often were not replicated. In the 1990s, the foundation also began capacity-building programs and offered resources to breathe life into the few nonprofits operating around the island. It helped form other local foundations, just as it had been formed and nurtured since 1985 through a collaboration of the National Puerto Rican Coalition and four U.S. foundations: Ford, MacArthur, Rockefeller, and C.S. Mott.

Since I assumed executive leadership of the foundation in 2000, it has broadened its perspective on how to best serve Puerto Rico, along with expanding its services. That year, the foundation had two donor-advised funds. By 2020, it had 102. Established with $10 million, it has reached $40 million in assets.

I like to look more at the community impact than at the money that has come in. Six thousand housing units for low-income families have been built in Puerto Rico, and thousands of jobs and small businesses have been created. The social return on investment from those organizations, in terms of economic development, is that every dollar the foundation invested generated nine dollars. And in housing, every dollar from the foundation generated $140. The foundation's Community Investment Fund, established in 2015, had made seventeen loans to fourteen nonprofits. Through economic hard times, political crises, and a temporary payment moratorium during the pandemic, some loan agreements had to be amended. But, at least through the spring of 2021, there haven't been any defaults on the $2.1 million in loans.

The foundation's biggest shift occurred following the disastrous 2017 hurricanes, Irma and Maria. Our Access, Management, and Ownership (AMO) strategy represents a ground-up approach to community organizing focused on delivering on the basic human right to healthcare, electricity, and clean water. In the process, the foundation has become a nonprofit leader in promoting solar energy.

Of course, we were not alone in addressing the crisis. In the aftermath, forty-two community foundations in the United States sent donations to the foundation, with the San Francisco Foundation's $4 million award being the largest from that funding group. In its year-later study, the island's Red de Fundaciones highlighted how the disasters led to major shifts for other foundations, on the island and off, particularly in the area of long-term investments:

- The Network identified "fair distribution of government resources, nonprofit capacity-building, and collecting and analyzing data for decision making as its three grantmaking priorities for the recovery and rebuilding supported through its FORWARD Puerto Rico Fund."
- Segarra Boerman e Hijos Foundation changed its focus areas in the immediate aftermath and has since allocated 78.6 percent of its funding to Puerto Rico's rebuilding and transformation.
- The New York-based and Diaspora-supported Hispanic Federation, as well as Oxfam and Save the Children, not only provided support in the aftermath but also have each established a physical presence in Puerto Rico for the first time.
- Open Society Foundations chose to target federal advocacy, Diaspora empowerment and engagement, and community organizing.

Participants in the Red de Fundaciones' study had established many funds to handle the donations. The top ten funds in the group were created by Red | Ventures, $100 million; Hispanic Federation, $43 million; Unidos por Puerto Rico, $38.2 million; Bravo Family Foundation, $25 million; Save the Children, $18.5 million; Flamboyán Foundation, $15 million; the Puerto

Rico Community Foundation, $13 million; GlobalGiving, $12.4 million; Hand in Hand, $11.6 million, and Foundation for Puerto Rico, $7 million.

The Community Foundation's New Approach

The foundation focuses on six areas that need to grow to promote equity throughout the island:

- Human capital, including access to quality healthcare and education, as well as saving lives by preventing young men from dying violently and girls from having unwanted pregnancies
- Social capital, in which nonprofit institutions take more of a leadership role in public life and a greater collaboration occurs between funders in Puerto Rico and those on the U.S. mainland
- Financial capital, when communities can create enterprises and jobs
- Housing and infrastructure, including recreation facilities and spaces suitable for people to relax and gather
- Cultural capital, allowing people to preserve their culture, write their history, and have access not only to their own arts and culture but also to works created elsewhere
- Conservation of natural and cultural resources, as well as increased awareness of ecology

Puerto Rico's core problems of inequality are due to deficits in these six factors, which together should constitute community capital. Within the United States, the Commonwealth of Puerto Rico is the jurisdiction with the greatest gap between the haves and have-nots. Simply put, very few have much, and many have very little. And it's not just social and economic inequality; it's about health, housing, ecology, and race and gender.

Early Results

Community Building. With $3 million in support from the W.K. Kellogg Foundation, the Obama Foundation's My Brothers' Keeper Alliance, and the Puerto Rico Community Foundation, a pool of funds was set up to provide mentoring, alternative education, scholarships, and job-creation opportunities targeting at-risk, unemployed young men in the Loiza area, along the coast east of San Juan.

Originally ruled by an Indigenous *cacica*, the fishing and agricultural area became a refuge for former slaves in the nineteenth century. Nowadays, it is the most impoverished municipality on the island. According to 2019 census estimates, 38 percent of *loiceños* self-identified as Black and 23.7 percent as White, the highest concentration of Blacks in Puerto Rico. Islandwide, 10.8 percent listed their race as Black and 67.4 percent listed White.

Access to Power and Water. After the 2017 hurricanes, Puerto Ricans quickly realized that aid from Washington was slow in coming. In addition to landslides and roofs' having been torn off many homes, the island's human services structure had suffered serious damage. Many clinics in the public health-center network were without power to refrigerate drugs, such as insulin, and to light medical procedures and switch equipment on.

The Puerto Rico Community Foundation partnered with the Puerto Rico Primary Care Association Network, an umbrella for sixty-eight of the clinics, and together with other funders created solar back-up systems so roughly half could operate through blackouts.

People from the Toro Negro community of Ciales contacted the foundation because access to their rural mountain town had been cut off by the hurricanes, and they had no electric power for eight months. Five members of the U.S. House Committee on Natural Resources, which has jurisdiction over U.S. territories, visited Comunidad Solar Toro Negro in March 2019, a month before I was to go before the committee to request greater funding for the island's recovery. The foundation had partnered with the private firm SOMOS Solar and students from Duke University's Nicholas School of the Environment, among others, to help the Toro Negro community design and install a twenty-eight-home energy-independent microgrid. Near-term plans were under way for at least a dozen more microgrids.

"Hurricane Maria left a massive trail of devastation," I told the committee. "The storm also saw the emergence of hundreds of unsung heroes, who saved countless lives. This generation of heroes is rising in Toro Negro, Humacao, Utuado, Villalba, Caguas, Adjuntas and many other towns in Puerto Rico. Their goal is to forge stronger and more resilient communities through renewable energy. This goal can be achieved by sustained support for infrastructure and leadership development in low-income communities."

We are helping people to own their energy and link each microgrid into a network of solar communities. We are doing the same with access to water.

The blackouts knocked out the pumps needed to distribute water from the system of 300 community aqueducts, impairing access to potable water. As it turned out, many of the existing aqueducts needed more than a backup power supply because they weren't certified in compliance with EPA standards. The foundation has worked with more than thirty aqueducts and their nearby community members to provide power backup and certification, while training the neighbors to manage and take ownership of those resources.

The Future

Community empowerment alone cannot dig the island out of bankruptcy nor set its government on a path toward efficiency, compassion, and respect for the rule of law. The government's budget is controlled by the Financial Oversight and Management Board of Puerto Rico, created by the U.S. Congress in 2016 under the Puerto Rico Oversight, Management and Economic Stability (PROMESA) Act, and the subsequent string of catastrophes only served to slow down the process and has kept the insular government in near-constant emergency response mode. Unless reorganization of the multibillion-dollar debt is completed fairly, we won't be in a very different place by 2030. Political action is needed. This is not about projects; this is about power.

The struggle for racial justice in Puerto Rico also remains. It is the struggle of Blacks on the mainland, of Indigenous and African descendants in Latin America, as well as the Spanish- and English-speaking Caribbean. And it has very real consequences that need to be acknowledged. It touches on social status, jobs, housing, education, and yes, even the sense of self-worth. At the crossroads of the Americas, Puerto Rico can be an important driver in moving racial justice forward, and perhaps in ten years Puerto Ricans will be able to tell their children about how the end of racism and colorism contributed to the island's recovery by harnessing untapped human and social capital and contributing to a flourishing arts environment and cultural pride.

Puerto Rico is perfectly situated to have a preeminent Racial Equity Building Institute of the Americas to support the next generation of Black leaders in the United States, the Caribbean, and Latin America, and to promote the rich cultural capital of Afro-descendant communities. An institution like this can be endowed as a research and leadership development center for thought leaders and racial justice movements throughout the Western Hemisphere, starting with the United States and its territories.

Of course, there is more that can be done. Candid, which resulted from the merger of the philanthropic research titans Foundation Center and GuideStar, tracked $4.2 billion in racial-equity funding committed by large funders by July 2020, a 22 percent increase over the $3.3 billion raised over the previous nine years.

The Andrew W. Mellon Foundation committed $15 million in September 2020 to fund the Institute for the Study of Global Racial Justice at Rutgers University, in New Jersey. It is important that such well-meaning and well-funded endeavors reflect the perspectives from Latin America and the Caribbean, given not only the struggles their racial minorities must face, but the Diasporas that maintain networks of relationships and influence throughout the Western Hemisphere.

Also, following the police killing of George Floyd, The Ford Foundation decided to focus its grantmaking on inequality in all its forms and to award 40 percent of its grantmaking budget to general operating support to strengthen nonprofits, rather than directing most funding to programs. Ford also announced that it would raise more than a billion dollars by issuing a taxable social bond and acknowledge the deadly toll the COVID-19 pandemic had on communities of color by joining other foundations to collectively increase their grantmaking during the global health crisis. The funders included, among others, the Doris Duke Charitable Foundation, the MacArthur Foundation, the W.K. Kellogg Foundation, and the Andrew W. Mellon Foundation.

In the short term at least, more funding will undoubtedly help build a brighter future for racial and ethnic minorities and contribute to increased productivity, citizen empowerment, and civic cohesion, where equal opportunity really means something. This vision is of a world where no one is afraid to leave home, where no one lives at risk because of the color of their skin or their accent.

I am very positive that change can happen from the ground up. Even in the pandemic, people were meeting online and forming networks, and in the community foundation's network of communities organized to prevent the spread of the virus, no one over age sixty-five—that was the goal—has died from COVID-19. In the same way, we can have microgrid networks so that communities have power, water, housing, business incubators, and interconnected cultural and ecological projects.

Our natural allies to realize this vision are the island's system of *cooperativas,* financial institutions that are similar to credit unions, as well as labor unions, progressive churches, other philanthropic entities, and some universities. At the ground level, the focus will have to be on community empowerment, on growing the human, social, financial, housing, cultural, and environmental capital—for all. And on achieving racial equality. Giving islanders the tools to become more empowered makers of their own destiny will be essential, along with funding and microfinancing efforts. That's how Puerto Rico will rise.

In 2030, there will be many flourishing towns and communities. Loiza will be vibrant. There will be parks and environmentally friendly housing, a Loiza like no one could have imagined decades ago. It's there, it's already starting to happen. Once the economic recovery occurs, Puerto Ricans who have slogged through the toughest times with resilience, humor, and care for their neighbors will make the island exceed all expectations. Yes, I see a much brighter future for Puerto Rico.

PART V

LATINES ARE GIVERS

Antonia Hernández is one of the few Latinas heading a major U.S. foundation, and a true force of community change. She is at home among children living in public housing in East L.A., among civil rights advocates, and among Senators in the halls of Congress.

From her modest but loving early childhood in Mexico, she recalled her parents encouraging their seven children to study, work hard, and persist. After completing her education, she fought as a lawyer for the rights of many Americans in the field of civil rights litigation and in the crafting of federal legislation—as a Counsel on a powerful Senate Committee chaired by the late Senator Edward "Ted" Kennedy. She is the President of the California Community Foundation and former President of the Mexican American Legal Defense and Educational Fund (MALDEF), a prominent nonprofit advocating for Latino civil rights. Throughout her career, she has fought for the empowerment of Latinos and other communities of color, advocating for fair treatment and level playing fields in education and the workforce.

Born in an *ejido* farming community, in northeastern Mexico's Coahuila state, Hernández was in the third grade when her parents, Manuel Hernández and Nicolasa Martínez, decided to move from Torreón, Coahuila, to California with their daughters in 1956. On their way, the family stayed near El Paso, Texas, and Juárez, Chihuahua, for a few weeks while their documents were finalized, and it was there in Texas that the eight-year-old Hernández first saw the discrimination leveled at immigrants: a sign in a restaurant window reading "No Dogs and No Mexicans."

"Always remember to be proud of who you are," Hernández recalled her father telling the four little girls afterward. "You're no better, you're no worse, but be proud of who you are." She has carried these words with her throughout her life.

Leadership Lesson #1: If others underestimate you, prove them wrong

Hernández grew up in the Maravilla housing project in East L.A. In 1965, when she was a student at Garfield High School, her class was assigned to write an essay about what they wanted to be when they grew up. For an East L.A. Chicana at the time, "Your dream was to become a secretary, a nurse, or a teacher," Hernández recalls, and so she wrote that she wanted to be a teacher, since there were teachers in her extended family.

Her high school teacher returned her paper with a sad face drawn on it. He thought that she was not college material. She would prove him wrong, eventually graduating from East Los Angeles College and the University of California, Los Angeles.

"I'm always overcoming barriers, you know, unlocking doors that have been locked."

When she obtained her bachelor's degree, she went back to her high school to see that teacher. "I showed him my degree and I said, 'If I hadn't been the person I am, you would have squashed my dream.' But I went to see him again, just to show him, you know, that he shouldn't do that."

Her desire to pursue higher education didn't stop there. After graduating from UCLA and obtaining her teacher's credential, Hernández anxiously broached the conversation with her parents about her future. As the eldest child of seven, she knew her parents expected her to get a job to help with the other kids. She remembers the conversation clearly.

"Dad, I've decided to go to law school . . ."

"But *mijita*," he replied in Spanish, "why do you want to do that? Lawyers are a bunch of thieves."

"No, Papi. Here in the United States there are good people, good attorneys who help people."

Ultimately, her parents supported her decision, and she enrolled in the UCLA School of Law. While there, she met her future husband, Michael Stern, who went on to work as a Justice Department attorney and serves as a judge on the bench of the State Superior Court in Los Angeles.

She graduated with her law degree in 1974, a banner year for Hernández, in which she also passed the California Bar exam and became a U.S. citizen. She went on to work in legal aid offices and became a staff attorney at the Los Angeles Center for Law and Justice and the Legal Aid Foundation.

Her teacher had indeed been wrong. She proved it to him and to herself.

Leadership Lesson #2: Trust your higher ambition

People close to Hernández recognized her talent in the legal profession, and it wasn't long before her longtime friend, Gloria Molina, started trying to recruit her into politics. Molina, who would go on to become a political giant in Southern California, first rose to the national stage in the 1970s, joining President Jimmy Carter's administration as Deputy for Presidential Personnel.

"Gloria would call me and say, 'Antonia, I've got this job! You gotta come.' Because there were so few Chicanos from California in Washington, DC, and the few Chicanos who were there were from Texas." But Hernández had recently married. "We were just starting our life," she said. "I loved the job that I had. I said, 'No.' I had no interest. I had no knowledge of politics or anything. I was a hippie legal aid lawyer, and I loved it."

She was eventually swayed when then-Senator Ted Kennedy became Senate Judiciary Committee Chairman and a vacancy opened in its corps of counsels, who advised the committee members on legislation.

Molina quickly phoned Hernández, who initially resisted but decided she couldn't miss the opportunity to work with someone of Kennedy's caliber and standing.

Hernández said that working for Kennedy was the experience of a lifetime, even more so because of all the bright people around him—including Chief Counsel Stephen Breyer, who is now an Associate Justice of the U.S. Supreme Court. Hernández advised the committee on immigration, civil rights, and judicial nominations. She worked alongside Kennedy, as the campaign's Southwest Coordinator, when he unsuccessfully challenged President Carter in the 1980 Democratic primaries.

When Ronald Reagan defeated Carter in the presidential election later that year, Republicans gained control of the Senate for the first time since 1954 and routinely took over all committee chairmanships. Since he and his team would no longer be running the Judiciary Committee, Kennedy gathered its staffers and promised to help them find jobs.

By that point, Hernández had forged a close personal friendship with Kennedy and his wife. He was unhappy when Hernández said that she wanted to work for the Mexican American Legal Defense and Educational Fund.

"He said, 'Antonia, you have broken a barrier that very few people have. You can go to the major law firms . . . you can do all of these things,'" she recalled. "'You can go to MALDEF after you've done all this stuff. But you have a unique opportunity to do that, and a responsibility.'"

"I said, 'Teddy, I went to law school to be a public interest lawyer to represent my people.'"

In 1981, she accepted a job directing MALDEF's Washington, DC, operations and stayed for twenty-three years—rising to Vice President and eventually assuming leadership as President and General Counsel. Under her leadership (and while she and Michael raised their three children), MALDEF fought for voting rights in California, Texas, Michigan, and Wisconsin, among others, and to redress unequal educational funding in public schools. In 1985, MALDEF sued successfully to prevent California's Proposition 187 from taking effect. It would have prohibited immigrants from receiving public benefits including education and medical services. Another major-impact case won by MALDEF in 2001 allowed undocumented students living in California to pay in-state tuition at the public universities. One of the longest-standing institutions focused on Latino civil rights, MALDEF continues to be a powerhouse in fighting injustice, using the law as a tool for advancing a vision of equity.

A Seat at the Table in Philanthropy

Hernández joined the Board of Directors of the Los Angeles-based California Community Foundation (CCF) in 2003. It partners with individuals of wealth, corporations, and other institutions to channel millions of dollars in grants each year to California nonprofits.

"One of the attributes of leadership is to not worry about what people say about you . . . if I had started thinking, 'Oh, my God, what do they think of me?' we would never have done a lot of the stuff that we got to do."

Seeing how she was driven by community needs, her fellow Board members recognized her potential as a trailblazing leader who could guide the foundation on a path for real change, and she was appointed President in 2004.

U.S. foundations hold over a trillion dollars of assets and often determine which issues and organizations get funding, which policies are promoted, what research moves forward, and more. There are few Latinos in top positions, and Latino communities receive a disproportionately low amount of investment from philanthropy. Though it was a departure from her legal career and from a beloved institution she had built up over two decades, she saw the potential to influence social change in a different way, through philanthropy. The choice was easy, and she said yes.

Leadership Lesson #3: Draw strength and resourcefulness from your family, culture, and community

Reflecting on her career, Hernández credits her family and upbringing for laying the groundwork for her success.

Young Antonia had an entrepreneurial streak from the beginning. As the oldest child, she was expected to help the family make ends meet. She began working at just age ten—crocheting and embroidering items along with her mother and sisters to sell in the housing projects and in swap meets, helping her father sell tamales in bars and local market stalls, and spending the summers doing migrant farm work alongside her family.

"Antonia, can you see yourself as President of CCF?" she was asked by the Board of Directors at the California Community Foundation. "I can see myself as President of the United States," she answered, "but can you see me as President of CCF?"

When Hernández graduated from high school, her father drove her to downtown Los Angeles and dropped her by a street bustling with retail stores.

"Go find a job," he said. She knocked on doors. "'Do you need help? I can do this, whatever.' First day, I couldn't find a job. The next day I found a job" at a lingerie shop as a summer substitute for a salesperson who had returned to her country.

Years later, that same resourcefulness was instrumental in her achievements on behalf of a number of organizations, including shaping MALDEF into an important national institution and her continued efforts to support communities through philanthropy at California Community Foundation.

In December 2017, Hernández's family gathered as her father's health failed and he was receiving hospice services at home. "We took care of him, and we made eighty-five pounds of tamales," she remembered. "If you go back to who we are, about who my family is, we were crying, we were laughing, my father was next door dying. But we were doing something jointly and that helped us with the knowledge that he was going." He died two days after Christmas.

Even though both her parents have passed away, Hernández and her sisters continue to gather every year at Christmas, surrounded by grandchildren, visiting relatives, music, and laughter, to assemble and steam tamales, although in 2018 they agreed to use just thirty pounds of *masa*.

When life gives you *masa*, you make tamales.

Looking Forward: A New Portrait of Being American

President of California Community Foundation for over seventeen years, Hernández remains committed to using her position to make real and lasting change for communities.

"I take my role as a Latina in philanthropy very seriously," Hernández stressed. "You know, when a White person fails, it's his or her failure. If a Latino fails, it's a community's failure. And I think that there is a unique burden on us to really be transparent and to try to be successful, because it's not just our failure or our success. It's a reflection of our community as we are evolving. It shouldn't be that way, but it is, and I think that is really something that leaders in the Latino community need to understand, and embrace the role that we play in opening doors for others."

Looking forward, she envisions a new portrayal of what it means to be an American.

"You have to look at me and say, 'Yeah, you're an American'—instead of saying, 'Where did you come from?' It happens to be that I came from Mexico, but I've lived here the better part of sixty-four years," she said. "For people to look at me and say, 'Yeah, you're an American,' that's the leap that we have to make."

She also expressed a hope for Latino communities in the United States to rise to their potential, which in her view will only happen by increasing opportunities for women.

"I've always said there are a lot of things of beauty in our *cultura*, and a lot of things that are not so beautiful," she says. "The community has to deal with the cultural issues that are inhibiting us from moving forward. Foremost is the sexism . . . the fact that we don't promote our women." She added that sexism and violence against women are universal issues in the general population that must be addressed.

"Secondly, we have to deal with the importance of family, however you define that structure," she said. "Not just Latinos but society really needs to focus on the importance of being part of a family and a larger community. We are going to make it, or not make it, on the concept of who we are as a community, as a nation, and [as] part of this human race."

14 ENVISIONING NEW PHILANTHROPY
IS THERE A LATINO DONOR?

ANA GLORIA RIVAS-VÁZQUEZ

The 2020 presidential election significantly raised awareness about the diversity of the U.S. Latino community, which came as a surprise to many people. During the campaign, we consistently heard leading news and political organizations speak of "the Latino vote" as if all Hispanics voted the same way. Anyone who believed that learned that the reality is otherwise.

Members of the Latino community in the United States have always known that we are not a monolithic group. We share a language, albeit with geographic nuances. Most of us are not immigrants, although our families hail from different countries, have different immigrant experiences, and vote differently. At the same time, however, Latinos do share strong cultural and family values regardless of the countries of origin.

What, if anything, does this mean for Latino charitable giving? Rather than focusing on the differences among Latinos as donors, it is important to understand the basic shared values that shape and inform philanthropy among Latinos. For years, Hispanics and non-Hispanics alike have repeated the myth that Hispanics don't give. The truth is that Hispanics do give and do so quite generously, but not always in ways that fit neatly within U.S. models of philanthropy. For example, much of our giving takes place within extended family networks, and the money sent back to family and communities in our countries of origin—remittances—has been amply documented.

The Shared Values of Latinos

"I think there is some commonality among Latinos that is relevant in philanthropy," says Washington, DC-based Dan Restrepo, who advises foundations and nonprofits on Latino engagement. "Even if there is no 'Latino voter,' that does not necessarily mean that there is no 'Latino donor'—because people's politics and philanthropy are informed by very different things."

Miami-based eMerge Americas CEO L. Felice Gorordo, who has a long history of raising money for charitable as well as political causes, agrees: "I think there is a Latino donor, but the Latino community is not monolithic. It's segmented by country of origin, socioeconomic status, and geography."

Restrepo, Gorordo, and others say that relationships and faith are both important for Latinos.

"Latinos are much more driven by relationship over time and their faith in their decisions about to whom and how to give back," Restrepo says.

"We are a diverse group, but we share values that shine through: our sense of family, our wanting to propel our kids forward, our sense of wanting to give back to our communities through remittances, our church . . ." says Boston-based philanthropist Aixa Beauchamp. There is a set of foundational values that we share, she added. "The differences are where we all come from."

Mark Hugo Lopez, Director of Global Migration and Demography at the Pew Research Center in Washington, DC, and a nationally recognized expert on U.S. Latinos, stresses the importance of one's relatives.

"It's that family-first component that is an important part of the Latino economic story," Lopez says. He explains that Latinos frequently have more responsibilities for family members, which may limit what they can do philanthropically. But he says that as Latinos in general and young Latinos in particular begin to make more money, there will be more opportunities for them to become more philanthropic.

"For Latinos with the capacity to give, there is an interest and a desire to give back and pay it forward, especially for those with a faith background. But I do think that trust is also important—establishing trust is key," Gorordo says. "There is a natural skepticism when it comes to institutional giving."

Developing that trust and those relationships with Latinos takes time. Restrepo says that patience is very important when engaging Latinos.

"First is patience," Restrepo says. "Second, real relationship building matters, and that doesn't just mean touching the donor multiple times, but actually getting to know who that person is, who their family is, what their values are, and how they see themselves in the society around them."

It's About Family

Latinos have a long history of giving—to family, to church, and to causes and organizations about which they care. But their giving is strongly tied to their relationships, which are deep and extensive. To understand this, we need to go no further than to think about the ties that Latinos have with both their immediate and their extended families. Given the cultural value placed on family, it makes sense that the concept of family plays an important role in Hispanics' philanthropy.

"You have to make a connection almost on familial terms," says Ramón Murguía, a Kansas City attorney who has decades of experience serving on nonprofit Boards. "A lot of nonprofits don't get that about us—if you really want to get us involved, you have to relate to us as family."

Murguía is a long-serving co-founder of the Greater Kansas City Hispanic Development Fund and a trustee of the W.K. Kellogg Foundation, which has given him additional experience with philanthropy in diverse communities.

"Our concept of family is much broader than the Anglo concept," says Murguía.

Beauchamp agrees: "My theory always has been that we need to make these institutions feel like family."

Giving for Beauchamp began with the example of her father. Although she grew up in what she describes as "humble beginnings" in Brooklyn, her father "did okay for the neighborhood." He would buy school supplies for Beauchamp's girlfriends and was always very generous with family members. Beauchamp says that she saw that generosity and participated. She attributes those experiences to her desire to go into a helping profession. Her undergraduate degree was in social work, and her first job was working for Catholic Charities in Brooklyn.

Eventually, Beauchamp found her way to a career in philanthropy, both at foundations and as a consultant. And, along the way, she and her husband became philanthropists. They focus their philanthropy on education because they feel that it has been the "big equalizer" in their lives. And they focus not only on Latino issues, but also on young people and on issues affecting all children of color.

In 2013, Beauchamp led the establishment of The Latino Equity Fund, the first Latino-focused fund in Greater Boston and a unique partnership between Latino philanthropists and leaders, as well as the Boston Foundation and Hispanics in Philanthropy. Not surprisingly, most of the photographs in the Latino Legacy Fund's brochure depict Hispanic families, and the text focuses on the importance of contributions made by Latino families.

"If we as a community don't step up and fund our own, no one else is going to step up to the plate," Beauchamp says about Latinos helping their communities.

As someone with extensive experience both as a professional in philanthropy and as a donor, Beauchamp would like organizations to understand that people need to be involved with the entities that seek their support.

"Nonprofits are just not getting it," Beauchamp says. "People want to put in their time and talent, not just their money." She acknowledges that Latinos are very philanthropic within their own families but are hesitant to support institutions. "We're very relational," she says.

Sergio González has been a fundraiser for twenty years. Previously with the University of Miami, he is the Senior Vice President for Advancement at Brown University in Rhode Island. During his tenure at the University of Miami, the university raised twenty-eight gifts of $1 million or more from Hispanic donors.

"The difference is that you need to make them feel really engaged with the organization," González says of working with Latino donors. He says that you have to "personalize" the giving experience more for them. Cultivation can take longer with Hispanic donors, which González says is tied to the "central theme of connectivity" for Latinos.

A Story of Family, Love, and Generosity

Carmen and Al Castellano also grew up with a strong sense of family and with examples of giving at home. Carmen called it a "generosity of heart."

Not surprisingly, when the Castellanos won the then-largest individual prize in the California Lottery—$141 million—in 2001, one of the first things that Carmen did was to make a list of the people they wanted to help.

The Castellanos soon established a family foundation. And, inspired by the examples of giving in their families growing up, Carmen and Al focused their giving on Latinos, and on families and the issues with which they grapple.

On the Castellano Family Foundation website, the Castellanos' focus on family is very clear: "The foundation's focus areas reflect the values of family, community and social change that stem from family members' love for each other and for their community." The Castellanos point out that Latinos are very generous, giving significantly to their families and to their churches. But that participation by Latinos in mainstream philanthropy is not something that you see in large numbers.

"We give in a nontraditional way, not mainstream," said Carmen, who passed away in July of 2020. "We are very generous-hearted people. . . . We tithe to our community."

The Castellano family tries to lead by example and hopes to inspire others to join it. The Castellanos also value the personal connections that they make through their giving.

"It's very fulfilling," Carmen said. "Once in a while, I'll be out somewhere and someone will tell me that a scholarship helped them." As do many Latinos, Carmen found it very gratifying to hear from people who had been impacted by the donations.

Although of modest means, the Castellanos were givers long before they won the California Lottery. But the winnings enabled them to increase and formalize their giving through the foundation, which is now led by their three children.

"We're taking the story and the love of my parents and creating change within the Latino community," says Armando Castellano, who runs the foundation with his two sisters.

The younger Castellano is committed not only to supporting Latino-led nonprofits, but also to engaging other Latinos in giving. He has been involved in many fundraising efforts and says that "when you are asked in a culturally appropriate way and in a correct linguistic way, without assumptions, we're all engaged."

Armando Castellano believes that there are things that bind U.S. Latinos together and that there is a lot that nonprofits can do to engage Latino communities. He says that it includes making sure that the nonprofits have Latinos on their Boards, that they have cultural competence on the fundraising team, and that they let go of stereotypes about wealth and capacity.

"It's expensive and time consuming, so are you ready for the journey or not?" Armando says. And for nonprofits that don't want to figure out how to engage Latinos, he says, "It's your loss, it's your failure, it's your bottom line."

Recommendations for Nonprofits Looking to Engage Latinos

As Armando Castellano points out, engagement of Latinos in philanthropy in the United States must include an understanding of Latino culture, including the all-important values of relationship and family. As Latinos, family is one of our core values, and we define family more broadly than do our non-Hispanic friends and neighbors.

First, nonprofit organizations that want to engage Latinos in their fundraising efforts need to assess their capacity to do this work in a meaningful way. They should look at the diversity, and specifically the inclusion of Latinos, on their Boards and staffs, particularly on the fundraising team. They also should evaluate their level of cultural competence in working with Latinos and whether they have the Spanish-language proficiency that may be necessary, or preferred, with a segment of the Latino community. Without these things in place, establishing connections with Latino donor prospects will be more difficult and not very effective.

Second, when engaging Latino donors, care must be taken to develop relationships that feel more familial than transactional. As fundraisers familiar with Hispanics acknowledge, this means a longer cultivation phase in which a relationship is developed with the donor so that she or he feels more like family. Both donors and fundraisers recognize that for Hispanics, the line between business and friendship is blurred. It is important to spend time talking and visiting with Latinos. And Hispanic donors will admit that they do not want to be solicited before a trusting relationship has developed with the solicitor and the organization. Most Hispanics will not mail in a large check without a significant connection to the people at the charitable organization. Even wealthier Latinos who may have more experience with being solicited require a high-touch approach.

Third, the cultivation, solicitation, acknowledgment, and stewardship of donors should take into account the familial relationships of the donor. Fundraisers should ask themselves questions such as: Which family members should be invited to cultivation events and solicitation moments? How can the family, including the extended family, be included in recognition events? How can thank yous be personalized to feel like family gratitude? What kinds of connections can be made between the donor and those whose lives are improved by the gift?

Fourth, given the connections that Latinos have to family and the fact that Latinos are still building wealth, consideration should be given to the possibility of creating opportunities that enable family members and families to join together to give to a particular cause. There are many examples of Latino families establishing scholarship funds. Early in my fundraising career, I worked on a million-dollar gift from three Latinos—two family members and a close business partner. These people had successfully accomplished much together in their business lives, so coming together to make a significant gift felt like one more joint family effort.

Fifth, as evidenced in the wisdom of the Latino Legacy Fund founders, materials used to cultivate and solicit Hispanics need to reflect not only Hispanics themselves, but also our cultural values. I have been told by more than one donor that they are put off when they don't see themselves in an organization's materials.

The bottom line is that engaging Latino donors is about developing real relationships. "You have to get to know and understand them," Restrepo says. "And not see them simply as the target from whom you want to extract something."

15 FUNDING SECTOR
DEMOCRATIZING PHILANTHROPY
FOR SOCIAL CHANGE

ANA MARIE ARGILAGOS

Setting the agenda for social movements and providing the funding to help them succeed; stepping in when the government fails to provide a safety net for our communities to ensure no one gets left behind; investing in the most innovative nonprofits and entrepreneurs solving the social issues of the day—this is philanthropy at its best.

Take, for instance, the civil rights organizing of the 1960s and the subsequent legislation that transformed our society. Yes, foundations were behind those movements. The Ford Foundation's intentional support of emerging Latino organizations built the infrastructure of a Latino civil sector that decades later is mobilizing civic engagement and more (organizations including MALDEF, Latino Justice, UnidosUS, and Southwest Voter Registration were birthed—opening the way for others to emerge). More recently, unprecedented action by five foundations (Doris Duke Charitable, W.K. Kellogg Foundation, Andrew Mellon Foundation, MacArthur Foundation, and The Ford Foundation) to collectively increase their annual grantmaking by $1.7 billion by issuing social bonds was creative and gutsy.

Strategic, ambitious, focused on social-change outcomes—that is philanthropy at its best.

In the United States, philanthropy is significant. Charitable giving totaled $410 billion in 2017; that's 2.1 percent of GDP.[1] With that money comes enormous power—power to truly shift entrenched systems that impact our country's diverse communities. And yet, in practice, philanthropy sometimes falls short, or perpetuates the same beliefs and practices that keep those systems in place. Too often, it is not setting a bold new agenda, but rather furthering the agenda that maintains the status quo.

Why the discrepancy between what philanthropy *could be*, and what it actually *is*? For one, consider *who* is setting the philanthropic agenda. People in the top 1 percent of income give a third of all charitable contributions in the United States.[2] On the surface, that seems laudable, except that the 1 percent does not include many Black, Brown, queer, trans, Indigenous, or disabled people. The top 1 percent does not include those who are most marginalized by society. For that matter, neither do the leadership teams or Boards of most of the foundations in the United States. So, the people setting the philanthropic agenda do not embody or represent the communities that philanthropy should be prioritizing.

I believe this can change, and I believe deeply that philanthropy can reach its best potential. Now is a perfect time to reimagine philanthropy. Donor Advised Funds (DAFs) are growing exponentially, micro-donors are changing the landscape of giving, and younger generations want to see the impact of their social investments. Even more important, there is a need to focus on the often ignored and massive charitable power and assets of people of color. We're at a seminal inflection moment—a shift that can build the power of the Latino community to create change from within, as well as in partnership with others.

What Could Be

Picture this: Next week, you walk into a meeting of investors discussing strategies to fund social enterprises. Who do you see around the table? How does the discussion start, and what perspectives does it include? Who is missing? What goes unspoken or unaddressed?

Now imagine this: You walk into a meeting of investors discussing strategies to fund civic power-building in the Latino community. Seated in a circle you see a trans community organizer; an Afro Latina investment banker from Puerto Rico; an *abuelo* who founded a Latine giving circle with his church community; a second-generation Mexican tech entrepreneur who is launching a new impact investment fund; a young, queer Latino from a Southwestern Indigenous tribe; and a White program officer from a major foundation. The meeting kicks off with a discussion of recent political and economic gains by Latinos across the country. Next, Latine organizers from the communities in which the group plans to invest present their strategies and needs. Finally, time for brass tacks: the group starts planning its investment strategy, focusing on building political and economic power from the ground up.

Now consider: What has shifted from how you pictured the first meeting and then what *could* be? I see a few key differences in the second scene:

- **Representation:** The decision makers are diverse across multiple identities and truly represent the communities in which they are seeking change. They are not just seated at the table; their voices are heard.
- **Focus on strength:** The group spotlights the strengths of the Latino community, instead of just its vulnerabilities.
- **Centering the community:** The investment strategy is built ground-up, based on the needs that the community expresses, rather than the needs that the investors perceive.
- **Democratizing giving:** The group of investors includes traditional philanthropists and high-net-worth individuals, but it also includes everyday community members who are invested in change.
- **Building power:** The core lens of the investment strategy is building power, which sets the community up for long-term prosperity.

This is my vision of the future of philanthropy, and I believe we can get there.

For things to change, we need to put philanthropic, civic, and economic power in the hands of our community. We need to launch a new era of Latinx philanthropy that is for, by, and about our community. We need to offer an alternative to the corporate and philanthropic behemoths and high-net-worth individuals who have been setting the agenda—their agenda—for too long. We need to build power from within the Latine community so that everyone, from my *abuela* to our Latino CEOs, is investing in change.

For that to happen, we need to expand and democratize the notion of philanthropy. Traditional philanthropy has left communities of color out—from high-net-worth individuals to the *tías* who donate to their local church but would never consider themselves "philanthropists." To engage these individuals, we need innovative, tailored strategies that harness new vehicles for philanthropy, from micro-giving to crowdfunding and impact investing. And we need to build funds that can do two things at once: first, provide the stability needed to build long-term civic power, and second, be flexible enough that we can be responsive to the urgent needs of our community as they arise.

These are big tasks, and the road will be challenging. But before we create a map, we need to chart the territory. Let's take a look at where we are today.

Taking Stock

Latinos are the largest ethnic minority in the United States, and we're growing. There were 60.6 million Hispanics in the United States in 2019, accounting for 18.5 percent of the total population.[3] The Census Bureau projects that, by 2060, 111 million Latinos in the United States will make up over 28 percent of the total population.[4]

Projected Hispanic Population, 2017 to 2060

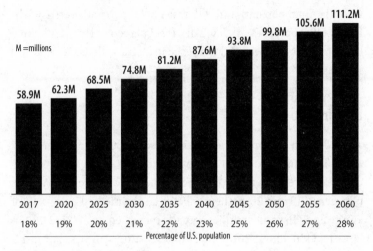

Source: U.S. Census Bureau, 2017 National Population Projections and
Vintage 2017 Population Estimates.

And yet, at both national and local levels, our community is
underrepresented in politics and in other halls of power, corporate and philanthropic alike. In our capitalist system, Latinos' lack
of power and influence goes hand-in-hand with our lack of wealth
and assets. To add to those challenges, our communities are under
attack and facing countless pressures, including systemic racism,
inequity, deportations, and natural and manmade disasters. Our
community also lags behind in a variety of socioeconomic indicators, from education to income and health. Looking at a snapshot
of the data, an image begins to emerge.

Political Power

Our numbers are growing, but that has come with uneven progress. As just one indicator, Latinos make up a small share of eligible voters in Southern states, even though these states have

experienced some of the fastest Latino population growth in the country.[5] Only about a third of Latinos are eligible to vote[6] in Georgia (34.8 percent) and Arkansas (34.6 percent), versus California (49.7 percent), or New York (53.2 percent). This results in a lack of political power and influence in states such as Georgia and Arkansas.

Economic Power

According to data from the Federal Reserve Board, between 2007 and 2016, Hispanic families' net worth rose more than 40 percent.[7] That trend seems promising, until you compare it to Whites: between 2013 and 2016, the gap between the median net worth of White and Hispanic families actually increased, from $132,200 in 2013 to $150,300 in 2016.[8] In 2016, Hispanic families had just a fraction of the wealth of White families.

In our democratic, market-driven system, wealth is intrinsically linked to political power; the wealthy can afford to support the campaigns of politicians who will represent their interests and, often, the status quo. In addition to political power, a lack of wealth also underlies many of the challenges facing the Latino community, including a lack of access to quality healthcare, education,

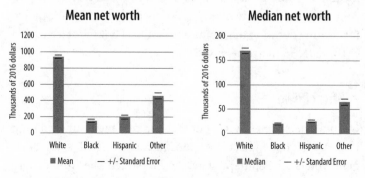

Net Worth by Race/Ethnicity, 2016

Source: U.S. Federal Reserve Board, Survey of Consumer Finances.

and employment opportunities, among others. And, of particular relevance to the field of philanthropy, limited wealth means a limited ability for Latinos to invest in their own communities.

Philanthropic Funding

In the United States, between 2013 and 2016, foundation funding for Latino communities decreased—from 1.1 percent to just 0.6 percent.[9] This is a steep decline, especially when you consider that the Latino population is booming. And these numbers mirror what we're seeing nationally in other spaces. Less than 2 percent of startup dollars go to Black and Brown social enterprises.

Our banks, angel investors, and venture capitalists are not investing in our Black and Brown entrepreneurs. And philanthropy, which is supposed to be championing equity—racial, health, and education—is just replicating the lack of investment. It's not even scratching the surface of the economic inequities that are keeping our community without access to what it needs most.

Why has philanthropy consistently underfunded Latinxs and other communities of color? For one, as I mentioned earlier, we are not represented among the high-net-worth individuals and foundation leadership circles that are making investment decisions. And when we are, we are often tokenized rather than truly heard. There are also structural systems that make it difficult for large foundations, which are set up to fund national groups, to reach and support local grassroots, Latino-led, Latino-serving organizations with small grants to younger, edgier locals in comparison to the multimillions that are appropriately awarded to the national groups. That leaves out entire segments of the next generation of leaders and ideas.

Root Causes of Inequality

The causes for these disparities are complex and interconnected, and are particularly difficult to parse for the Latino community in the United States, which includes a diverse array of nationalities, races, and immigration histories. One factor is clear, however: we have been made invisible. Latinos have been in the United States for more than five hundred years, and our Indigenous people have been here far longer. And yet we are not included in history books. In fact, we are often painted as though we are new immigrants, even though by 2015 nearly two-thirds (65.6 percent) of Latinos in the United States were born here, according to 2015 U.S. census data.

For those of us who are newer to the United States, immigration status and language and cultural barriers play important roles in understanding where we, as a community, are today. This has also been the case with institutionalized racism, that often invisible mechanism that limits power and resources to communities of color through gerrymandering, lack of enforcement of housing laws, and illegal employment screening. Even as the number of juvenile court cases declined by more than half (55 percent) nationwide from 2005 to 2018,[10] aspects of institutionalized racism create a vicious cycle of inequality that impacts communities of color for generations. These include the school-to-prison pipeline, which funnels boys of color into the criminal justice system at shockingly disproportionate rates.

When we look at the macro picture, it's easy to get overwhelmed. The Latino community in the United States faces immense challenges, and barriers like institutionalized racism can seem entrenched and immovable. But focusing only on U.S. Latinos' challenges and vulnerabilities obscures an important reality—the Latino community has incredible strength, resilience, and power. Here are just a few examples:

In 2016, Hispanics' buying power in the United States was $1.4 trillion—and that was projected before the pandemic to grow to $1.8 trillion by 2021.[11]

- America's total economic output (or GDP) is more than 13 percent higher than it would be without the Latino contribution. The nominal GDP of U.S. Latinos reached $2.3 trillion in 2018, according to the *2020 Latino Donors Collaborative U.S. Latino GDP Report*. If U.S. Latinos were a separate country, its GDP would be larger than Italy, Brazil, or South Korea, the report noted, adding that it grew at a faster rate than India or China in 2018, which bodes well for the post-pandemic recovery.

- Families' remittances to Latin America and the Caribbean reached nearly $100 billion in 2019, despite an 8 percent drop from the year before.[12]
- A U.S. Trust study, "The 2018 Study of High Net-Worth Philanthropy," found the volunteering rate among Hispanic respondents was 60 percent, the highest level found in any demographic.[13]
- 2020 saw the highest number of Latinos elected to Congress, with thirty-nine House members and six Senators, making up 9 percent of the House and 6 percent of the Senate.[14]

This is enormous economic strength, and it's growing—which means the Latino community is becoming more powerful.

So, the question for philanthropy is, how can we effectively support this growth and power?

Vision for Change: Building Power Through Philanthropy

One thing is clear—the traditional philanthropy of today isn't philanthropy at its best. Latino communities are not getting the funding they need, and the diverse voices of the community are not being heard and considered in the decision making about what to fund and how.

My vision, my hope, is something much different: a philanthropy that is truly *led by* the community—by the Black, Indigenous, queer, trans, disabled Latinos who have been at the margins and who deserve to be in charge of their own communities' destinies;

a philanthropy that is diverse in its vehicles so that nonprofits do not need to rely solely on grants from the top foundations but can access funds from venture philanthropists, crowdfunding, giving circles, and other innovations we haven't even thought about yet. And I envision a philanthropy that doesn't just focus on short-term, stop-gap solutions but that truly builds power for the long term.

At Hispanics in Philanthropy, we're thinking deeply about how to foster this new era of philanthropy. As we have developed our model, we've looked for inspiration to other communities that have blazed the trail before us. We've found some excellent examples of organizations that are offering flexible and accessible options for different types of donors:

- The Horizons Foundation fuels the LGBTQ movement in California by giving donors a variety of options that include giving directly to the foundation, opening a donor-advised fund (DAF), leaving a legacy gift, joining a giving circle, and joining a Young Professionals for Equality group.
- The Korean American Community Foundation allows donors to give stocks and appreciated securities.
- The Center for Arab American Philanthropy provides extensive services and four options of fund types so donors have flexibility in donating.

Now let's consider the goals, audience, and strategies for shifting philanthropic resources to more efficiently target Latino communities and remake Latinx philanthropy.

I propose three big power-building goals:

1) **For Voice:** Increasing power and influence in the Latino community so that families have a voice in public decision making. This must include funding for voter registration

and mobilization, an accurate 2020 census, leadership development, and grassroots power-building strategies.

2) **For Opportunity:** Investments that build and promote education and entrepreneurship and address the deep wealth gap. Many donors are interested in giving back to the community to give the next generation a leg up in achieving success. By building education and entrepreneurship, people can start thriving, not just surviving. This can then become a virtuous circle of success and investment.

3) **In Crises:** Funding for resilient, equitable communities that prepare for the future and are can effectively respond to crises, including natural disasters, political strife, and migration surges.

Who Will Be the Change Makers?

A few groups are particularly promising:

- **High-Net-Worth Individuals:** The priorities, interests, and experiences of high-net-worth donors of color are largely invisible in discussions within mainstream philanthropy, but there are now more than one million high-net-worth people of color—and that includes 514,260 Hispanics.[15] These donors are largely concerned with building their wealth, are philanthropically engaged, and are very generous, according to research in *The Apparitional Donor: Understanding and Engaging High Net Worth Donors of Color.*[16] However, the report finds that these donors remain isolated from each other, that they are not present within existing donor networks of high-net-worth individuals, and that the funding these donors provide remains less widely known even to organizations in the fields of work in which they are giving.

The absence of high-net-worth donors of color as an organized force in philanthropy has consequences. It renders critical experience, resources, and talent missing at a moment in which our society requires new ideas, investment, and innovation. As traditional philanthropy also seeks answers in finding better ways to achieve equity, now is the time to harness these donors—both to change dynamics within philanthropy and to achieve better outcomes and solutions for communities that need attention.

- **Traditional Philanthropy:** The philanthropic sector is keenly aware that equity needs to be elevated, but the sector is slow to change. Nevertheless, traditional philanthropy can seed funding to make this change happen and catalyze investment to transform how resources are distributed to communities that need it most.

- **The General Public:** With about 60 million Latinos now in the United States and with a buying power of more than $1.4 trillion, just a fraction of that could address issues that prevent Latinos from fulfilling our potential and securing our future. Microgiving has tremendous potential and is growing exponentially in charitable and political circles. The largest transfer of generational wealth in U.S. history is beginning to occur, and younger donors are looking to invest their money in ways that benefit society.

- **Corporate Social Responsibility:** These programs are growing in prominence and scale—especially in the aftermath of COVID-19 and the protests sparked by the 2020 murder of George Floyd in Minneapolis. It is yet to be seen whether corporate funders will move out of their safe space (sponsoring conferences and events) and be more willing to take risks and invest in systems-change work that builds equity (tackling the wealth gap, leadership development, and movement organizing).

What Strategies Can Get Us There?

Latinos have a tremendous culture of generosity—from churches to family to remittances—and now is the time to harness that generosity to showcase our collective giving power.

To meaningfully engage the community, the same old techniques will not do; philanthropy needs a new toolbox. Luckily, two important forces are aligning now: technological innovation and mass movements of marginalized people claiming their power and stepping up to lead.

Here are a few of the tools and strategies that have tremendous potential to democratize Latino philanthropy, both by including a diverse new variety of donors and by providing alternative sources of funding for community nonprofits:

- **Giving Circles:** Giving circles allow everyday people to work together to invest in the changes they want to see in their community. A Giving Compass report found that giving circles are becoming more diverse, especially among Latinos; new members are more diverse across age, race, and income.[17] The report also noted that members of giving circles "give more, give more strategically and proactively, give to a wider array of organizations, volunteer more, and are more likely to engage in civic activity."[18]

- **Crowdfunding:** Since crowdfunding took off as a fundraising tool two decades ago, it has had an immense impact: worldwide, $34 billion has been raised through crowdfunding.[19] And in the social sector, crowdfunding has given nonprofits access to new donor audiences outside of more traditional fundraising: $5.5 billion in donations have been raised globally, and 71 percent of millennials have donated to a crowdfunding campaign for a nonprofit.[20] A few years ago, HIP identified a critical gap in this market: there were no crowdfunding platforms

for Latino nonprofits to raise money from bilingual,
transnational donors. That's why, in 2014, Hispanics in
Philanthropy founded HIPGive.org, the first-of-its-kind
platform serving Latino nonprofits in the United States
and throughout Latin America. Since then, more than
six hundred nonprofits have raised more than $2 million
from twelve thousand individual donors. We're exploring
ways to make the platform even more relevant and impactful.

- **Impact Investing:** Impact investing allows profit-driven
  individuals to receive a return on their investment while
  also creating a positive social impact.
- **Donor-Advised Funds:** We must take advantage of the
  enormous wealth moving into donor-advised funds and
  similar vehicles by networking with wealth advisors, finding opportunities through impact-investment vehicles,
  and tapping into the ways in which philanthropy will continue to evolve.

Conclusion

In Puerto Rico, a year after Hurricane Maria, communities were
struggling. People lacked access to food, clean water, and electricity. Grupo Guayacán, a nonprofit startup accelerator, took action.
It invested in entrepreneurs whose ideas would help the island
recover. One of those entrepreneurs was José Nolla-Marrero, who
in 2018 was a fifteen-year-old high school student.

José saw a problem in need of a solution. The rural *campesinos* had food, the restaurants in Old San Juan needed the food,
and there was no infrastructure connecting them. So, José created
e-Farm, an app to redeploy the taxi drivers who had no tourists to
bring the food from the *fincas* in the mountains to the restaurants
and the markets in the cities.

The idea is brilliant. It creates economic opportunity for the
restaurants, the campesinos, the taxi drivers, and—of course—

for him, the entrepreneur. One app helps a vital part of the retail economy to flourish again. And yet, the chance that José would have been able to get this idea funded without Grupo Guayacán is slim-to-none.

This is where the new, innovative philanthropy I imagine steps in. At that moment, when Puerto Rico needs us the most, we invest in tangible support that helps first responders, nonprofits, small businesses, allowing entrepreneurs to use their passion, talent, and time to thrive and support their communities.

This is OUR philanthropy. By us, and for us. When there's a crisis, we respond—with or without traditional partners. We're not asking for permission to invest in our communities anymore. OUR philanthropy is Brown, Black, Indigenous, queer and trans, young and old, and differently abled. Together, we will invest in our own economic power, in our own political power. We will fund the brilliant young entrepreneurs, such as José, who traditional funders have turned away. We will fund the nonprofits that are innovating to change systemic and historic racism in our country. Their success is OUR success.

This is my vision: to deploy capital for change and to build our power.

Right now, there is no denying that we still face immense challenges. We are seeing the clear legacy of colonization in our community every day. We are also seeing the other side of that coin—the resilience of people who refuse to be pushed aside. Just imagine how that resilience, that strength, that brilliance will flourish with our deepened investment.

IF WE WANT TO WIN TEACHING GUIDE

Leading Discussion and Encouraging Reading of the Essays

We hope you will spread the messages of these Latine leaders and expose your colleagues and students to the lessons they can teach all of us. Here are some suggestions for discussion questions that you can use in your classroom or conference room. Perhaps they will prompt discussion of some big ideas that relate to your group or organization.

The readings can be separated into two main categories: profiles and topics of interest to Latines. The lesson ideas are applicable to many different age groups. Topics addressed in the anthology essays include community organizing, environmentalism, feminism, immigration reform, and political organizing, among others.

Here are some ways to use the stories in this book to help promote ideas or themes that you are interested in conveying to your classroom or organization.

Pre-Reading: The purpose of a pre-reading discussion is to bring up knowledge individuals already have about the topic and develop their interest in the reading. A discussion about the topic can stimulate what members of the group already know, but also show the leader the limits of the students' knowledge and what areas to review with the group before reading.

Discussion: Choose the topic of discussion. Giving participants a few minutes to brainstorm ideas on their own papers is likely to increase participation. Then call on them for ideas and write their answers on a board. Discuss the topics with the students. Assess their knowledge during the discussion and provide information as necessary. This discussion is a preview of the more in-depth conversation that will follow the reading. It hopefully will pique their interest in the topic and compel them to read the text.

Example:
Foundation/Philanthropy
Recipients (Who Receives Money)
Donors (Who Donates Money)
Fundraising Campaign (How Money Is Collected)
**Awarding Grants (Decision Making About Distribut-
ing Money)**

After-Reading Discussion: If you have a mature audience, then discussion rules are probably unnecessary. If you are working with a younger group, consider promoting a set of expectations to enhance the success of the discussion. For example, to discourage individuals from monopolizing the discussion or interrupting one another, indicate whether it will be necessary for students to raise their hands and be called on before speaking; this decision will depend on your preference and on the size of the group. See the Washington University of St. Louis's "Teaching with Discussion" web page for more ideas: https://teachingcenter.wustl.edu /resources/teaching-methods/discussions/

Questions to Follow the Reading

Profiles

1. What early experiences in the lives of the people who were profiled do you think influenced some of the life decisions they made? Why?

2. What lessons do you think the person profiled hopes that you will learn from his or her life? Why?

3. What characteristics or achievements in this book are admirable? What do you think contributed to personal success? Can the methods of achieving success be copied? How can we encourage individuals to emulate some of these leaders or their actions? What motivates people to treat others as they themselves would like to be treated?

Topical Essays

1. Philanthropy represents the promotion of the welfare of others, primarily through the donation of money to good causes. Is this necessary for democratic societies? How can we encourage more people to donate?

2. Doing good works for other people is often cited as a key to happiness in life. Do you agree? Why or why not?

3. What makes the United States a powerful country? Is democracy a key factor? What about democracy contributes to the success of the country? Do individuals have a role in promoting democracy? What role do Latines play in upholding U.S. democracy?

4. What are factors that affect the economic status of developing countries? Why are some countries in Latin America more successful economically than others? Are some of these influences due to cultural factors? What aspects of Latino culture encourage or hold back development in economic or social issues?

5. Do you think there is a general U.S. Latino culture? Compare Latino culture(s) to American culture. What are their pros and cons? What can non-Hispanic Americans learn from Latino culture(s)? What aspects of Latino culture(s) should be promoted? What can Latino culture(s) add to American democratic ideals? To social justice?

YOUR SOCIAL CHANGE NARRATIVE WORKSHEET

Envisioning Your Story and Message

As you've seen in reading *If We Want to Win*, narrative is a powerful tool for social change, and you can be a part of envisioning the next decade for yourself, your community, our country, and our homelands in Latin America. Start now, start where you are, and find the authentic story that compels that change.

Here, we provide tips to encourage you, the members of your group, or your students, to write a story in a way that promotes messages about issues you and your community care about.

Consider holding writing or script-planning sessions for your organization or community to give your members opportunities to develop their narratives. Providing actual time to write, rather than hoping your colleagues or students will do it in their free time, can be the difference between success and failure.

The Message

What is the message you want to convey as an individual or a group? Most writers use a central message. Ask yourself why that message is important, how it is unique, and who it impacts.

What is my message?

_____

_____

_____

Who is my audience?

_____

_____

_____

Why is this message important, unique, or impactful?

_____

_____

_____

A Call to Action

Sometimes writers simply allude to what they hope readers will do as a result of reading a text. But often, you must be specific and tell your audience exactly what you want them to do. Be aware of this call to action and how you want to present it to your audience.

What is your call to action, the change you want to see?

_____

_____

_____

_____

Personal Narrative

Personal narratives can be more powerful than fiction and often illustrate in emotional ways the message you're trying to get across. Aim to create images in the reader's mind. The more vivid the details, the better.

Sharing an experience that changed you can be educational for both the writer and the audience members. Writing about an emotional experience can provoke empathetic responses from the audience.

If you work for a nonprofit, choose an experience that may reflect your organization's larger issue, such as lack of housing, hunger, racial inequality, or poverty. A personal experience that made you aware of a social justice issue, or motivated you to work for a nonprofit, could be a good writing topic.

What is your story?

_____

_____

_____

How does it connect with your message?

_____

_____

_____

Structure of Writing

When starting to write, keep in mind that the beginning is the most important aspect. Start with a compelling experience or anecdote that will capture the audience members' interest. In today's distraction-packed world, drawing the audience's attention is more than half the battle.

What is your beginning?

_____

_____

_____

After you have caught the audience's attention, get into the gist of the story. Explain in detail what happened and how you (the author) feel about it. Many beginning writers choose to tell a story chronologically, but that's not always the most interesting approach. Start with the most important or compelling aspect of the experience, then go back and color in the background and provide detail, without forgetting the key references that relate to your central message.

What is the body of your story?

_____

_____

_____

_____

All good stories require a conclusion. Wrap up your topic and make sure the message is clear to your audience members.

What is your conclusion?

_____

_____

_____

Many websites are available to help writers. Consult the Purdue Online Writing Lab (owl.purdue.edu) or Writers Digest (writersdigest.com) for more tips.

Publication

Sometimes writing for its own sake, to help individuals work through an issue or express themselves, is sufficient. Writing can help further your organization's objectives. But other times, publication is the goal. Provide some discussion or time for your writers to contemplate publishing their work. There are so many options today. One simple method could be for your organization to prepare a script for a podcast, or to self-publish small booklets for distribution within the organization or to a small community. The writing can also be published on a company website or in a blog. Online publishing is very easy, and it is often free.

BIOGRAPHIES

CONTRIBUTORS

Alexandra Aquino-Fike

A highly experienced development and program management leader, Alexandra Aquino-Fike oversees donor stewardship as the Vice President of Development at the East Bay Community Foundation in the San Francisco Bay Area. Previously, she was the Vice President of Development at Hispanics in Philanthropy. Aquino-Fike holds a Juris Doctor degree from the University of California, Berkeley, a Harvard Kennedy School master's degree in public policy, and a bachelor of arts from Wellesley College. She is a member of the State Bar of New York. Aquino-Fike chairs the Mauricio Aquino Chacón Foundation Board of Directors and serves on the Boards of SHARE El Salvador Foundation and Common Future.

Ana Marie Argilagos

Ana Marie Argilagos has paved the way for a new era to democratize philanthropy from her position as President and CEO of Hispanics in Philanthropy (HIP), a national and transnational philanthropic network dedicated to strengthening Latinx communities. In addition to HIP, through her work with The Ford Foundation, the U.S. Department of Housing and Urban Development, UnidosUS, and the Annie

E. Casey Foundation, she bridges diverse agendas. Argilagos's trajectory is a testament to her entrepreneurial spirit that seeks to center Latinx voices and leadership. She currently resides in Washington, DC, with her husband, Rodger, and cat, Alfie.

Carmen Barroso

A lifelong women's movement and movement-building supporter, Carmen Barroso started her career as professor and founder of a women's studies center in Brazil. In 1990, she became the first MacArthur Foundation Director of the Population and Reproductive Health Program, which supported women's organizations in Latin America, Africa, and Asia. She has retired as Director of the Western Hemisphere Region of the International Planned Parenthood Federation, but continues to write, consult, and serve on international panels to advocate for reproductive and sexual rights. She holds a PhD from Columbia University and did post-doctoral work at Cornell University. She has received the 2016 UN Population Award, the 2019 Women Deliver Award, and the Fred Sai Award for lifetime commitment to sexual and reproductive health and rights.

Nelson I. Colón

As President and CEO of the Puerto Rico Community Foundation, Nelson I. Colón has launched initiatives to build community-level equity and racial justice. After Hurricane Maria, the foundation centered its strategy on accelerating equitable access to social and economic resources. A former college professor, Dr. Colón has taught at major universities in Puerto Rico and lectured on five continents. He has served on several Boards, including the Puerto Rico Civil Rights Commission. Dr. Colón was named Emeritus Chair of Hispanics in Philanthropy in 2018. He holds a bachelor's degree in sociology from the University of Puerto Rico, a master's degree in cultural anthropology from the State University of New York Binghamton, and a doctorate in education from Harvard University.

Anjanette Delgado

Puerto Rican writer and journalist Anjanette Delgado authored a 2009 Latino International Book Award winner, *The Heartbreak Pill* (Simon and Schuster, 2008), as well as *The Clairvoyant of Calle Ocho* (Kensington Publishing & Penguin Random House, 2014). She has contributed to numerous anthologies, *The Kenyon Review*, *Pleiades*, *Vogue*, the *New York Times* ("Modern Love"), the *Hong Kong Review*, National Public Radio, and HBO. A Bread Loaf Conference alumnus, she won an Emmy Award for writing in 1994 and served as a 2015 Flannery O'Connor Short Fiction Award judge and as a 2016 Peter Taylor Fellow in Fiction. Her short story "Lucky" was a 2020 Pushcart Prize nominee. She holds a Florida International University master's degree in creative writing and lives in Miami.

Reavey Fike

As an inclusive educator living in Brooklyn, New York, Reavey Fike teaches first grade at a public, inquiry-based charter school. She expected to complete her master's degree in elementary inclusive education at Teachers College at Columbia University in the fall of 2021. Fike previously worked as Development Coordinator at Global Kids Inc., a youth development nonprofit that brings international education and leadership opportunities to students from underserved communities. She has also served as a grant writer and researcher at a variety of nonprofit and philanthropic organizations.

Olga Garay-English

Independent arts consultant Olga Garay-English is Senior
Advisor for International Affairs to Chile's Fundación Teatro
a Mil and producer of Festival Internacional Santiago a Mil.
She is a former Executive Director of the Ford Theatres, a Hollywood Hills amphitheater. She was Senior Advisor to France
Los Angeles Foundation (2014–2019) and to Staging Change,
a joint New York University–University of Pennsylvania arts
research project. From 2007 to 2014, Garay-English served
as Executive Director, City of Los Angeles Department of
Cultural Affairs. For seven years, she was founding Program
Director for the Arts for the Doris Duke Charitable Foundation, with $145 million awarded. She was named a Chevalier
dans l'Ordre des Arts et Lettres in 2012. Born in Santa Clara,
Cuba, and a U.S. citizen since 1978, she is the widow of Dr.
Kerry English, a developmental pediatrician who long served
abused and foster children in South Los Angeles.

Nellie Gorbea

The Honorable Nellie Gorbea has served as Rhode Island's Secretary of State since 2015, when she became the first Latine candidate to be elected to a statewide office in New England. She
was previously Executive Director of Housing Works RI and,
from 2002 to 2006, served as Deputy Secretary of State. She has
worked with the Governor's Committee on Children's Services
Planning for New Jersey and served as an economic advisor to
the Governor of Puerto Rico. Gorbea, who was born in Puerto
Rico, holds a bachelor's degree from Princeton University and
a master's in public administration from Columbia University.

Mónica C. Lozano

Mónica C. Lozano is President and Chief Executive Officer
of the California-based College Futures Foundation, which

works to close equity gaps and increase college completions. She previously served for twenty years as Editor and Publisher of *La Opinión*, the leading Spanish-language daily founded by her grandfather. Lozano became CEO of the parent, ImpreMedia, until retiring from the business in 2017. She sits on Apple's Board of Directors and California Governor Gavin Newsom's Task Force on Business and Jobs Recovery. She served as a University of California Regent for fifteen years, including two as Chair, as well as a University of Southern California Trustee and a State Board of Education member. Lozano was inducted into the American Academy of Arts and Sciences in 2016.

Julio Marcial

Julio Marcial is Vice President at the Liberty Hill Foundation. In this capacity, Marcial oversees foundation relations and partnerships with government and other sectors. In addition, Marcial guides the foundation's youth justice portfolio, including grantmaking and public policy, which are focused on reducing the size of Los Angeles County's justice system. He began his grantmaking career in 1988 at The California Wellness Foundation, a $1-billion health equity-focused foundation. Most recently, Marcial served as a Cal Wellness Program Director, where he managed more than $60 million in grants focused on criminal justice and other public health issue areas.

Markos Moulitsas Zúniga

Political activist, well-known blogger, and businessman Markos Moulitsas Zúniga founded Daily Kos, the nation's largest progressive online community, and is co-founder of Vox Media and Civiqs, a data and analytics firm. He is the author of three nonfiction books, among other writings. He is the Chicago-born son of a Greek father and a Salvadoran mother.

When he was a child, his family lived in El Salvador for four years until the civil war there forced them to flee. As an adult, he transitioned from being a Republican to being a Democrat while serving in the U.S. Army. He holds a bachelor's degree from Northern Illinois University and a law doctorate from Boston University.

Hector Mujica

Hector Mujica leads the economic opportunity portfolio at Google.org—Google's philanthropy arm—across the Americas. Prior to Google, Mujica worked, among other jobs, performing constituent casework at the office of U.S. Representative Debbie Wasserman Schultz in South Florida and in bilateral relations at the U.S. Embassy in Tokyo. Mujica holds a bachelor's degree in international business from Florida International University, a certificate in social entrepreneurship from the Stanford University Graduate School of Business, and a master's degree in public administration from the University of California, Berkeley. Outside of work, Mujica serves on the Boards of Directors of Hispanics in Philanthropy and the Hispanic Federation. The Venezuelan-born philanthropy executive grew up near Fort Lauderdale, Florida, and now resides in Berkeley, California.

Matt Nelson

Colombian-born and Midwestern-raised, Matt Nelson serves as Executive Director of Presente.org, the nation's largest online Latinx organizing group, which advances social justice with technology, media, and culture. Nelson also served as the Organizing Director at ColorOfChange.org and has co-founded several cooperative enterprises in the Midwest. He is a long-serving community organizer and campaign strategist who was featured in the book *Ferguson Is America:*

Roots of Rebellion. He contributed to the book *Welcome to the Revolution: Universalizing Resistance for Social Justice and Democracy in Perilous Times* and is an editor of *Turnout! Mobilizing Voters in an Emergency* (Routledge, 2020). He has also completed a book on how Latinx organizing and cultural power are reshaping U.S. politics (Routledge, 2021).

Daniel Parnetti

Daniel Parnetti is the Emerging Markets Foundation (EMpower) Senior Program Officer for Latin America, responsible for Argentina, Brazil, Colombia, Mexico, and Peru. Previously, he served as Director of Relations with Affiliates at International Planned Parenthood Federation/Western Hemisphere Region. He also worked for the Inter-American Parliamentary Group on Population and Development. Parnetti is a political scientist who earned a master's in public administration from the New York University Robert F. Wagner Graduate School of Public Service.

Ana Gloria Rivas-Vázquez

A nationally recognized expert on Latino philanthropy, Ana Gloria Rivas-Vázquez has worked in philanthropy for more than twenty-five years. An attorney and former journalist, Rivas-Vázquez is the Director of Catholic Relief Services' Hispanic Development Unit. She previously served as Vice President and Chief Philanthropy Officer of Hispanics in Philanthropy and Vice President of Development and External Relations at St. Thomas University. Rivas-Vázquez earned bachelor's and master's degrees from Georgetown University and a law degree from the University of Miami School of Law. She is the co-founder of the Key Biscayne Community Foundation and serves on the Chronicle of Philanthropy's Advisory Committee.

Robert K. Ross, MD

Robert K. Ross, MD, is President and Chief Executive Officer for The California Endowment, a health foundation. Before his July 2000 appointment, Dr. Ross served as Director of the Health and Human Services Agency for San Diego County. His past service also includes Philadelphia Department of Public Health Commissioner, clinical medicine instructor at Children's Hospital of Philadelphia, and San Diego State University's School of Public Health faculty. He serves on the President's Advisory Commission on Educational Excellence for African Americans and as Co-Chair of the Diversity in Philanthropy Coalition. Dr. Ross was a member of the Rockefeller Philanthropy Advisors Board, National Vaccine Advisory Committee, and the Board of Grantmakers in Health. He is an American Academy of Pediatrics Diplomate. He was a Council on Foundations Distinguished Grantmaker of the Year for 2008.

Mary Skelton Roberts

Mary Skelton Roberts is Senior Vice President, Programs, of the Energy Foundation. She envisions major urban areas in which affordable, transit-oriented development forms a low-carbon, resilient cities. She previously worked as Co-Director of the Climate Change Program at the Boston-based Barr Foundation. Skelton Roberts has a master's degree in city planning from MIT. She also holds mediation and facilitation accreditations from the Program on Negotiation at Harvard Law School and from the Center for Dispute Resolution in London, where she served as lead faculty. Prior to joining Barr in 2009, Skelton Roberts was a consultant specializing in collaborative problem-solving and dispute resolution. She is a native Spanish speaker of Afro-Cuban heritage. Skelton Roberts serves on, among others, the Massachusetts Governor's Latino Commission and chairs the Hispanics in Philanthropy Board.

NUESTRA AMÉRICA FUND TEAM

Diana Campoamor

Diana Campoamor is an editor, an advisor to philanthropists, and a mentor to change makers. She founded the Nuestra América Fund (NAF) to support a new narrative of Latine leadership. She was the founding President of Hispanics in Philanthropy (HIP) through 2017. Campoamor served on the Boards of the Council on Foundations, Independent Sector, and the International Planned Parenthood Federation/Western Hemisphere Region. Among her honors, she received the Council's Scrivner Award for Creative Grantmaking, the Maestro Award from Latino Leaders magazine, and was named consecutively among *The NonProfit Times* "Top 50 Leaders." She previously edited *Nuevos Senderos: Hispanics and Philanthropy.*

Cheryl Brownstein-Santiago

Having served as a Director on U.S. national and local nonprofit Boards, Cheryl Brownstein-Santiago is the Principal of Tucson-based CBS Consulting Group, which specializes in management consulting, communications, and fundraising. She honed internal corporate-relations skills and efficient project management during a long journalism career in which she served as an Editorial Board member/Op-Ed Editor, line editor, staff reporter, assistant city editor, and copy editor. She worked for the *Los Angeles Times,* where she shared in three staff Pulitzer Prizes, the *Boston Globe, Miami News,* and the Spanish-language *El Miami Herald.* She is bilingual, Puerto Rican, and well traveled.

Kelly Ortiz

Born and raised in Los Angeles, Kelly Ortiz is a multimedia writer and digital and social media specialist, with years of nonprofit-sector experience. She has served as a project manager and communications liaison, as well as assisted in the development of this anthology. Prior to Nuestra América Fund, she received her bachelor's degree in English with a focus on postcolonial studies from Mills College. She has served in Latinx voter outreach, copy editing, and writing for various campaigns. She hopes that her work in digital organizing and storytelling will contribute to the liberation of her communities.

WRITERS / RESEARCH SUPPORT TEAM

Cynthia Chavez

Cynthia Chavez (she/her/hers) is a nationally respected organizational strategic planning consultant, leadership coach, and author. With a career in public policy, philanthropy, and the social sector, Chavez has successfully spearheaded national and place-based programs grounded in racial equity, leadership development, and personal transformation. As founder and former Executive Director of Oakland-based LeaderSpring, she and her team invested over seventeen years in leadership and organizational development for over two hundred community-based organizations, many on the front lines of fighting poverty. Chavez earned a bachelor's degree in government from Pomona College and a master's degree in Latin American studies from Stanford University.

Camila Güiza-Chávez

Camila Güiza-Chávez, a Nuestra América Fund writer and editing assistant, graduated from Yale University in 2019 with a bachelor's degree in ethnicity, race, and migration. Within her major, she focused on U.S. state violence in Latin America and against Latinx communities within U.S. borders. She took special interest in learning about the varied modes of resistance that Latin Americans have employed across generations in defining their social and political circumstances on their own terms. She is now the Fellowship Director at Havenly Treats, a New Haven, New Jersey, community cafe that builds power with refugee and immigrant women through paid education, job training, and collective action.

Laura Sarvide Alvarez Icaza

A full-time committed citizen and social critic, Laura Sarvide Alvarez Icaza has influenced development of many institutions, promoted lasting cross-sector dialogue, and focused on her life's passion: citizen engagement. In addition to offering conferences, fairs, and micro-theater performances, she hosts a public radio show on social justice issues from Mexico City on IMER 660 AM. She was founding President of the Malinalco Community Foundation, founding President of the Comunalia Partnership for Community Foundations in Mexico, and Social and Private Sector Program Network Coordinator. She authored *Ciudadanía intermitente. ¿Hasta cuándo?* (*Intermittent Citizenship: Until When?*), published in 2016. Her second book is to be published in 2022.

Danielle Sherman

Danielle Sherman is a writer and fundraising consultant based in Portland, Oregon. Her career has centered on helping organizations that are driving social change and promoting equity and justice. She was formerly the Director of Development at Hispanics in Philanthropy, and, as a consultant and volunteer, she has worked with organizations that include the Puerto Rico Community Foundation,

Neighborhood Funders Group, Emerging Practitioners in Philanthropy, Portland Public Schools, and Oakland Unified School District.

Nancy Zubiri

Nancy Zubiri is an author and journalist in Los Angeles. She is the author of *Travel Guide to Basque America* and is Editor of the Euskal Kazeta news website, which covers the Basque community in the United States. She is a former high school teacher for the Los Angeles Unified School District. She was the longtime Journalism Advisor at Venice High School and also taught English and Spanish. Prior to becoming a teacher, she was a reporter at several newspapers in Northern California, including the *Oakland Tribune*.

ACKNOWLEDGMENTS

Early in the planning of this book, a colleague cautioned that assembling a collection of essays was more work than writing a book oneself. While there is some truth to that, the opportunity to work with and write about almost two dozen outstanding leaders is a rare and delightful opportunity, one worth all the effort. Moreover, at this historic moment, when the Americas seek to reaffirm values of democracy, tolerance, and justice, a chorus of voices is ever more powerful and appropriate than a solo.

It goes without saying that the book was a collaboration among a distinguished, visionary, and diverse group of thought leaders. As activists and practitioners on the front lines of social change, their vision for the next decade is a blueprint, an agenda that proposes specific steps to progress on our unfinished democratic experiment in the Americas. In a country that has hardly valued the assets that Latines bring, this narrative is an important tool for social justice.

Alexandra Aquino-Fike's efforts to organize orphans of the war in El Salvador reminds us that there is no peace without truth and reconciliation. Ana Marie Argilagos cautions that philanthropy's promise is in democratizing the field itself; Ana Gloria Rivas-Vázquez discusses what compels Latine philanthropy; Carmen Barroso and Daniel Parnetti's summary of sexual and reproductive rights in Latin America connects the South/North work at an inflection moment in the region; Nelson Colón sees a Puerto Rico that heals from racism and where power returns to citizen activists and innovators; Anjanette Delgado's chilling account of

ACKNOWLEDGMENTS

domestic violence is a timely reminder to confront hidden truths and systemic crimes; Olga Garay-English's insights reveal the imperative role of the arts in imagining a better world; Nellie Gorbea's account of political life encourages others to consider public office; Mary Skelton Roberts sees untapped environmental movement resources in the Latine experience throughout the Western Hemisphere; Mónica Lozano's envisions how to accelerate Latino college education; Julio Marcial compels us to think of a future where juvenile justice is indeed, just; Hector Mujica's assessment of identity and politics reveals messages and strategies for Latino political engagement; Markos Moulitsas Zúniga's assessment of Trump and his voters charts the intersection of racism, xenophobia, and misogyny; and Matt Nelson contributes an assessment of the successful organizing of Latine voters. I also want to thank Julio Copo and Oscar Chacon, who shared their expertise with the contributors group.

The loving essay written by Dr. Robert Ross about his lost colleague, the incomparable Beatriz Solis, is the triumph of a life and legacy devoted to redressing health disparities. In that same spirit, Dr. Ross, one of the few Afro Latino leaders in philanthropy, informs all the portraits and essays by taking us back to our families and rich heritage, the source of our resilience.

The profiles of leadership we selected are a small sample of our Latine/Latin American human capital. These are examples of the pioneers upon whose shoulders our future visions stand. Having had the privilege to work with each one of them, I can attest to their inspired contributions and how, in small and large ways, they've changed the landscape of the Latine civil sector, advocacy, and philanthropy. Early in my own career, one of these leaders whose counsel I sought in a challenging moment advised, "It's not what happens but how you handle it." Restoring power to the person and changing mindsets were common denominators to all these leaders.

Our Nuestra América Fund (NAF) team was small but abundant in talent, creativity, and joy. My co-editor and project manager, Cheryl Brownstein-Santiago, deserves the biggest applause. As a seasoned journalist and editor, a veteran of prestige newspapers, her skillset, instincts, and direction were essential to this anthology. Kelly Ortiz, social media expert, researcher, planner, coordinator, was a continuous thread throughout the project. Her youth, patience, and joy lit the path for everyone who worked on this book. We offer our appreciation for Danielle Sherman, writer and fundraiser extraordinaire, as well as a colleague from my tenure at Hispanics in Philanthropy (HIP), and Nancy Zubiri, our teacher and wordsmith. And additional thanks to Marilse Rodríguez García and Rachel Seaborn. The talented Stephanie Ruiz, also a former colleague from HIP days, designed this book's cover with artwork by Pablo Soto-Campoamor.

Ben Woodward, our editor at The New Press, has been the essential servant leader, thoughtfully shepherding the project from its infancy. His insights and direction were invaluable as we moved forward through the chaos, the pandemic, the reeling economy, the disruptions to our daily lives, and the changes in the publishing business. Ben also has a lovely virtue for anyone, but especially for an editor: diplomacy and respect for others' work. Thank you, Ben.

The funders who believed in this project deserve our thanks as well: California Community Foundation, The Ford Foundation, Hispanics in Philanthropy (HIP), the Marguerite Casey Foundation, Rockefeller Brothers Fund, and several anonymous donors. Our gratitude to our fiscal sponsor, Feed the Hunger Fund (FTHF), and its leader, Patti Chang.

A number of others have also lent support, among them Cheryl's spouse, Cosette Thompson; Marta Jimenez at The California Endowment; Chris Cardona at Ford; Ben Rodríguez-Cubeñas and Betsy Campbell at Rockefeller Brothers Fund; Julie Rodrigues Widholm, Director of the Berkeley Art Museum and Pacific Film Archive (BAMPFA); Alma Flor Ada and Isabel Campoy, award-winning authors/editors and dear friends; Mary Ellen Kapek and Sue Hallgarth, authors and publishers; Gara LaMarche, Antonia

Hernández, Nancy Pearson, Laura Sarvide, Gracia Goya, Luis Pérez-Tolón, Adelaida Mejía, Arturo Vargas, and Thomas Saenz.

My wife, Margarita Gandia, was an integral part of the project, lending tech support, encouragement, advice, and so much more. My son, Pablo, an artist and teacher, my daughter, Kiana Chang-Campoamor, my granddaughters, Mayelí and Soraya, and my brother and sister-in-law, Robert and Halcyon, all provided inspiration and support.

Last, to the innumerable Latine heroes whose stories deserve to be recognized as part of the fabric of our collective narrative: rise and tell your truth, for the change we seek starts there.

Diana Campoamor
San Francisco, 2021

NOTES

Ch. 1 Politics: Latine Paths to Political Leadership

1. National Association of Latino Elected and Appointed Officials (NALEO).

2. Dianna M. Náñez, "Latinos Make Up Only 1% of All Local and Federal Elected Officials, and That's a Big Problem," *USA Today*, Jan. 6, 2020.

3. Susan Milligan, "Women Turn the Tide," *U.S News and World Report*, Nov. 7, 2018.

4. Rakesh Kochhar and Anthony Cilluffo, "How Wealth Inequality Has Changed in the U.S. Since the Great Recession, by Race, Ethnicity and Income," Pew Research Center, Nov. 1, 2017.

5. Kira Sanbonmatsu, Kathleen Rogers, and Claire Gothreau, "The Money Hurdle in the Race for Governor: Center for Women and Politics at Rutgers University, 2020.

6. Phil West, *Secrets and Scandals—Reforming Rhode Island 1986–2006* (Westford, MA: Courier Westford, 2014), 482.

Ch. 3 Community Organizing: Powering Civic Engagement

1. Nicole Acevedo, "Young Latino Voters in Pennsylvania, Florida Could Tilt Race for Trump, Biden," *NBC News*, Oct. 23, 2020.

2. "The Latino Vote," *Latino Decisions*, Nov. 3, 2020. https://latinodecisions.com/blog/the-latino-vote-ready.

3. Acevedo, "Young Latino Voters in Pennsylvania."

4. "The Latino Vote," *Latino Decisions*.

5. "Juan González: Mainstream Media Has Missed the Real Story About Latinx Voter Turnout," *Democracy Now*, Nov. 11, 2020.

6. U.S. Elections Project, Nov. 23, 2020. https://electproject.github.io/Early-Vote-2020G/index.html.

7. See targetsmart at: https://targetearly.targetsmart.com/?view_type=National&demo=Race%20+%20Education&demo_val=Hispanic&demo2=Age.

8. "Juan González: The Media Has It Wrong. Record Latinx Turnout Helped Biden. White Voters Failed Dems," *Democracy Now*, Nov. 5, 2020.

9. "Juan González: Mainstream Media."

10. Suzanne Gamboa, "'Building for the Last Four Years: Pennsylvania Latinos Were Pivotal for Biden," *NBC News*, Nov. 7, 2020.

11. "Juan González: Mainstream Media."

12. Abby Budiman, Luis Noe-Bustamant, and Mark Hugo Lopez, "Naturalized Citizens Make Up Record One-in-Ten U.S. Eligible Voters in 2020," Pew Research Institute, Feb. 26, 2020.

13. Jens Manuel Krogstad, Mark Hugo Lopez, Gustavo López, Jeffrey S. Passel, and Eileen Patten, "Millennials Make Up Almost Half of Latino Eligible Voters in 2016," Pew Research Institute, Jan. 19, 2016.

14. Uth Igielnik and Abby Budiman, "The Changing Racial and Ethnic Composition of the U.S. Electorate," Pew Research Institute, Sept. 23, 2020.

15. Jens Manuel Krogstad, Antonio Flores and Mark Hugo Lopez, "Key Takeaways About Latino Voters in the 2018 Midterm Elections," Pew Research Institute, Nov. 9, 2018.

16. Nicole Acevedo, "Candidates Need Young People to Boost Latino Voter Turnout. Here's Why," *NBC News*, March 1, 2020.

17. "New CMC Latino Religions and Politics National Survey 2020 Released," Claremont McKenna College (blog).

18. "The Latino Vote," *Latino Decisions*.

19. "Juan González: Mainstream Media."

20. National Research Council, *Hispanics and the Future of America* (Washington, DC: The National Academies Press, 2006).

21. Jens Manuel Krogstad, "Key Facts About the Latino Vote in 2016," Pew Research Institute, Oct. 14, 2016.

22. See *2020 Election Handbook*, NALEO Educational Fund.

23. "Juan González: Mainstream Media."

24. See Latino Decisions website, https://latinodecisions.com/wp-content/uploads/2020/08/Xtabs-Somos-Unidos-Aug-Svy.pdf.

25. Melissa Gomez, Vanessa Martínez, and Rahul Mukherjee, "Biden and Trump Offer Latino Voters Different Visions of America—and of Each Other," *L.A. Times*, Sept. 29, 2020.

26. Jose A. Del Real, "Democrats Lose Ground with Latino Voters in Florida and Texas," *Washington Post*, Nov. 4, 2020.

27. "Young Latinx Voters Dominate Early Vote Across Battleground States Heading into Election Day," *Voto Latino*, Nov. 3, 2020. https://votolatino.org/media/press-releases/young-latinx-voters-dominate-early-vote-across-battleground-states-heading-into-election-day.

28. Charles Derber, Suren Moodliar, Matt Nelson, et al., *Turnout! Mobilizing Voters in an Emergency* (New York: Routledge, 2020), Chapter 28.

Ch 4. Identity: A Family of Diverse Communities

1. See Schooldigger website: https://www.schooldigger.com/go/FL/schools/0018002081/school.aspx.

2. See Florida International University website: https://datausa.io/profile/university/florida-international-university.

3. See Google's Annual Diversity Report 2018: https://static.googleusercontent.com/media/diversity.google/en//static/pdf/Google_Diversity_annual_report_2018.pdf.

4. Judith A. Morrison, "Behind the Numbers: Race and Ethnicity in Latin America," *Americas Quarterly*, Aug. 5, 2015. https://www.americasquarterly.org/fulltextarticle/behind-the-numbers-race-and-ethnicity-in-latin-america.

5. Edward Telles and Stanley Bailey, "Understanding Latin American Beliefs About Racial Inequality," *American Journal of Sociology* 118, no. 6 (2013): 1559–595.

6. Telles and Bailey, "Understanding Latin American Beliefs."

7. "Afro-descendants in Latin America: Toward a Framework of Inclusion," *World Bank*, Aug. 29, 2018. https://www.worldbank.org/en/region/lac/brief/afro-descendants-in-latin-america.

8. Paul Taylor, Mark Hugo Lopez, Jessica Martínez, and Gabriel Velasco, "When Labels Don't Fit: Hispanics and Their Views of Identity," Pew Research Institute, April 4, 2012.

9. Mark Hugo Lopez, Ana Gonzalez-Barrera, and Gustavo López, "Hispanic Identity Fades Across Generations as Immigrant Connections Fall Away," Pew Research Institute, Dec. 20, 2017.

10. Ibid.

11. Joint Economic Committee, "The Economic State of the Latino Community in the United States." Oct. 2016.

12. Mark Hugo Lopez, Ana Gonzalez-Barrera, and Jens Manuel Krogstad, "More Latinos Have Serious Concerns About Their Place in America Under Trump," Pew Research Institute, Oct. 25, 2018.

13. Antonio Flores and Mark Hugo Lopez, "Among U.S. Latinos, the Internet Now Rivals Television as a Source for News," Pew Research Institute, Jan. 11, 2018.

14. "2020 Hispanic Digital Fact Pack." H Code Hispanic Digital Consumption Survey. https://hcode.docsend.com/view/xas6nutdcm/d/tgfkpwt.

15. Mark Hugo Lopez, Ana Gonzalez-Barrera, and Jens Manuel Krogstad, Pew Research Center FactTank, Sept. 11, 2018. https://www.pewresearch.org/fact-tank/2018/09/11/latinos-are-more-likely-to-believe-in-the-american-dream-but-most-say-it-is-hard-to-achieve.

16. See *Digital Hispanics: The Role of Culture and Language Online*, Google, 2015.

Ch. 5 Domestic Violence: Against Abuse in Latin America and in the United States

1. National Domestic Violence Hotline. https://www.thehotline.org/stakeholders/domestic-violence-statistics.

2. World Health Organization, *World Report on Violence and Health*, Chapter 6, pp. 151–153. 2002. https://www.who.int/violence_injury_prevention/violence/global_campaign/en/chap6.pdf.

3. Hope M. Tiesman, Kelly K. Gurka, Srinivas Konda, Jeffery H. Coben, and Harlan E. Amandus, "Workplace Homicides Among U.S. Women: The Role of Intimate Partner Violence." *Annals of Epidemiology* 22, no. 4 (2012): 277–284. https://doi.org/10.1016/j.annepidem.2012.02.009.

4. Statistics from the National Domestic Violence Hotline.

5. United Nations Office on Drugs and Crime, *Global Study on Homicide 2019*, p. 10. https://www.unodc.org/documents/data-and-analysis/gsh/Booklet_5.pdf.

Ch. 6 Gender Rights: Bodily Autonomy and Democracy

1. Liz Plank, *For the Love of Men: A Vision for Mindful Masculinity* (New York: St. Martin's Press, 2019).

2. See National Center for Immunization and Respiratory Diseases (NCIRD), "Health Equity Considerations and Racial and Ethnic Minority Groups," Centers for Disease Control and Prevention, July 24, 2020. https://www.cdc.gov/coronavirus/2019-ncov/community/health-equity/race-ethnicity.html#fn2; also, Pippa Stevens, "Women Are Disproportionately Impacted by Coronavirus Job Losses, Costing Global Economy $1 Trillion, Says Citi," CNBC, May 29, 2020; Talha Burki, "The Indirect Impact of COVID-19 on Women," *The Lancet* 20, no. 8, Aug. 1, 2020; Lucy Erikson, "The Disproportionate Impact of COVID-19 on Women of Color," *Society for Women's Health Research* (blog), April 30, 2020.

3. Jens Manuel Krogstad and Mark Hugo Lopez, "Coronavirus Economic Downturn Has Hit Latinos Especially Hard," Pew Research Institute, Aug. 4, 2020; Patricia Cohen and Ben Casselman, "Minority Workers Who Lagged in a Boom Are Hit Hard in a Bust," *New York Times*, June 6, 2020.

4. Equal Measures 2030, "Harnessing the Power of Data for Gender Equality," *Equal Measures 2030 Global Report 2019*. https://www.equalmeasures2030.org/wp-content/uploads/2019/07/EM2030_2019_Global_Report_English_WEB.pdf.

5. Sebastián Essayag. "From Commitment to Action: Policies to End Violence Against Women in Latin America and the Caribbean," UN Development Program/UN Women Regional Analysis Document, 2017.

6. Paula Tavares and Otaviano Canuto. "No Women, No Growth: The

case for Increasing Women's Leadership in Latin America," *World Bank* (blog). https://blogs.worldbank.org/latinamerica/no-women-no-growth -case-increasing-women-s-leadership-latin-america.

7. Guttmacher Institute, "Adding It Up: Investing in Contraception and Maternal and Newborn Health in Latin America and the Caribbean," *Guttmacher Institute.* https://www.guttmacher.org/fact-sheet/adding-it-up -contraception-mnh-2017-latin-america-caribbean.

8. Jonathan Bearak, Anna Popinchalk, Bela Ganatra, Ann-Beth Moller, Özge Tunçalp, Cynthia Beavin, Lorraine Kwok, Leontine Alkema, "Unintended Pregnancy and Abortion by Income, Region, and the Legal Status of Abortion: Estimates from a Comprehensive Model for 1990–2019," *The Lancet Global Health* 8, no. 9 (Sept. 1, 2020): E1152–E1161. Published online, July 22, 2020. https://www.thelancet.com/journals/langlo/article/PIIS2214 -109X(20)30315-6/fulltext.

9. Pan American Health Organization, United Nations Population Fund, and United Nations Children's Fund, "Accelerating Progress Toward the Reduction of Adolescent Pregnancy in Latin America and the Caribbean," 2017. https://iris.paho.org/bitstream/handle/10665.2/34493 /9789275119761-eng.pdf?sequence=1&isAllowed=y&ua=1.

10. "Our Future: A Lancet Commission on Adolescent Health and Wellbeing," *The Lancet,* May 11, 2016. https://www.thelancet.com/commissions /adolescent-health-and-wellbeing; Independent Accountability Panel, "Transformative Accountability for Adolescents," *Independent Accountability Panel 2017 Annual Report.* http://iapreport.org/2017.

11. "Innovative Litigation Filed Against Three Countries to Protect Girls' Rights in Latin America," *Center for Reproductive Rights,* May 29, 2019. https://reproductiverights.org/press-room/innovative-litigation-filed -against-three-countries-to-protect-girls%E2%80%99-rights-in-latin-ame.

12. Nicholas Kristof, "We Interrupt This Gloom to Offer You . . . Hope," *New York Times,* July 19, 2020.

13. Marisa Franco, "Mijente," *New York Times,* Nov. 17, 2020.

14. Laura D. Lindberg, Alicia VandeVusse, Jennifer Mueller, and Marielle Kirstein, "Early Impacts of the COVID-19 Pandemic: Findings from the 2020 Guttmacher Survey of Reproductive Health Experiences," Guttmacher Institute online. https://www.guttmacher.org/report/early-impacts-covid -19-pandemic-findings-2020-guttmacher-survey-reproductive-health.

15. Guttmacher Institute, "Unintended Pregnancy and Abortion Worldwide," Guttmacher Institute online, July 2020. https://www.guttmacher.org /fact-sheet/abortion-latin-america-and-caribbean.

Ch. 8 Education: Access to College Degrees

1. In 2016, Latino high school graduates enrolled in college at a rate of 72 percent, compared with 70 percent for White high school graduates.

"Latinos in Higher Education: Enrollment and Completion," UnidosUS, March 2019.

2. Michael Mitchell, Michael Leachman, and Matt Saenz, "State Higher Education Cuts Have Pushed Costs to Students, Worsened Inequality," Center on Budget and Policy Priorities, Oct. 24, 2019.

3. UnidosUS, March 2019.

4. Mitra Toossi, "Projections of the Labor Force to 2050: A Visual Essay," U.S. Bureau of Labor Statistics, Oct. 2012.

5. "American College President Study 2017," American Council on Education, 2017.

6. Jacqueline Bichsel and Jasper McChesney, "Pay and Representation of Racial/Ethnic Minorities in Higher Education Administrative Positions: The Century So Far," College and University Professional Association for Human Resources, March 2017.

7. Deborah A. Santiago and Matthew Cuozzo, "College Completion Through a Latino Lens," Excelencia in Education, April 2018. https://www.edexcelencia.org/research/issue-briefs/college-completion-through-latino-lens.

8. Renee Stepler, "Hispanic, Black Parents See College Degree as Key for Children's Success," Pew Research Center, Feb. 24, 2016. The survey also found that 49 percent of Latinos and 49 percent of Blacks say that a college education is a requirement to be part of the middle class, compared with 22 percent of Whites.

9. Margaret W. Cahalan, Laura W. Perna, Marisha Addison, Chelsea Murray, Pooja R. Patel, and Nathan Jiang, *Indicators of Higher Education Equity in the United States: 2020 Historical Trend Report* (Washington, DC: The Pell Institute for the Study of Opportunity in Higher Education, Council for Opportunity in Education [COE], and Alliance for Higher Education and Democracy of the University of Pennsylvania [PennAHEAD], 2020). http://pellinstitute.org/indicators.

Profile: Douglas X. Patiño

1. It is reported that 85 percent of foundation Board members are White, while 7 percent are African American and only 4 percent are Hispanic. Owen Jones, "We Don't Want Billionaires' Charity. We Want Them to Pay Their Taxes," *The Guardian*, Oct. 26, 2018.

2. The Pew Research Center, June 26, 2014, and July 8, 2019.

3. J. McCray, "Is Grantmaking Getting Smarter? A National Study of Philanthropic Practice," Grantmakers for Effective Organizations, 2017. https://ncg.org/sites/default/files/resources/GEO_IsGrantmakingGettingSmarter_2014_field_study.pdf.

Ch. 9 Criminal Justice: Youth System Transformation

1. Justice LA, "Care First LA Budget, Fiscal Year 2020–2021." https://justicelanow.org/wp-content/uploads/2017/08/CareFirstLABudget_2020.pdf.

2. W. Hayward Burns Institute, "Los Angeles County Youth Justice Reimagined: Recommendations of the Los Angeles County Youth Justice Work Group," Oct. 2020.

3. Jemima McEvoy, "At Least 13 Cities Are Defunding Their Police Departments," *Forbes*, Aug. 13, 2020.

4. See Terrie E. Moffitt, "Adolescence-Limited and Life-Course-Persistent Antisocial Behavior: A Developmental Taxonomy," *Psychological Review* 100, no. 4, 674–701; Charles E. Irwin and Susan G. Millstein, "Biopsychosocial Correlates of Risk-Taking Behaviors During Adolescence: Can the Physician Intervene?" *Journal of Adolescent Health Care* 7, no. 6, Suppl., 82–96; and Frank F. Furstenberg and Mary Elizabeth Hughes, "Social Capital and Successful Development among At-Risk Youth," *Journal of Marriage and Family* 57, no. 3, 580–592, among others.

5. Danielle Kaeble and Mary Cowhig, "Correctional Populations in the United States, 2016," *Office of Justice Programs Bulletin*, April 2018. https://www.bjs.gov/content/pub/pdf/cpus16.pdf.

6. Prison Policy Initiative, Dec. 19, 2019. https://www.prisonpolicy.org/reports/youth2019.html.

7. "United States: World Prison Brief Data," World Prison Brief, Institute for Crime and Justice Policy Research database, Birkbeck—University of London. https://www.prisonstudies.org/country/united-states-america.

8. Bryan Stevenson, "The Power of Proximity," talk at CEO Initiative 2018.

9. National Research Council, "Reforming Juvenile Justice: A Developmental Approach" (Washington, DC: The National Academics Press, 2013).

10. Anna Aizer and Joseph J. Doyle Jr., "Juvenile Incarceration, Human Capital and Future Crime: Evidence from Randomly-Assigned Judges," National Bureau of Economic Research, June 2013.

11. National Research Council, "Reforming Juvenile Justice."

12. California Endowment, Poll: Californians Support Closing Youth Prisons, 2017.

13. Justice LA, "Care First LA Budget, Fiscal Year 2020–2021."

14. Eduardo B. Torre Cantalapiedra, review of Frank D. Bean, Susan K. Brown, and James D. Bachmeier, *Parents Without Papers: The Progress and Pitfalls of Mexican American Integration* (New York: Russell Sage Foundation, 2015), in *Estudios Demográficos y Urbanos* 33, no. 1, 267–272; Kalina M.

Brabeck, Erin Sibley, Patricia Taubin, and Angela Murcia, "The Influence of Immigrant Parent Legal Status on U.S.-Born Children's Academic Abilities: The Moderating Effects of Social Service Use," *Applied Developmental Science* 20, no. 4, 237–249.

15. H. Yoshikawa, C. Suárez-Orozco, and R.G. Gonzales, "Unauthorized Status and Youth Development in the United States: Consensus Statement of the Society for Research on Adolescence," *J Res Adolesc* 27, no. 1, 4–19.

Ch. 10 Environment: A Diversity Lens on Transit Policy

1. Joseph Romm, *Climate Change: What Everyone Needs to Know* (New York: Oxford University Press, 2015).

2. See Center for Climate and Energy Solutions website: https://www.c2es.org/content/international-emissions.

3. See Climate Action Tracker website: https://climateactiontracker.org/global/temperatures/.

4. The Intergovernmental Panel on Climate Change, "Special Report: Global Warming of 1.5 Degrees Celsius." https://www.ipcc.ch/sr15.

5. Juliet Ellperin, "Trump Rolled Back More Than 125 Environmental Safeguards," *Washington Post*, Oct. 30, 2020.

6. Rachel Morello-Frosch, Manuel Pastor, James Sadd, and Seth B. Shonkoff, "The Climate Gap: Inequalities in How Climate Change Hurts Americans & How to Close the Gap," University of South Carolina, May 2009.

7. Doug Struck, "Pollution, Poverty and People of Color: Falling into the Climate Gap," *Scientific American*, June 19, 2012.

8. Shannon Dooling, "'Hit First and Worst': Region's Communities of Color Brace for Climate Change Impacts," WBUR.org, July 26, 2017.

9. Neela Banerjee, "Q&A: A Harvard Expert on Environment and Health Discusses Possible Ties Between COVID and Climate," *Inside Climate News*, March 12, 2020.

10. National Center for Immunization and Respiratory Diseases, "Health Equity Considerations and Racial and Ethnic Minority Groups," Centers for Disease Control and Prevention, July 24, 2020.

11. Jose A. Del Real, "In an Immigrant Community Battling Coronavirus, 'Essential' Means 'Vulnerable,'" *Washington Post*, May 9, 2020.

12. April Ehrlich, "Wildfires Leave the Most Lasting Impacts on Minority Populations," *Center for Health Journalism*, March 29, 2019. https://centerforhealthjournalism.org/2019/03/13/wildfires-leave-most-lasting-impacts-minority-populations.

13. Lorena Estrada-Martínez, Paul Watanabe, and Katsyris Rivera-Kientz, *Views That Matter: Race and Opinions on Climate Change of Boston Area Residents*, The Sustainable Solutions Lab at the University of Massachusetts Boston, September 2020. https://www.umb.edu/editor_uploads/images

/centers_institutes/sustainable_solutions_lab/SSL_Views_That_Matter_9
-2020.pdf.

14. Anthony Leiserowitz, Matthew Cutler, and Seth Rosenthal, *Climate Change in the Latino Mind*, Yale Program on Climate Change Communication, Sept. 27, 2017.

15. See Green2.0 website: https://www.diversegreen.org.

16. James Eilperin and Annie Linskey, "How Biden Aims to Amp Up Fight Against Climate Change," *Washington Post*, Nov. 12, 2020.

17. Christina Cauterucci, "'Demographics' Did Help Ocasio-Cortez Win, and That's a Good Thing," *Slate*, July 1, 2018.

18. See *The New Climate Economy: The 2018 Report of the Global Commission on Economy and Climate* at: http://newclimateeconomy.report/2018.

19. See the U.S. Environmental Protection Agency website: https://www.epa.gov/transportation-air-pollution-and-climate-change/carbon-pollution-transportation.

20. Mary Skelton Roberts and Aaron S. Bernstein, "How Do We Avoid a Transportation Relapse? We Need to Restore Confidence in Public Transit," *CommonWealth*, Aug. 7, 2020.

21. Mark Arsenault and John R. Ellement, "Roads, Cars Submerged: Storm Raged with Snow, Floods," *Boston Globe*, Jan. 21, 2018.

22. Ibid.

23. See Metro De Medellín website: https://www.metrodemedellin.gov.co/cultura-metro.

24. Amitabh Barthakur and Ignacio Montojo, "Leveraging Transportation Investments to Create Inclusive Cities," *MyLiveableCity*, October 2018.

25. See the Boston BRT website: http://www.bostonbrt.org/the-brt-report.

26. Richard Stone, "Cuba Embarks on a 100-Year Plan to Protect Itself from Climate Change," *Science*, Jan. 10, 2018.

27. Funders Network on Transforming the Global Economy, *A Perfect Storm: Lessons from the Defeat of Proposition 23*, September 2011. https://edgefunders.org/wp-content/uploads/2015/09/Prop23CaseStudy_000.pdf.

28. Debra Kahn, "Environmental Justice: From the Margins to the Mainstream," *E&E News*, Nov. 28, 2016.

29. California State University, Los Angeles, Office of Communications and Public Affairs, "L.A. County Latino Voters Poised to be Defining Force in General Election, New Poll Finds." https://calstatela.patbrowninstitute.org/wp-content/uploads/2016/11/PBI-Latino-Poll-Press-Release.pdf.

30. Steve Scauzillo, "Millennials, Latinos Voted for Measure M in Huge Numbers," *San Gabriel Valley Tribune*, Nov. 16, 2016.

31. See the Neighbor to Neighbor website: https://www.n2nma.org/en/who-we-are.

Ch. 11 Arts and Culture: Our Voices and Images Matter

1. PolicyLink, "Creating Change through Arts, Culture, and Equitable Development: A Policy and Practice Primer" (2017). https://www.policylink .org/resources-tools/arts-culture-equitable-development.

2. American Association of Museums, "Demographic Transformation and the Future of Museums" (2010). https://www.aam-us.org/wp-content /uploads/2017/12/Demographic-Change-and-the-Future-of-Museums.pdf.

3. Elizabeth Méndez Berry and Mónica Ramírez, "How Latinos Can Win the Culture War," *New York Times*, Sept. 2, 2020.

4. Paulo Freire, *Pedagogy of the Oppressed* (New York: Herder and Herder, 1970).

5. Ibid.

6. M. Mustakova-Possardt, "Is There a Roadmap to Critical Consciousness?" *One Country* 15, no. 2.

7. Jim Key, "Why Seeing Marginalized Communities in Pop Culture Matters," *University of Southern California* (blog), https://dornsife.usc.edu /news/stories/2954/marginalized-communities-in-popular-culture.

8. Carlos Aguilar, "The American Latino Experience: 20 Essential Films Since 2000," *New York Times*, Oct. 1, 2020.

9. "Two-spirit" refers to a person who identifies as having both a masculine and a feminine spirit, and is used by some Indigenous people to describe their sexual, gender, and/or spiritual identity.

10. Alvaro Tallarico, "Isto é um Negro?" *Critica, Vivente Andante* online, February 2020. https://viventeandante.com/critica-isto-e-um-negro-teatro.

11. See Helicon Collaborative, "Not Just Money: Equity Issues in Cultural Philanthropy" (2017), https://heliconcollab.net/wp-content/uploads/2017/08 /NotJustMoney_Full_Report_July2017.pdf; and "Fusing Art, Culture and Social Change" (2011), https://heliconcollab.net/our_work/our-work-test.

12. The Ford Foundation, "Sixteen Major Donors and Foundations Commit Unprecedented $156 Million to Support Black, Latinx, Asian and Indigenous Arts Organizations," The Ford Foundation website, Sept. 24, 2020, https://www.fordfoundation.org/the-latest/news/sixteen-major-donors -and-foundations-commit-unprecedented-156-million-to-support-black -latinx-asian-and-indigenous-arts-organizations.

13. Méndez Berry and Ramírez, "How Latinos Can Win the Culture War."

14. Jaroslav Andel, "Why Democracy Needs Arts and Culture," *World Policy Journal*, Oct. 29, 2015.

Ch. 12 Central America: A Model of Diaspora Activism

1. Migration Policy Institute, UNHCR 2017. https://www .migrationpolicy.org/article/central-american-immigrants-united-states -2017.

2. Ibid.

3. "Nayib Bukele's Power Grab in El Salvador," *The Economist*, May 9, 2020

4. Susan Bibler Coutin, "Falling Outside: Excavating the History of Central American Asylum Seekers," *Law & Social Inquiry* 36, no. 3 (Summer 2011): 569–596.

5. Storer H. Rowley, "American Aid Can't Guarantee Victory in Salvadoran Civil War, *Chicago Tribune*, Oct. 15, 1989.

6. Raymond Bonner, *Weakness and Deceit: America and El Salvador's Dirty War*, 2nd ed. (OR Books: 2016).

7. Christina Steenkamp. "In the Shadows of War and Peace: Making Sense of Violence After Peace Accords," *Conflict, Security & Development* 11, no. 3 (2011): 357–383.

8. Cecilia Menjívar and Andrea Gómez Cervantes. "El Salvador: Civil War, Natural Disasters, and Gang Violence Drive Migration," Migration Policy Institute, Aug. 29, 2018. https://www.migrationpolicy.org /article/el-salvador-civil-war-natural-disasters-and-gang-violence-drive -migration.

9. Anna Catherine Brigida, "Showdown in El Salvador Shows Growing Role of Military in Latin American Democracies," *Washington Post*, Feb. 11, 2020.

10. See Amnesty International, "El Salvador: Repression and Broken Promises, the Face of the Country after One Year of President Bukele's Government," *Amnesty International*, June 1, 2020; Mariana Alfaro, "The Daily 202: Human Rights Group Sounds Alarm over Government Crackdowns During Coronavirus," *Washington Post*, April 29, 2020.

Ch. 15 Funding Sector: Democratizing Philanthropy for Social Change

1. "Giving Statistics," *Charity Navigator*. https://www.charitynavigator .org/index.cfm?bay=content.view&cpid=42.

2. "Who Gives Most to Charity?" Philanthropy Round Table. https:// www.philanthropyroundtable.org/almanac/statistics/who-gives#:~:text =People%20are%20generally%20more%20philanthropic,26%2D45%20 years%20old.

3. "Hispanic Heritage Month 2020," U.S. Census Bureau, Aug. 11, 2020. https://www.census.gov/newsroom/facts-for-features/2020/hispanic -heritage-month.html.

4. "Hispanic Population to Reach 111 Million by 2060," U. S. Census Bureau, Oct. 9, 2018. https://www.census.gov/library/visualizations/2018 /comm/hispanic-projected-pop.html.

5. "Ranking the Latino Population in the States," Pew Research Center: Hispanic Trends, Sept. 8, 2016. https://www.pewresearch.org/hispanic/2016

/09/08/4-ranking-the-latino-population-in-the-states.

6. Antonio Flores and Mark Hugo Lopez, "Key Facts About Latinos in the 2018 Midterm Elections," Pew Research Center, Oct. 15, 2018. https:// www.pewresearch.org/fact-tank/2018/10/15/key-facts-about-latinos-in-the -2018-midterm-elections.

7. "Recent Trends in Wealth-Holding by Race and Ethnicity: Evidence from the Survey of Consumer Finances," Federal Reserve, Sept. 27, 2017. https://www.federalreserve.gov/econres/notes/feds-notes/recent-trends -in-wealth-holding-by-race-and-ethnicity-evidence-from-the-survey-of -consumer-finances-20170927.htm.

8. Ibid.

9. "Funding Trends of Foundation Funding for Latinxs in the U.S.," Latinx Funders. https://latinxfunders.org/funding-trends.

10. "Delinquency Cases in Juvenile Court 201," U.S. Office of Juvenile Justice and Delinquency, August 2018. https://ojjdp.ojp.gov/library /publications/delinquency-cases-juvenile-court-2018#:~:text=In%20 2018%2C%20juvenile%20courts%20in,person%2C%20and%20drug%20 law%20violation.

11. "Hispanic Consumers Continue to Drive U.S. FMCG Dollars." Based on Nielsen data. July 2017. http://multivisionmediagroup.com/hispanic -consumers-continue-to-drive-u-s-fmcg-dollars.

12. "Remittances to Latin America and the Caribbean in 2019." The Inter-American Dialogue. https://www.thedialogue.org/analysis/remittances-to -latin-america-and-the-caribbean-in-2019-emerging-challenges.

13. "The 2018 U.S. Trust Study of High Net Worth Philanthropy: Por-traits of Generosity," U.S. Trust. https://www.privatebank.bankofamerica .com/articles/2018-us-trust-study-of-high-net-worth-philanthropy.html.

14. "Latinos Show Record Gains in Congress, Though Numbers Are Still Low," *NBC News*, Nov. 15, 2018.

15. Urvashi Vaid and Ashindi Maxton, *The Apparitional Donor: Understanding and Engaging High Net Worth Donors of Color* (The Vaid Group, 2017). https://thevaidgroup.com/hnwdonorsofcolorreport -download.

16. Ibid.

17. "Report on Giving Circle Membership: How Collective Giving Impacts Donors," Giving Compass, Nov. 13, 2018. https://givingcompass .org/partners/gender-and-giving/giving-circle-membership.

18. Ibid.

19. "Crowdfunding Statistics," Fundly, 2020. https://blog.fundly.com /crowdfunding-statistics/#general.

20. Ibid.

INDEX

ABOUT THE EDITOR

Diana Campoamor is an editor, an advisor to philanthropists, and a mentor to change makers. She founded the Nuestra América Fund (NAF) to support a new narrative of Latine leadership. She was the founding President of Hispanics in Philanthropy (HIP) through 2017. Campoamor served on the Boards of the Council on Foundations, Independent Sector, and the International Planned Parenthood Federation/Western Hemisphere Region. Among her honors, she received the Council's Scrivner Award for Creative Grantmaking, the Maestro Award from Latino Leaders magazine, and was named consecutively among *The NonProfit Times* "Top 50 Leaders." She previously edited *Nuevos Senderos: Hispanics and Philanthropy.*

PUBLISHING IN THE PUBLIC INTEREST

Thank you for reading this book published by The New Press. The New Press is a nonprofit, public interest publisher. New Press books and authors play a crucial role in sparking conversations about the key political and social issues of our day.

We hope you enjoyed this book and that you will stay in touch with The New Press. Here are a few ways to stay up to date with our books, events, and the issues we cover:

- Sign up at www.thenewpress.com/subscribe to receive updates on New Press authors and issues and to be notified about local events
- Like us on Facebook: www.facebook.com/newpressbooks
- Follow us on Twitter: www.twitter.com/thenewpress
- Follow us on Instagram: www.instagram.com/thenewpress

Please consider buying New Press books for yourself; for friends and family; or to donate to schools, libraries, community centers, prison libraries, and other organizations involved with the issues our authors write about.

The New Press is a 501(c)(3) nonprofit organization. You can also support our work with a tax-deductible gift by visiting www.thenewpress.com/donate.